Department of Economic and Social Affairs
Division for the Advancement of Women

BRINGING INTERNATIONAL HUMAN RIGHTS LAW HOME

Judicial Colloquium on the Domestic Application
of the Convention on the Elimination
of All Forms of Discrimination against Women
and the Convention on the Rights of the Child

United Nations • New York, 2000

NOTE

The designations employed and the presentation of the material in this publication do not imply the expression of any opinion whatsoever on the part of the Secretariat of the United Nations concerning the legal status of any country, territory, city or area or of its authorities, or concerning the delimitation of its frontiers or boundaries. The term "country" as used in the text of this publication also refers, as appropriate, to territories or areas.

Symbols of United Nations documents are composed of capital letters combined with figures.

United Nations Publication
Sales No.E.00.IV.3
ISBN 92-1-130204-8

Contents

iii

Preface

The twentieth anniversary of the adoption of the Convention on the Elimination of All Forms of Discrimination against Women and the tenth anniversary of the adoption of the Convention on the Rights of the Child in 1999 were celebrated by many Governments, non-governmental organizations and women's rights activists in all parts of the world. The Division for the Advancement of Women, the substantive office within the United Nations charged with the development of policies for the promotion of women's human rights, and the Secretariat of the Committee on the Elimination of Discrimination against Women, sought to join these celebrations with an event of its own.

In recent years, judges in many jurisdictions based their decisions on the Women's Convention or the Convention on the Rights of the Child, while others have referred to these treaties in the course of their judgements. We thus resolved to invite senior judges and magistrates from around the world to join us for a discussion on how to use international human rights law, and in particular the two Conventions, in domestic decision-making to further the quest for equality for women. Almost 100 judges and magistrates from 65 countries and all regions of the world accepted our invitation to come to Vienna for three days of legal discussion. They, together with the six resource persons who guided us in our discussions, brought to the event a true spirit and commitment to women's and girls' human rights.

While the Women's Rights Unit of the Division for the Advancement of Women assumed responsibility for organizing the event, it would not have been possible without the support of many actors. My deep appreciation goes first and foremost to those whose financial contribution made the judges' participation possible. I would like to thank very warmly our colleagues in the United Nations system, UNICEF, UNFPA and UNDP, who supported the attendance of a number of participants from developing countries and countries with economies in transition. Particular thanks are due to the country offices of these organizations who worked with the staff of the Division so that critical logistical arrangements could be made. I would also like to express my gratitude to Ms. Angela King, Special Adviser on Gender Issues and Advancement of Women for supporting the Division in this endeavour.

A number of Governments deserve our special gratitude for their financial support, encouragement and positive feedback. They are Austria, Belgium, Canada, France, Germany, Ireland, the Netherlands, New Zealand, Norway and Sweden.

Warm words of appreciation are addressed to our colleagues at the United Nations Office at Vienna and its Director-General, Mr. Pino Arlacchi, for hosting us at the Vienna International Centre and for providing us with excellent facilities. The kindness of the highly professional and efficient staff of the Centre who helped service the colloquium made our stay memorable.

Special thanks go to Ms. Benita Ferrero-Waldner, the Austrian State Secretary for Foreign Affairs at the time and now her country's Foreign Minister, for her support and her participation in the opening of the colloquium, and for her generous hospitality to the participants.

The judicial colloquium was the first such event organized at the international level. It drew inspiration from the judicial colloquia that had been administered since 1988 by the Commonwealth Secretariat. The first of these took place in Bangalore, India, in 1988, and the Bangalore Principles adopted there have become widely known and used in judicial and human rights circles. This was followed by five further colloquia between 1989 and 1993.

The Division is proud to present this publication of the proceedings of the judicial colloquium. The six keynote papers and 28 workshop presentations and case studies show the creativity with which senior judges and magistrates have used international human rights norms in their decision-making.

The Division hopes that this publication will constitute a rich resource for those who seek to use international human rights law at the domestic level and an inspiration for others in their efforts to promote the human rights of women and girls.

Yakin Ertürk
Director
Division for the Advancement of Women
August 2000

Introduction

On 18 December 1979, the United Nations General Assembly adopted the Convention on the Elimination of All Forms of Discrimination against Women. Ten years later, on 20 November 1989, it adopted the Convention on the Rights of the Child. To commemorate the anniversaries of these two Conventions, the judicial colloquium on the application of international human rights law at the domestic level was convened in October 1999.

As at October 1999, the Women's Convention had been ratified or acceded to by 165 States, while the Convention on the Rights of the Child is the most widely accepted international human rights treaty with 191 States parties. Both Conventions have been acknowledged for their important contribution to the quest to improve the status of women and girls worldwide, as well as for their positive impact on efforts to achieve equality for women and girls in the family, the community and society at large.

The Women's Convention provides a definition of discrimination against women, and identifies measures required to ensure women's right to equality and non-discrimination in the enjoyment of civil, political, economic, social, and cultural rights. It requires States parties to pursue a policy of eliminating discrimination against women, and to take all appropriate measures to eliminate such discrimination, whether committed by public authorities or by any person, organization or enterprise.

The Convention on the Rights of the Child requires States parties to protect the rights of each child, defined as a human being below the age of eighteen. Among the Convention's general principles are the best interest of the child, a child's rights to life, survival and development, and respect for the views of the child. The protection and promotion of the rights of the girl child is guaranteed through the Convention's principle of non-discrimination.

Together, these two instruments provide a solid basis upon which to create, through law, policy and practice, an enabling environment that allows women and girls to enjoy their civil, political, economic, social and cultural rights without discrimination. Twenty and ten years respectively of the applicability of these two instruments in a large majority of States bear witness to the centrality of the legal norm of women's and girls' equality with men and boys, and of the right to non-

1

ation in the enjoyment of human rights and fundamental free-

The principles of both Conventions have inspired Governments to examine closely their domestic framework for the promotion of the rights of women and girls, including remedies against violations of their provisions. Many Governments have introduced new laws, or amended those which discriminate against women and girls. They have adopted policies and programmes to bring their domestic framework into line with their legal obligations under these instruments, and have sought to harmonize customary principles and prescriptions with the requirements of international law relating to women's rights and non-discrimination on the basis of sex. They have expanded the opportunities women have to seek redress at the domestic level, and have improved and simplified access to courts and tribunals, created mediation and conciliation procedures, and instituted Ombudspersons. Governments have also spearheaded legal literacy campaigns so that women are aware of their rights and the means available to enforce them. At the international level, the adoption of the Optional Protocol to the Convention on the Elimination of All Forms of Discrimination against Women by the General Assembly on 6 October 1999, provides the opportunity for individual women and groups of women to petition an independent expert body, the Committee on the Elimination of Discrimination against Women, in cases where there are violations of its terms.

The expert bodies established to monitor implementation of the Conventions in States parties, the Committee on the Elimination of Discrimination against Women, and the Committee on the Rights of the Child, are particularly concerned with the effect of the Conventions in domestic legal systems. Both Committees have advocated the practical realization of the principles of these instruments through their incorporation into national constitutions, as well as through legislation and regulations.

Both Committees have stressed the relevance of the Conventions and the jurisprudence of the Committees in domestic litigation. Courts in different countries, and from different legal traditions have increasingly drawn on international human rights treaties and jurisprudence to achieve the goals of those instruments. Academic literature, covering both domestic decisions and decisions of international and regional human rights bodies, especially of the European Court of Human Rights, the Inter-American Court of Human Rights, and the United Nations Human Rights Committee, has traced these developments. An

2

impressive body of jurisprudence, both international and national, concerning human rights, including with regard to women and children, now exists. Efforts have been undertaken by various bodies, including the Council of Europe, the United Nations Development Programme (UNDP), and the Commonwealth Secretariat, to increase judges' awareness and knowledge of the domestic application of international human rights norms. The United Nations Division for the Advancement of Women sought to build on those efforts by convening this colloquium.

Government action is essential for the implementation of the obligations of international human rights treaties. At the same time, courts and the judiciary have critical roles to play in ensuring that the legal framework is applied fully, justly and evenly, and benefits all individuals equally. Proper application of the legal framework can only be achieved where judicial decision-makers are aware of, and sensitive to, the realities of the lives of those who seek the protection and remedies that the law offers. Judicial decisions can take a narrow path and be based upon a restrictive interpretation of domestic law. However, judges also have the power to approach their important task in an expansive and open manner which takes account of principles derived from international human rights law and the legal obligations of States as a result of accepting human rights treaties. International human rights law, and particularly that derived from the principles of the two Conventions whose anniversary was marked by the judicial colloquium, provide the framework for judicial decision-making based upon openness, receptiveness and real justice. This body of law allows those responsible for applying and enforcing the law to take into account the often very different needs and experiences of women and girls.

The colloquium provided an opportunity for judicial practitioners from around the world to examine the potential for using international human rights law at the domestic level to achieve equality for women and girls. It provided a forum for a discussion of cases where international human rights norms have been relied on to benefit women and girls, and to assess how courts in different legal systems utilize international human rights treaties to ensure that women and girls are guaranteed their rights to equality and non-discrimination. Judicial officers from both common and civil law systems presented strategies for more creative and widespread use of international human rights norms contained in the Women's Convention and in the Convention on the Rights of the Child at the domestic level.

3

Participants in the judicial colloquium addressed three themes. Each theme was introduced at the colloquium by a keynote speaker, providing the basis for further discussion and case study presentations in working groups. The issues of nationality and marriage and family relations are dealt with in detail in the Women's Convention, but continue to pose challenges at the national level. Violence against women has emerged as a major concern of international and regional human rights law though it is not addressed specifically in the Women's Convention. Violence is the subject of a general recommendation by the Committee on the Elimination of Discrimination against Women, as well as the Declaration on the Elimination of Violence against Women, adopted by the United Nations General Assembly in 1993. Women's right to work and work-related rights have long been a concern in international law, as can be seen from the international human rights instruments adopted by the International Labour Organization.

The relationship between international law and domestic law was a recurrent theme in many working group presentations. In her case study on this topic, Katherine O'Regan showed how South Africa's constitutional principle mandating courts or tribunals to consider international law when interpreting that country's bill of rights is beginning to be implemented in practice by that country's courts.

Arline Pacht took up an issue that had frequently arisen in the presentations and discussions, namely the need for judicial training in international human rights law in general and in the two Conventions in particular to move towards a jurisprudence of equality. She described the training programmes implemented by the International Association of Women Judges, and the International Women Judges Foundation. The importance of judicial education was also prominently reflected in the communiqué adopted by participants.

Nationality: Marriage and family relations

Nationality defines an individual's relationship with a State, and gives rise to rights and duties under international and domestic law. In her keynote presentation on nationality in international and regional human rights law, Christine Chinkin examined the impact of nationality laws on the lives of women. She showed the legal and social disadvantage women suffer through the application of discriminatory laws. Her discussion of international legal provisions with respect to nationality, their particular relevance to women, as well as the emerging international and regional jurisprudence on this topic provided the basis to

4

identify the nature of States' obligations to ensure women's enjoyment of nationality rights.

Marriage and family relations, while having been the topic of international legal instruments preceding the Women's Convention, continue to be the source of discrimination against women, and treated insufficiently in domestic law and jurisprudential practice. In her keynote presentation on this topic, Emna Aouij noted that major reservations had been entered to article 16 of the Women's Convention on marriage and family relations. She reviewed the legislative and policy approach taken by the countries of the Maghreb region to the Convention's provisions in this area, and concluded that family relations remain based much more on cultural practices and custom than on concepts of equality.

Nationality issues were taken up in two case study presentations. Unity Dow presented the ruling by the same name of the High Court of Botswana, where the Court with specific reference to the Women's Convention found in favour of the plaintiff deciding that the Botswana Citizenship Act discriminated against women. The inequities of the practices of immigration officers in Zimbabwe to deny permanent residence permits to alien husbands married to Zimbabwean citizens were reported on by Antony Gubbay in cases decided by the Zimbabwe Supreme Court.

Emna Aouij's conclusion about the continuing preponderance of cultural practice and custom was borne out by several working group presentations. Several also underlined opportunities for judges to use international human rights provisions to support positive change towards equality for women. While customary law practices remain in effect in many jurisdictions, examples were provided where courts clearly found their non-applicability in cases where they discriminated against women. Gwen Phillips discussed Pacific Islands cases where the Constitution was found to take precedence over customary law in favour of equality for women. The examples of women's inheritance and succession rights in countries such as Zimbabwe (Elizabeth Gwaunza), Benin (Conceptia Ouinsou), and Nepal (Krishanajung Rayamahji) highlighted continuing difficulties for courts and legislatures to balance international human rights law and constitutional provisions on equality on the one hand, with customs and traditions on the other. In these three cases, the presenters gave examples how courts in their countries have resolved such conflicts, not always to the benefit of the equality principle. Florence Array gave examples of how courts in Cameroon have protected women's property rights in marriage and upon divorce. Tassaduq Hussain Jilani highlighted a decision in which an adult woman's right to enter into marriage without the consent of her father or guardian was clearly affirmed within the framework of Pakistan's commitment to gender equality and in accordance with the norms of the Women's Convention.

Within the theme of family relations, a number of presentations dealt with the best interests of children. They focused both on judicial decisions within a given legal framework, as well as on court procedures to uphold the best interest of children. Referring to decisions of the Supreme Court of Canada, Michel Bastarache discussed opportunities for courts to incorporate the values of the Convention on the Rights of the Child in their decision-making, especially in jurisdictions such as Canada where treaties cannot be invoked as direct source of rights and obligations, but can serve as an interpretive aid. Cases from Uruguay (Marta Battistella de Salaberry) and Uganda (Stella Arach-Amoko) demonstrated how the incorporation of the concept of the best interests of the child in legislation, together with the Convention on the Rights of the Child, gives judges the space to arrive at satisfactory decisions in family relations involving minors. Odette Murara discussed the difficult task of judges in Rwanda to reconcile the need to prosecute and punish alleged perpetrators of crimes, including genocide, with the need to limit the criminal liability of minors as defined in the Convention on the Rights of the Child. Ameurfina Melencio-Herrera reviewed the proposals of the Philippine Judicial Academy for a revision of that country's rules of court, based on the Convention, to accommodate better the special needs and vulnerabilities of children, especially concerning the reception of testimony from children.

Violence against women

The issue of violence against women was considered from two specific perspectives during the colloquium. Claudio Grossman discussed the international legal framework as it pertains to domestic violence, reflected in the provisions of the Women's Convention, the Committee's General Recommendation 19 on violence against women, and the United Nations General Assembly Declaration on the Elimination of Violence against Women. He also gave an overview of the Inter-American system, especially the Inter-American Convention on the Prevention, Punishment and Eradication of Violence against Women, and of specific steps taken by countries in the region to achieve implementation.

Navanethem Pillay's keynote presentation focused on the development, justification, strengths and weaknesses of international law as it pertains to State-sponsored violence against women. Emphasizing State responsibility to respect and ensure the rights of all citizens, as well as the principle of individual criminal responsibility, she outlined the evolution of international human rights and humanitarian law and their attention to gender-based violence. She reviewed the statutes and case law of the International Criminal Tribunals for the former Yugoslavia and for Rwanda with regard to such violence.

Participants presented a range of case studies within the theme of violence against women. Catherine Fraser presented a Canadian case that centred on the question of consent in instances of sexual violence. The case showed how the Women's Convention has relevance at every step of the analysis of facts and law. Emphasizing the fact that the Indian Supreme Court had repeatedly invoked international human rights law in support of its decisions, Sujata Manohar described a case affirming women's right to freedom from sexual harassment in the work place, where the Court, in the absence of specific legislation, relied on the Women's Convention and the Committee's General Recommendation 19 and laid down guidelines to secure women's rights in this context.

Khandker M. Hasan discussed the Bangladeshi judicial practice of sending minor girls to so-called safe custody in jail, with the stated intention of protecting the welfare of the minor, and recent challenges to this practice based on the Convention of the Rights of the Child. Nasir-ul-Mulk highlighted the need to apply international human rights law in Pakistan to address so-called "honour killings" of women, and to abolish the introduction of evidence of "honour killings" as a mitigating circumstance in murder cases or as a basis for reduction of penalties.

A.K. Badrul Huq stressed that legislation including that specifically introduced to benefit women would remain ineffective unless judges considered it in a gender-sensitive manner when dispensing justice. On the basis of a decision of the Supreme Court of Bangladesh, he showed how judges in rape cases can ensure a victim's rights in the interpretation of corroborative evidence. Stella Dabutha discussed the Botswana Penal Code (Amendment) Act of 1998 concerning rape and questioned whether this legislation met the demands of international human rights law and by providing sufficient protection for women. Petra Smutny argued that in Austria, court action based on adequate legislation and

7

good policies had led to concrete changes and effective results in the context of trafficking in women and children.

The strengths and weaknesses of the legislative framework and administration of justice with regard to violence against women with regard to Ecuador, Latvia and Venezuela were discussed by Maria Leonor Jimenez de Viteri, Anita Usacka and Maria Cristina Parra de Rojas, respectively.

Work and work-related rights of women and girls

The third theme of the judicial colloquium, women's right to work and work-related rights, allowed for a focus on affirmative action. Krisztina Morvai described the constraints women face in the labour market because of the persistence, in most societies, of separate public (male) and private (female) spheres. She outlined opportunities for domestic courts to apply the Women's Convention and by providing an interpretive guide to those articles of particular relevance to women's and girls' work-related rights, she demonstrated the type of analysis required from judges to ensure consistency and compliance of domestic decisions with international human rights law, in particular the Women's Convention.

Marc Bossuyt's discussion of affirmative action was based on the general understanding of the concepts of equality and prohibition of discrimination contained in international and regional human rights instruments, as well as a review of cases decided by international and regional judicial and quasi-judicial bodies clarifying the meaning of these concepts. The jurisprudence of the United States Supreme Court, the Belgian Court of Arbitration, and the Court of Justice of the European Communities on the meaning and purpose of affirmative action was also discussed.

Three participants presented case studies on work-related rights. Jenny E. Goldschmidt gave a synopsis of the relevance of the Women's Convention to the work of a semi-judicial authority such as the Equal Treatment Commission of the Netherlands, and also noted a reluctance of Dutch courts to apply the provisions of the Convention. Consuelo Ynares-Santiago pointed out that the Philippine Supreme Court had so far made reference to the Women's Convention in only two decisions. Hamida Laarif gave an overview of the Tunisian Labour Code and its special provisions for women, as well as the role of courts in the protection of the rights of working women.

Several recurrent issues emerged throughout the three-day colloquium. One common conclusion was the importance of an adequate legislative framework, in accordance with international treaty law, to support judges' efforts to ensure just and equitable outcomes for all those who seek redress for their grievances. There was also a sense that notwithstanding constitutional and legislative provisions on equality and non-discrimination, in many jurisdictions statutory law continued to coexist with customary law, rules and traditions which sometimes conflicted with the general law. Here, finding a balance between women's claims for justice, and a community's desire to maintain its traditions presented a significant challenge. International human rights treaty law was regarded as a powerful tool for resolving such conflicts and advocated for a more expansive use of this body of law in order to arrive at decisions to overcome systemic and widespread discrimination against women and girls. The relationship between international human rights law and domestic law, including traditional forms of incorporation and new opportunities for judges to draw on international law were recurrent themes. All agreed on the need for judges' greater awareness and knowledge about international human rights law and its relevance for domestic judicial processes.

The communiqué adopted by participants at the end of the colloquium stressed the critical role played by an independent judiciary in interpreting and applying national laws in a positive manner in the light of human rights principles. Applicable in all countries and in all cultural contexts, participants emphasized that no pretext of culture, custom or religious considerations could be allowed to undermine human rights principles. They recommended measures for increasing awareness and knowledge among the judiciary of international human rights law and the two Conventions, and their domestic use, and called for wider availability of, and accessibility to significant human rights decisions.

In addressing participants at the closing session of the colloquium at which the communiqué was adopted, Emna Aouij expressed her hope that "the recommendations that have arisen from the colloquium will be taken into consideration in your various countries, both in the practice of judicial institutions and in civil life". She continued that she had "no doubt of the effectiveness of the work carried out by the judges who are my colleagues throughout the world, or of their strong contribution to the application of human rights principles in their respective domestic legal systems, in accordance with the norms of the international conventions that their countries have signed".

9

Communiqué

Almost 100 judges and magistrates from most legal cultures and traditions met at the United Nations Office in Vienna to consider the application of international human rights law at the national level as a strategy to advance the rights of women and children, particularly girls.

Recalling the Vienna Declaration and Programme of Action adopted at the World Conference on Human Rights in 1993, and the Beijing Declaration and Platform for Action, adopted at the Fourth World Conference on Women in 1995, participants confirmed that the human rights of women and the girl-child are an inalienable, integral and indivisible part of universal human rights and that the eradication of all forms of discrimination on grounds of sex and gender is a priority objective of the international community.

Participants called on the remaining States which had not ratified the Convention on the Elimination of All Forms of Discrimination against Women to do so as soon as possible so that the goal of universal ratification by the year 2000 could be achieved. They also urged speedy ratification of the optional protocol to the Convention. Participants strongly encouraged the incorporation of universal principles of human rights, elaborated in international human rights treaties, into the national legal system.

Participants recognized that domestic legal provisions were usually gender-neutral and their application could be discriminatory in a non gender-sensitive environment. They drew attention to areas where women and girls are particularly vulnerable, emphasizing the persistence of gender-based violence against women and girls in many settings. They stressed the importance of measures to improve women's and girls' access to justice as well as the importance of the composition of the judiciary reflecting the population it serves. Accordingly, they called for strategies to ensure gender balance in national, regional and international judicial systems.

Participants recognized the universality of human rights - inherent in women and men - and the critical role that an independent judiciary plays in interpreting and applying national laws in a positive manner in the light of human rights principles. They underscored the fact that these human rights principles are applicable in all countries and in all cultural contexts and emphasized that no pretext of culture, custom or religious considerations should be allowed to undermine these principles. They also emphasized the importance of an enlightened and forward-looking interpretation of existing legal texts with a view to achieving equality for women and girls and their enjoyment of human rights without discrimination.

Participants agreed that international human rights principles and the developing jurisprudence within international, regional and national systems enshrine values and principles long recognized as essential to human dignity, well-being and happiness. These international instruments have inspired many of the guarantees of fundamental freedoms and rights in national constitutions and other legislation. These guarantees and provisions, including those which prohibit discrimination, should be construed generously and purposively.

Participants agreed that it was essential to promote respect for and adherence to international and regional human rights norms, particularly those affecting women and girls. They underscored the compatibility and complementarity of international and regional human rights guarantees and recommended that such guarantees must be considered as intrinsic to domestic law in national courts. Participants recommended that all judicial officers be guided by international human rights instruments, including the Convention on the Elimination of All Forms of Discrimination against Women (CEDAW) and the Convention on the Rights of the Child (CRC), in the interpretation and application of national constitutions, laws and practices, including customary law.

Participants agreed that all citizens, especially judges and lawyers, must be aware of and responsive to international human rights law. Judges and lawyers have a responsibility to familiarize themselves with the growing international jurisprudence of human rights, especially that on the protection and promotion of the human rights of women and children. Participants underlined that enduring law reform requires concerted and consistent professional legal activity. They called for all judges to engage in an on-going process of comprehensive, indepth and credible judicial education to integrate CEDAW, CRC and other international human rights instruments into domestic law and decision-making to enhance the social, political and economic lives of women and children and to eradicate violence against them. To that end, participants called on Governments to support the judiciary in these efforts, including through the provision of adequate resources.

Participants recommended that educational establishments, especially law schools and continuing legal education bodies include in their curricula education on CEDAW, CRC and other international human rights instruments and their use domestically.

Participants urged the United Nations to explore the creation of an international judicial education centre to assist countries in the design, development and delivery of judicial education programmes on international human rights instruments and jurisprudence, involving NGOs in this process.

Participants recommended the creation of an international resource centre to advise and assist law-makers, judicial officers, prosecutors and lawyers in developing specific practices and processes required to implement and integrate international human rights instruments into their domestic legal systems. This resource centre should assume responsibility for the collection of significant human rights decisions and make them available to judges worldwide through all available means, including the Internet.

The participants committed themselves to advocate the substance of this communiqué at national level and proactively to promote its application.

Keynote presentations

Nationality: Marriage and family relations

Nationality in International and Regional Human Rights Law*
Christine Chinkin

> *If identity is defined as an awareness of self, national identity would appear to imply the awareness of self within a defined national context.*[1]

The paper attempts to do three things in leading the discussion with respect to women and nationality. First it examines the impact of nationality laws on the lives of women to show the ways in which women have suffered legal and social disadvantage through the application of discriminatory laws. Second it outlines the existing international law regime with respect to nationality, in particular human rights law, and the emerging international and regional jurisprudence on the topic. Third it briefly examines the nature of States' obligations to ensure women's enjoyment of nationality rights.

Nationality, citizenship and women

Nationality defines an individual's relationship with one (or more) nation state(s). Bestowal of nationality is an attribute of state sovereignty that gives rise to rights and duties under international law, as well as domestic law. Under the international law principle of diplomatic protection a State accords its protection to its national if that national suffers a violation of international law in a foreign State that is attributable to the foreign State. The most recognized signifier of nationality is the right to a passport. In state law the closely related concept to nationality is citizenship, that is the relationship between the State and the individual that operates to accord rights and obligations

---

*   This paper draws on the report of the International Law Association (ILA), Committee on Feminism and International Law, Preliminary Report, Taipei, May, 1998, *Women's Equality and Nationality in International Law.* The author (who chairs the Committee) especially thanks the Rapporteur, Dr Karen Knop, for the enormous amount of work and inspiration she has put into the ILA Report.

[1]   Salma Sobhain, 'National identity, fundamentalism and the women's movement in Bangladesh', in V. Moghadam, *Gender and National Identity* (1994), p. 63.

internally. Citizenship, and the rights and obligations that accompany it, depend for the most part on nationality.

Both nationality and citizenship are contested and contingent concepts and both are especially problematic for women. Linguistically, frequent reference to nation-states as the primary actors of international law blurs the distinction between them. Thus nationality (the external association between the State and the individual) gives rise to citizenship rights. However this is not always the case and a distinction can be drawn between citizenship that links an individual to a political entity defined by international law as a sovereign State and nationality that links a person to a sub-state unit based upon ties such as those of ethnicity, culture, or religion. Individuals may claim membership of a nation separate to that of their citizenship of a State. A person may be a citizen of the United Kingdom but identify her or himself as having Welsh, Scottish or Irish nationality. Citizens of the former Yugoslavia had, *inter alia*, Serbian, Croatian, Macedonian nationality.

Claims of nationality, in this sub-state sense enter international law through a number of concepts that are constructed around issues of identity. One example is the right to self-determination. The incompatibility between territorial claims of the republics of the former Yugoslavia and the peoples-based claims of the nations of the former Yugoslavia, both made in the name of self-determination, was at the heart of the conflicts there. Another is genocide where people may be targeted for destruction because of their affiliation to a nation. A third is the claims of indigenous peoples to sovereign rights for their nation. A fourth is the concept of the human rights of national minorities. All such claims are of necessity pitted against the sovereign State and as such are controversial areas of international law. Assertions of women's rights all too frequently become subsumed and lost in these other claims. For example the Council of Europe Framework Convention on National Minorities[2] makes no reference to the ways in which being a female member of a national minority differ from being a male member. Differences based on sex are lost in the emphasis upon the collective, the rights of the national minority, in a way that is not necessarily for the benefit of women's human rights guarantees.

---

[2]   ETS 157, 1 February 1995. As of October 1999, the Convention has not yet entered into force.

The social construction of citizenship raises issues of exclusion and identity for women. The internal political concept of citizenship was traditionally played out in the public arena and derives from membership of the *polis* from which women were excluded. Feminist critique has shown how western liberal philosophy located women in the private realm of the family, excluded from the public arena of politics, law and business. Within that private realm women were denied rights by their subordination to the male family members – husbands, fathers or other relatives. Even when women were included, understandings of the essential attributes of citizenship ensured that they remained 'second class' citizens. For example, two of the quintessential rights and duties of citizenship – payment of taxes and some form of military service - remain problematic for women. Much of women's work is deemed unproductive and is accordingly unpaid. Where it is paid women are frequently in low-paid occupations. Their tax contribution is accordingly low, their economic importance to the State undermined and their citizenship less highly regarded.

Much of the traditional discourse of citizenship centres on the notions of loyalty and preparedness to fight for one's State, which reflect a male understanding of citizenship. Non-participation in military activities places women as lesser citizens. A major feature of women's struggles has been to secure the right to participate in public life through suffrage (possibly a duty to do so such as compulsory voting in Australia). More recent campaigns around women's right to serve in the military on a basis of equality with men, including in combat roles, have an underlying assumption that equal citizenship requires this. (The desirability of a concept of citizenship that assumes conflict and willingness to use force is another debate.) Much of the underlying agenda of women's rights as human rights has been aimed at reconfiguring the concept of citizenship to encompass and to value women's civic position within the State.

More recently the idea of supra-national citizenship has entered the debate, for example through citizenship of the European Union, shared by all nationals of the individual states of the Union.[3] These broad issues of what is encompassed by a gendered analysis of nationality and citizenship and how we could ensure that women's rights are fully guar-

---

[3] European Community Treaty, article 8: (1) Citizenship of the Union is hereby established. Every person holding the nationality of a Member State shall be a citizen of the Union.

anteed within all their configurations merit further consideration. However, the rest of the paper considers the narrower problem of state conferral of nationality upon individuals and the denials of rights of citizenship that follow denial of nationality. Nationality is understood in the following sense:

> *Nationality can be deemed to be the political and legal bond that links a person to a given state and binds him to it with ties of loyalty and fidelity, entitling him to diplomatic protection from that State.*[4]

The problem

A number of links between the State and the individual have become the recognized basis of States' bestowal of nationality upon individuals. The most common are those through birth in a territory, or through birth to a national. The particular issue of the nationality of married women has long been on the agenda of international law and was brought to the fore by feminist campaigners in the League of Nations. The widely accepted principle, the law in all but a handful of States at the end of the first decade of the twentieth century, rested upon the apparently natural assumption that a woman's legal status is acquired through her relationship to a man – first her father and subsequently her husband. Accordingly a woman acquired the nationality of her husband upon marriage, which normally entailed the loss of her nationality of birth. It was considered that her loyalties would be divided if she retained her own nationality and that all her loyalty should be accorded to her husband. This position links with the importance of military duty to a construction of citizenship through the underlying expectation that there might be conflict between the States in question. Thus dual nationality with split loyalties was not regarded as a viable option.

The consequence of this legal position was that a woman could be living in her own country of birth with a foreign husband and no longer have her own nationality. A woman's identity and sense of belonging to a State, and of being important to that State, were disregarded through her reduced status within the place she called home. The State's disinterest in her contribution is indicated by its willingness to let her go. If

---

[4]   *Proposed Amendments to the Naturalization Provisions of the Constitution of Costa Rica*, Inter-American Court of Human Rights, 1984.

the husband acquired a new nationality through naturalization, a choice that was his to make, her nationality also changed. Termination of the marriage would result in her losing her husband's nationality. She would revert to her own nationality, provided the laws of that State so allowed. If they did not (the usual situation) statelessness would be the consequence, and she would be denied rights resting upon nationality in her own homeland. Truly under this regime women have no country, as was famously asserted by Virginia Woolf.

In a state-oriented system of international law a stateless person falls outside the ambit of diplomatic protection of any State and hence statelessness is to be avoided. An interesting gendered example of this is found in the very earliest arbitration claims between the United States and Britain in the 1910 Pecuniary Claims Arbitration procedure under the auspices of the Hague Convention on the Peaceful Settlement of Disputes, 1907. The arbitration concerned claims to land by Americans whose lands had been confiscated by the Lands Claims Commission established by Fiji's British colonial governor. The claims were taken up by the US and Britain on behalf of their own nationals. Then the British played a trump card. The Americans are informed:

> 'That among the American claims advanced in Fiji some, ... were put forward by ... the American con-sul on behalf of the bastard offspring of native women who, *of course*, are not American citizens' (emphasis added).

The commentator continues:

> 'Without citizenship there can be no contest, for ac-cess to international law must depend upon the trans-formation of rightful citizens' claims into those of the representative State. The surprise proves effective: On this basis, the Department of State reduces the number of claims from fifty three to only ten.'[5]

The other 43 claimants remained without a State to take up their claims. The colonial context may have changed but the importance of nationality to international claims has not.

---

[5]   A. Riles, 'The view from the international plane: perspective and scale in the architecture of colonial international law', in E. Darian-Smith and P. Fitzpatrick, *Laws of the Postcolonial* (1999) 127, at p. 130.

Accordingly international campaigns with respect to the nationality of women originally focused upon the necessity to avoid statelessness as a consequence of automatic and forced change of nationality upon marriage. The goal was to ensure that women retained a choice that would allow them to retain a right to a separate nationality. This debate preceded the growth of human rights law, was not framed within the discourse of rights and was not dependent upon concepts of equality. It was an issue of conflicts of laws and as such was the focus of those provisions relevant to women in the Hague Convention on Certain Questions relating to the Conflict of Nationality Laws, 1930.

By the 1930s these concerns had been sufficient to induce considerable change with a number of States now allowing women the right to retain their nationality independent of their marital status. The change was not universal however, and as previously colonized States became independent after the Second World War some imposed such limitations upon the retention of a separate nationality by married women. However recognizing the right of married women to an independent nationality caused conflict with other rights and has entailed some undesirable consequences. These have had their most obvious manifestations in the contexts of immigration, residency rights and the nationality of children.

As States have increasingly restricted entry through immigration controls and visa requirements, different nationalities within a single family unit have created problems. These problems have two dimensions – the position of a woman who marries a man with another nationality and wishes to live with him in her State of nationality, and the woman who wishes to marry a foreign national and to live in his State. The legal issues revolve primarily around rights of entry and residency and abode.

A wife who retains an independent nationality from that of her husband may not have an independent right of residency in his State. She may be able to acquire it through satisfying residency requirements but until she satisfies these requirements she will suffer the legal disadvantage of non-citizenship. Her freedom of movement may be restricted, for example if the marriage terminates through death or divorce, or if the relationship becomes violent. She may find herself trapped in a violent situation until the residency requirements are satisfied for fear of being deported if she leaves the relationship. If the State imposes additional requirements such as language proficiency or knowledge of the country and its history, women may be at a further disadvantage.

Worldwide higher rates of illiteracy are recorded for women and confinement within the family in the new country may be an obstacle to learning the language. The very assumptions that make States more willing to admit foreign wives of national men may work against her ability to become a national. This has been suggested to be especially applicable to older women.

Accordingly, a further campaign at the international level has been to persuade States to ease the residency requirements to enable women married to foreign men to acquire their husband's nationality, voluntarily through facilitated procedures. Thus the Convention on the Nationality of Married Women, 1957 (prepared through the United Nations Commission on the Status of Women) provides:

> Article 3 (1): Each Contracting State agrees that the alien wife of one of its nationals may, at her request, acquire the nationality of her husband through specially privileged naturalization procedures; the grant of such nationality may be subject to such limitations as may be imposed in the interests of national security or public policy.
>
> (2): Each Contracting State agrees that the present Convention shall not be construed as affecting any legislation or judicial practice by which the alien wife of one of its nationals may, at her request, acquire her husband's nationality as a matter of right.

The Convention has not been widely ratified with just over 60 States parties in 1999.

The reverse position is also problematic, that is where the married couple live or wish to live in the State of the wife's nationality. It is in this situation that discrimination is most visible. The laws of a number of countries require a longer residency period for a man to acquire the nationality of his wife than for a wife to acquire that of her husband. Closely connected are discriminatory laws against the entry of the spouses or fiances of women nationals, as opposed to those of male nationals. Although the legal impact falls upon the man, - he may not be allowed entry, or be allowed entry on a restricted basis, he may be deported for wrongdoing, he may not be entitled to the benefits of citizenship, for example security benefits, - it is as a result of sex-based discrimination. The assumption still remains that the wife will follow her husband, that the place of joint residency will be that of his nationality and that there is no need to address the opposite situation. The legal situation is fuelled by gender stereotypes of immigrants. On the one hand there may be an underlying suspicion of arranged 'non-genuine' marriages. On the other, there is an assumption that male immigrants will seek work in the paid workforce, may increase unemployment and be a burden upon the State while women immigrants coming in to marry a male national will be dependant upon him and thus not constitute a burden upon the State. There may also be fears of dilution of the national identity by the entry of alien men. There is the underlying idea that men determine the constitution of the *polis* and that this is distorted by the selection of alien spouses by women nationals, whereas the choice of a foreign wife does not impinge upon this. The foreign wife is assumed to belong to the husband's family, lessening the importance of her relationship with the State.

If the husband does gain entry to the State of his wife's nationality and as a non-national is subsequently deported for some wrongdoing, the wife again faces the dilemma of going with him to a country where she has not got nationality, or separation. The dilemmas are heightened where there are children of the relationship in what have been termed second-generation nationality/equality issues. The problem typically arises through discriminatory laws with respect to the bestowal of nationality. In many States nationality is patrilineal and a child has a right to her or his mother's nationality only if the mother is unmarried, the father is unknown, or is stateless. Again the emphasis is upon ensuring that the child is not stateless, not on ensuring the mother's access to her children. There is still an underlying assumption of the priority of men's rights over the children of a marriage. A mother whose child has a different nationality from her own might have to choose between staying within the relationship or losing custody of the child. If the father leaves her State of nationality and returns to his own, taking the child with him, any rights of access are severely undermined. If the child does not have the same nationality as the mother, the rights of her State to take up claims on her behalf are limited. Even if the mother and child are living in her State of origin the child might be legally regarded as a foreigner and thus be ineligible for rights such as access to State education, the position in the famous *Unity Dow*[6] case. Siblings living with the same mother may have different nationalities and thus different entitlements.

---

[6] *Unity Dow v. A-G Botswana* [1991] LRC (Const.) 575; [1992] LRC (Const.) 627.

It need hardly be added that in many of these situations there is an interlocking of gender and race discrimination. Restrictive immigration and residency requirements often have racially discriminatory underpinnings. The conflation of these with gender stereotyping and patriarchal assumptions about the place of a woman as subordinate to her husband, as not entering the paid workforce and as free to move as he determines, play out in the legal systems of many States. These dilemmas shift the debate from that of conflicts of laws and concerns about statelessness to those of non-discrimination and equality, the language of human rights. The scale of the movements of peoples at the end of the twentieth century and the gendered dimensions of those movements have added to the practical consequences of these problems. There is insufficient time to look fully at these but the millions of women migrating to seek work in foreign States and the horrific levels of trafficking in women indicate the numbers of women who are potentially in foreign States, often in positions of powerlessness and increased vulnerability. They become susceptible to violent relationships but entering into one may still incur loss of their own nationality. The incident of forms of sexual violence against such women, including rape, adds another dimension to the problem, especially in the context of the nationality of children. A woman may also marry a migrant man but may then have to face his legal exclusion from her State of nationality.

Treaty provisions in international and regional human rights law

Mainstream human rights treaties

The Universal Declaration of Human Rights states in its article 15 (1): Everyone has the right to a nationality. Article 15 (2) states: No one shall be arbitrarily deprived of his nationality nor denied the right to change his nationality.

Article 15 asserts a right to nationality in the abstract, not the right to nationality determined in any particular way. The bestowal of nationality remains a state prerogative, although with some limitations imposed by international law, notably that there must be a 'genuine link' between the person and the State according nationality.

The International Covenant on Civil and Political Rights states in article 24 (3): Every child has the right to acquire a nationality.

Although the right to nationality is included within the Universal Declaration it is not in the International Covenant on Civil and Political Rights, 1966. Article 24 does not assert which State's nationality the

25

child has a right to – that of birth, or descent from the mother or the father, or both. This provision creates a rights holder, but no state with the corollary duty. The Convention on the Rights of the Child, article 7 reiterates this principle. Only the Inter-American Convention on Human Rights, 1969, article 20 (2) (see below) and the African Charter on the Rights and Welfare of a Child, 1990, article 6 (4) provide a fall-back situation, that is that a child with no other nationality entitlement acquires that of her or his place of birth.

In General Comment 17 on article 24, the Human Rights Committee stated:

> …..

> 8. Special attention should also be paid, in the context of the protection to be granted to children, to the right of every child to acquire a nationality, as provided for in article 24, paragraph 3. While the purpose of this provision is to prevent a child from being afforded less protection by society and the State because he is stateless, it does not necessarily make it an obligation for States to give their nationality to every child born in their territory. However, States are required to adopt every appropriate measure, both internally and in cooperation with other States, to ensure that every child has a nationality when he is born. In this connection, no discrimination with regard to the acquisition of nationality should be admissible under internal law as between legitimate and children born out of wedlock or of stateless parents or based on the nationality status of one or both of the parents. The measures adopted to ensure that children have a nationality should always be referred to in reports by States parties.

General Comment 17 makes no reference to laws that discriminate between the mother and father with respect to bestowal of nationality.

Claims have been brought under other articles of the International Covenant on Civil and Political Rights, notably the free-standing discrimination provision of article 26, the right to privacy of article 17, and the protection of the family of article 23.

Regional conventions

Neither the European Convention on the Protection of Human Rights and Fundamental Freedoms, 1950, nor the African Charter on Human and Peoples' Rights, 1981 have an article on nationality. Both contain articles prohibiting discrimination with respect to the rights guaranteed within the respective treaty.

The African Charter states in article 18 (3): The State shall ensure the elimination of every discrimination against women and also ensure the protection of the rights of the woman and child as stipulated in international declarations and conventions.

This is a unique provision that allows the 'reading in' of any other international declaration or convention that guarantees women's rights to be free from discrimination, including the Convention on the Elimination of All Forms of Discrimination against Women.

The American Declaration on the Rights and Duties of Man, 1948 states that every person has the right to the nationality to which he is entitled by law and to change it, if he so wishes, for the nationality of any other country that is willing to grant it to him.

The American Convention on Human Rights, 1969, states in article 20 (1): Every person has the right to a nationality. Article 20 (2) states that every person has the right to the nationality of the State in whose territory he was born if he does not have the right to any other nationality.

Article 20 (3): No one shall be arbitrarily denied of his nationality or of the right to change it.

Convention on the Elimination of All Forms of Discrimination against Women, 1979 (The Women's Convention)

The fullest guarantee with respect to the nationality of women is contained in the Women's Convention.

> Article 9 (1): States Parties shall grant women equal rights with men to acquire, change or retain their nationality. They shall ensure in particular that neither marriage to an alien nor change of nationality by the husband during marriage shall automatically change the nationality of the wife, render her stateless or force upon her the nationality of the husband.

Article 9 (2): States Parties shall grant women equal rights with men with respect to the nationality of their children.

Article 9 (1) addresses the need for women to retain an independent nationality and not to be rendered stateless, while article 9 (2) addresses bestowal of nationality upon children. However both (1) and (2) also address the question within the framework of equality. They do not guarantee to women the right to choose their nationality, nor that of their children. They give women the same rights as men in these matters. Thus if the State denies nationality through descent to both parents, relying upon place of birth, the mother cannot claim from that State the right to bestow her nationality upon the child (unless it is allowed by the law of her own State).

Article 9 goes to the core of States' relationships with individuals and reaches into the private domain that is deemed outside the scope of human rights law by many governments. That this remains unacceptable to many States is shown by the number of reservations that have been entered to it. As of May 1999 the following States had made reservations or interpretive declarations to either article 9 (1) or (2), or both: Algeria; Bahamas; Cyprus; Egypt; Fiji; France; Iraq; Jordan; Kuwait; Lebanon; Malaysia; Morocco; Singapore (without explicit reference to article 9); Tunisia; Turkey. In addition to these reservations directed towards nationality as such, other States have made broad reservations that subordinate the Convention to their national law or religion, for example Pakistan.

These reservations vary with respect to their precision and the giving of reasons for them. The fullest explanation is provided by Egypt:

> Reservation to the text of article 9, paragraph 2, concerning the granting to women of equal rights with men with respect to the nationality of their children, without prejudice to the acquisition by a child born of a marriage of the nationality of his father. This is in order to prevent a child's acquisition of two nationalities where his (sic) parents are of different nationalities, since this may be prejudicial to his future. It is clear that the child's acquisition of his father's nationality is the procedure most suitable for the child and that this does not infringe upon the principle of equality between men and women, since it is custom-

ary for a woman to agree, upon marrying an alien, that her children shall be of the father's nationality.

This replicates, without comment, many of the assumptions discussed above: that not being able to bestow her nationality upon her children is not prejudicial to the child or the mother; that it is in some sense 'natural' for the child to receive the father's nationality; and that it is 'customary' for the mother to agree to this (Where? Among how many States? What form does this agreement take?).

The lack of any right of individual petition to the Committee on the Elimination of Discrimination against Women (the CEDAW Committee) has meant that the Committee has not been able to develop any contextual understanding of article 9 on the basis of claims made under it. It has however prepared a General Recommendation that refers to article 9. General Recommendation 21, Equality in marriage and family relations (13th session, 1992) stresses the significance of the article for the status of women within the family (precisely the reason for its large number of reservations). Paragraph six of General Recommendation 21 states:

> Nationality is critical to full participation in society. In general States confer nationality on those who are born in that country. Nationality can also be acquired by reason of settlement or granted for humanitarian reasons such as statelessness. Without status as nationals or citizens, women are deprived of the right to vote or to stand for public office and may be denied access to public benefits and a choice of residence. Nationality should be capable of change by an adult woman and should not be arbitrarily removed because of marriage or dissolution of marriage or because her husband or father changes his nationality.

This asserts women's rights to their own nationality based on the denial of civil status and the enjoyment of other civil and political rights and social and economic rights if they are denied nationality. It does not address the question of bestowal of nationality upon children. In the context of article 15 (equality before the law), the General Recommendation, paragraph 10 continues that:

> Migrant women who live and work temporarily in another country should be permitted the same rights as

men to have their spouses, partners and children join them.

The CEDAW Committee has also questioned States on their application of article 9 in the reporting process and has referred to their non-implementation of it in concluding comments. In both General Recommendation 21 and its concluding comments, the CEDAW Committee has stressed the need for legislative, administrative and judicial conformity with article 9 for those States that have not reserved it, and for withdrawal of reservations and subsequent compliance for those that have reserved it. In addition some States have objected to reservations to article 9 in accordance with the terms of article 28 of the Women's Convention and article 19 of the Vienna Convention on the Law of Treaties, that is that they are incompatible with the object and purpose of the treaty (e.g. Denmark, Finland, Germany, Mexico, the Netherlands, Norway and Sweden). However since the objecting States maintain that the Convention remains in force as between themselves and the reserving States, objection amounts to little more than an official record of displeasure.

There has been some success in that the following States have removed reservations to article 9: Ireland, Jamaica, Liechtenstein, Republic of Korea, Thailand and the United Kingdom.

Other

Attempts have been made to minimize the adverse effects for individuals living within States whose nationality they do not have. One approach has been to agree to human rights standards for non-nationals. The human rights treaties discussed above are not restricted to nationals. For example the International Covenant on Civil and Political Rights is applicable 'to all individuals within [the State Party's] territory' (article 2 (1)). The International Convention on the Protection of the Rights of All Migrant Workers and Members of their Families, 1990 covers a particular group of non-nationals. This Convention, which is not in force, addresses the particular human rights abuses suffered by those who work in another State as migrant workers, many of whom are women. While it attempts to cover some of the disadvantages referred to above for women it does not confer any nationality rights as such.

a)   Human rights of all migrant workers and members of their families

> Article 29: Each child of a migrant worker shall have the right to a name, to registration of birth and to a nationality.

This provision again is focused on the undesirability of statelessness and does not address the question of which State should accord nationality (place of birth, mother's State of nationality, father's State of nationality.) The provision provides an entitlement without any duty holder. The non-discrimination clause again is with respect to the rights set forth in the Convention and is not free-standing.

More detailed rights are accorded to migrant workers whose presence in the State of employment is 'documented' or 'regular.'

b) Other rights of migrant workers and members of their families who are documented or in a regular situation

> Article 44 (2): States Parties shall take measures that they deem appropriate and that fall within their competence to facilitate the reunification of migrant workers with their spouses or persons who have with the migrant worker a relationship that, according to applicable law, produces effects equivalent to marriage, as well as with their minor unmarried children.

Such documented workers are accorded equality with nationals with respect to a number of rights, including access to education, health and some social services.

> Article 50 (1): In the case of death of a migrant worker or dissolution of marriage, the State of employment shall favourably consider granting family members of that migrant worker residing in that State on the basis of family reunion an authorization to stay; the State of employment shall take into account the length of time they have already resided in that State.

While this provision attempts to redress the lack of residency entitlements of family members of a migrant worker it focuses on the death of the migrant worker. It would not therefore cover a woman migrant worker who marries a national who dies; her continued residency would rest upon her own status. Further, the Convention does not bestow a right of continued residency, only a right to having the question examined 'favourably' by the State.

The General Assembly Declaration on the Human Rights of Individuals Who are not Nationals of the Country in Which They Live (GA Res. 40/144, 1985) provides a catalogue of fundamental rights for aliens including the right of the spouse of an alien lawfully in the territory to accompany, join and stay with the alien. However, as a General Assembly resolution, the Declaration is not legally binding. This provision is also weakened by the assertion that it is subject to national legislation and due authorization and the limited rights recommended for non-nationals do not equate with those for citizenship.

Other international law treaties also deal with the question of nationality. The Montevideo Convention on the Nationality of Women, 1933 states that there shall be no distinction based on sex as regards nationality, in their legislation or in their practice. The Montevideo Convention on Nationality, 1933 notes that neither matrimony nor its dissolution affects the nationality of the husband or wife or of their children. These provisions show that treaty law in the Americas was the first to emphasize the importance of non-discrimination in nationality laws.

The European Convention on Nationality, 1997 states in article 4 (d): Neither marriage nor the dissolution of a marriage between a national of a State Party and an alien, nor the change of nationality by one of the spouses during marriage, shall automatically affect the nationality of the other spouse.

Article 5 on non-discrimination of the same Convention states in paragraph (1): The rules of a State Party on nationality shall not contain distinctions or include any practice which amounts to discrimination on the grounds of sex, religion, race, colour or national or ethnic origin.

Article 6 requires States to facilitate the acquisition of nationality for spouses of nationals (with no differentiation between husband and wife); and children of one of its nationals (again with no gender differentiation). The European Convention takes a forward-looking approach to dual, or multiple, nationality as the appropriate solution and provides a framework for cooperation between States in this regard. As of this writing, it was not yet in force.

Jurisprudence of human rights bodies

The Human Rights Committee

As stated, the CEDAW Committee has not had an opportunity to apply article 9 in a contested situation. Since there is no equivalent provision to article 9 in other human rights treaties, such situations have been argued in the terms of other provisions. The first time the Human Rights Committee had to address the question showed the interlocking of questions of nationality and ethnicity. The case of *Lovelace v. Canada* (1981) concerned nationality in the sense of belonging to a substate unit, in this case membership of the Maliseet Indians of Canada. Sandra Lovelace was born a member of the band but upon her marriage outside the band, in accordance with the terms of the Canadian Indian Act, she lost her right of abode on the Indian reserve. This would not have been the case for a male member of the band who had married a non-Indian woman. Lovelace brought a case under the First Optional Protocol to the International Covenant on Civil and Political Rights and argued that this violated articles 2, 3 (equal enjoyment of the rights under the Covenant), 23 (the right to family life), 26 (the free-standing equality provision) and 27 (the right of individual members of a minority to enjoy their own culture).

The Human Rights Committee analyzed the case solely in terms of article 27 and found that Canada was in breach of this position. It found that Lovelace was entitled to claim the benefits of article 27 and that it was 'natural' as an ethnic Maliseet Indian that she would seek to return 'to the environment in which she was born' on the dissolution of her marriage. Refusing her this right was not necessary to preserve the identity of the tribe.

The Committee was therefore able to avoid considering article 26 – the question of equality. Three points might however be noted. First, the decision did not have to address the situation where she wanted to live on the reservation during her marriage, either with or without her husband. The factual situation illustrates how group identity resists the inclusion of 'alien' men through marriage with national women. There may have been the added concern that the band had no jurisdiction over men who were not members of it. Again, jurisdiction over women is readily asserted as women are absorbed into the legal structures of their husband's society while men retain their own identity. Second, this was the case even though Lovelace asserted that her band was organized on matrilineal principles and denied that there was any Indian tradition of patrilineality. Third, the case raised contested notions of equality in that

33

Lovelace, a Maliseet Indian, claimed sex-based equality over the claims of the tribe to determine its own members – the latter claim supported by the dominant community, the Canadian Government, despite domestic equality laws.

The second case concerned the question of entry of foreign husbands as opposed to foreign wives into Mauritius. In *Aumeeruddy-Cziffra v. Mauritius* (1981) Mauritian women complained that the restrictions imposed upon the right of entry of foreign husbands constituted discrimination under articles 2, 3 and 26 of the ICCPR and also violated articles 17, 23 and 25. The first question was who constituted victims of the alleged violations. The Committee found that 17 women who had not married foreign husbands could not be considered victims of discrimination since their right to marry under article 23 (2) or the right to equality of spouses under article 23 (4) were not affected.

This is a narrow perception of 'victim' that ignores the fact that the existence of such laws might in fact restrict choices and impose upon Mauritian women restraints that do not exist for Mauritian men. In the later case of *Toonen v. Australia* (concerning the existence of laws criminalizing homosexuality) the Committee held that the applicants had standing even though the laws had not been applied to them. The existence of discriminatory laws was sufficient to establish breach of equality requirements. It is hoped that if the present case were brought today, this approach would be taken.

In the Mauritian case the Committee found that 'not only the future possibility of deportation, but the existing precarious residence situation of foreign husbands in Mauritius represents ... an interference ... with the family life of the Mauritian wives and their husbands.' Since this was in accordance with Mauritian law it was not unlawful, so consideration had to be given to whether, in any other way, it contravened the Covenant. It was found to be discriminatory. In what is perhaps the strongest language of the case the Committee held that 'the authors [of the complaint to the Human Rights Committee] who are married to foreign nationals are suffering from the adverse consequences of the statutes discussed above only because they are women'. The statutes do not apply the same degree of control to foreign wives. Despite this strong statement of a free-standing principle the Committee then turns again to the implications of the discrimination on family rights, thus reinforcing the focus upon the protection of the family. The case finds sex-based discrimination, but in conjunction to family rights under article 23. The same underlying concerns about the entry of foreign husbands came to the fore yet again in this case. The Government suggested that foreign men were associated with subversive activities with the assumption that their wives would not be able to control them.

Regional human rights bodies

The institutions established under the European Convention on the Protection of Human Rights and Fundamental Freedoms have faced similar issues. In *Family K and W v. The Netherlands* (1985) the State allowed the alien wives of Dutch citizens to obtain nationality but not husbands of Dutch wives. A spouse with Dutch nationality could not be expelled. However since the European Convention does not provide a right to nationality, the European Commission on Human Rights found that article 14 (the non-discrimination provision) did not apply. It is only discrimination with respect to one of the rights conferred by the Convention that is prohibited. Thus it is important to peg the claim to a substantive provision such as article 8. This was done in a case brought against the United Kingdom. In *Abdulaziz, Cabales and Balkandi* (1985) the Government had presented statistical and social data to show why it was reasonable to take restrictive measures against the entry of foreign husbands. In this case the wives too were non-nationals but had residency rights. The Government had submitted that differences of treatment on the basis of sex were reasonable and that the measures were proportionate to the ends sought. Thus it argued that the measures protected the domestic labour market at a time of high unemployment: men were more likely to seek work than females and thus male immigrants would have a greater impact on the employment situation than women. Further, restrictions on the entry of foreign men would lessen the strains on society imposed by immigration. In response it was pointed out that this reflects an outmoded understanding of the role of both women and men in the labour force, and that the racial prejudice of the population of the United Kingdom could not be used to justify racial discrimination.

The Court noted that 'advancement of the equality of the sexes is today a major goal in the member States of the Council of Europe. This means that very weighty reasons would have to be advanced before a difference of treatment on the ground of sex could be regarded as compatible with the Convention.' The Government had not satisfied this high standard and accordingly there was discrimination contrary to article 14 that amounted to a violation of article 8 (the right to family life). In its analysis of what constitutes discrimination the Court used the 1967 United Nations Declaration on the Elimination of Discrimination against Women. In one of the most 'mean-spirited' responses to a judgment of the European Court, the Government amended the rules to remove from foreign wives and fiancées the privileges of entry that they had previously enjoyed. This form of 'equalizing down' removed the discriminatory elements from the regulations, but to no-one's benefit.

The need to find a 'peg' upon which article 14 can be attached has led the European Court (with some inconsistency in its jurisprudence) to allow alien husbands of national wives to stay where to exclude them would violate the right to family life under article 8. For example, *Berrehab v. The Netherlands* (1988) involved the exclusion of a Moroccan husband from the Netherlands. There was violation of article 8 because this would deny him access to his Dutch daughter. In response, the Dutch Government made promises of compliance but offered no legal guarantees. In *Beldjoudi v. France* (1992) the Court held that to deport a long-settled Algerian whose residence in France rested upon his French wife's nationality would disregard his family life. In this case one judge referred to a concept of 'integrated aliens' who should be assimilated to nationals because of their long and established family life. Again such reasoning emphasizes family life which may place pressure on a wife to maintain it against her own best interests.

None of these cases tackle the question of nationality directly, a clear result of the fact that women's right to equality in nationality questions is not specified in the relevant human rights treaties. The tying of non-discrimination to a right under the International Covenant on Civil and Political Rights gives an emphasis, for example on family life, which feeds into traditional understandings of the role of women within the family, as well as the nature of the family. This basis excludes any consideration of the nationality rights of unmarried women, or of women in non-traditional family relationships, for example lesbian relationships. In many cases the disadvantage is felt by men, but is based on discrimination against national women.

The question of women's nationality was squarely in issue in the *Proposed Amendments to the Naturalization Provisions of the Constitution of Costa Rica,* an advisory opinion of the Inter-American Court of Human Rights. Costa Rica was seeking amendments to its Constitution with respect to the acquisition of nationality through naturalization. The provision of the existing Constitution that is relevant to the nationality of women stated:

> Article 14: The following are Costa Ricans by naturalization:

> (5) A foreign woman who by marriage to a Costa Rican loses her nationality or who indicates her desire to become a Costa Rican.

The amendment proposed by the Special Committee of the Legislative Assembly (intended to restrict naturalization) stated:

> Article 14: The following are Costa Ricans by naturalization:

> (4) A foreign woman who by marriage to a Costa Rican loses her nationality or who after two years of marriage to a Costa Rican and the same period of residence in the country, indicates her desire to take on our nationality;

Another proposed amendment to the amendment presented by the Deputies of the Special Committee stated:

> A foreigner, who by marriage to a Costa Rican loses his or her nationality or who after two years of marriage to a Costa Rican and the same period of residence in the country, indicates his or her desire to take on the nationality of the spouse.

The Court noted that the proposed amendments did not purport to withdraw nationality from any person, nor to deny the right to change nationality. They therefore were not contrary to article 20. It recognized that proposed amendment 14.4 would impose some hardship in that a foreigner who loses nationality upon marrying a Costa Rican national would have to wait at least two years before naturalization because of the residency requirement. In the meantime that person would be stateless. The period would be even longer for foreigners who had to leave the country and thus would not satisfy the two year period. They 'would continue to be stateless for an indefinite period until they have completed all the concurrent requirements.' The Court advised that proposal did not directly violate article 20 however, in that it did not purport to create statelessness, which would be caused by the laws of the State whose nationals lose nationality upon marriage to a Costa Rican. The Court did 'reflect on current trends of international law' including the Convention on the Nationality of Married Women referred to above and commented that the proposal ran counter to the intention of that Convention.

However the Court advised that the proposed amendment would be discriminatory. Article 24 of the American Convention makes all persons 'equal before the law.' Draft article 14 was discriminatory in that it gave women but not men who marry Costa Ricans special status before the law. The Court noted that this position was influenced by two assumptions: that members of the family should have the same nationality and notions of paternal authority. The assumption is that it is the husband who is privileged by the law to determine the place of domicile and to administer marital property. The Court then looked at the history of opposition to these notions, based on the emerging human rights principles of non-discrimination and concluded that the 'different treatment envisaged for spouses... cannot be justified and must be considered as discriminatory.' The Court also advised that the alternative proposed amendment was, however, based upon equality between spouses and was therefore consistent with the Convention.

Conclusion

The paucity of human rights provisions directly addressing questions of non-discrimination in the acquisition and enjoyment of nationality and the fact that the Women's Convention (with its more far-reaching article 9) is not subject to individual complaints has meant that there has not been an opportunity to address the questions that have been faced in domestic courts, such as in *Unity Dow*. However, taking the provisions on nationality together with the norm of non-discrimination gives a clear direction with respect to the requirements of international law. Ensuring women's full enjoyment of their human rights through appropriate nationality laws cuts across both civil and political rights and economic, social and cultural rights and requires positive State action.

Following the methodology for the application of human rights obligations which presents duty holders with multilayered obligations, States are required to respect, protect and fulfil human rights.[7] The primary duty to respect requires States to refrain from direct violations of rights, for example not to enact discriminatory legislation or to uphold discriminatory judicial decisions. It also requires them to take positive steps to ensure appropriate legislation and practices. The duty to protect imposes a secondary obligation to prevent third parties from violating

---

[7]   Henry Shue, Basic Rights, Subsistence, Affluence and United States Foreign Policy (1980).

38

rights and the duty to fulfil denotes a tertiary obligation to provide the necessary resources for achievement of the right. Unlike so many other violations of women's human rights, the denial of nationality to women or their children on an equal basis with men involves no non-state actor. It is within the hands of Governments to fulfil their obligations by such actions as passing and implementing appropriate legislation, by complying with the spirit as well as the decisions of human rights bodies; by providing gender training to immigration officials, by incorporating the Women's Convention with the inclusion of article 9 into their domestic law; by becoming parties to the Optional Protocol to the Women's Convention; and by giving effect to dual nationality as the most just and fair way of addressing these questions. Above all States need to understand how the denial of nationality rights for women undercuts their enjoyment of other human rights through the denial of the basic legal protections of citizenship, of equality within the family, of identity and belonging, and of personal security and freedom from violence.

Marriage and Family Relations
Emna Aouij

Introduction

Since its adoption by the United Nations General Assembly in December 1979, already 20 years ago, the Convention on the Elimination of All Forms of Discrimination against Women has constituted the main basis for formulating international, regional and national policies and programmes to promote the implementation of the basic rights of women. The Convention is therefore a driving force for slow but far-reaching change and a factor that promotes the liberation of women throughout the world.

The Convention on the Elimination of All Forms of Discrimination against Women, like any human rights convention, cannot exist simply at the international level; its overall effectiveness depends on its validity within domestic legal systems and is determined to a large extent by the will of States to ensure the complete application of international law at the national level.

The United Nations system rests on the principle that States which ratify international human rights instruments do so in good faith and are prepared to accept that their domestic legislation and policies in the field of human rights are subjected to international monitoring.

This monitoring is carried out through the procedure of submitting reports, which constitutes the sole framework within which senior officials are called upon to provide information on the laws and policies applied by their Governments in the area of human rights.

Although the obligation to submit a report to a treaty body does not oblige States parties to remedy all forms of discrimination and inequality that still exist in their domestic law — the mechanism of reservations comes into play — it is encouraging to note that many States take their obligations under the human rights instruments seriously and introduce major changes in, and amendments to, their legislation and machinery to meet their international obligations.

In the light of the reports submitted by the countries of the Maghreb region, Tunisia, the Libyan Arab Jamahiriya, Morocco and Algeria, after their accession to the Convention, it is possible to judge progress made in the process of emancipating women and identify obstacles still to be overcome in order to achieve the objectives of the Convention. These countries ratified the Convention with major reservations relating, in particular, to article 16 concerning marriage and family relations.

Some of these countries have made significant changes in their codes and laws on family status in order to bring certain legal provisions into line with international law. The family status of women in the Maghreb is subject to a dual requirement: that of affiliation with a cultural identity and an Arab-Muslim civilization, on the one hand, and that of being open to the universal values of the modern world and the needs of development, on the other. This ambivalence has an impact on legal systems in the area of personal status. The principal source of inspiration for these rules will remain Muslim law, although adapted to the circumstances of the particular period and of modernity.

In order to gain an overall view of the matrimonial rights of women in the Maghreb, we shall briefly consider these rights as a marriage is concluded, during marriage and upon its dissolution and view them within the context of the application of private international law.

Entering into marriage

Wife's age

Regulating the marriage age is an important factor in the lives of girls because it protects them against early marriage and safeguards their health and right to an education.

The marriage age for girls throughout the countries of the Maghreb varies, according to their legislation, from 15 to 17, while it is 18 years of age under international law.

Major amendments were made to the Tunisian Personal Status Code under the Act of 12 July 1993.

Tunisian legislation has introduced a new provision which emancipates young wives of 17 years of age and will enable them to come of legal age as a result of the marriage: new article 53 provides that "Minors may attain majority through marriage if they are older than 17 years of age and this status shall relate to the management of their civil or commercial affairs". This new situation places the two spouses on an equal footing.

Husband's religion

Women do not have the right to marry non-Muslims, whereas men of the Muslim religion may marry Christians, Jews or women of any other religion. This prohibition is set forth in domestic legal regulations, and judges have the right to dissolve any marriage between a Muslim woman and a non-Muslim man: in Morocco, this type of marriage is prohibited under article 29 of the Moudawana (Code of Personal Law); in Algeria, article 31 of the 1981 Family Code is also categorical in this regard in that it provides that a Muslim woman may not marry a non-Muslim man. This also constitutes an obstacle to marriage in Tunisia, but was introduced through administrative means, namely a circular issued by the Ministry of Justice in November 1973 making it impossible for civil registry officers to perform such a marriage. Nevertheless, in Algeria and Tunisia, this prohibition is lifted if the husband converts to Islam. In the Libyan Arab Jamahiriya, the same prohibition against the marriage of a Muslim woman and a non-Muslim man exists.

Although this type of prohibition can be explained on the basis of the logic of Muslim law, it is nevertheless not compatible with the provisions of the international human rights instruments (declarations, covenants and conventions) which recognize that women have the same right as men to choose a spouse.

The obligation of the matrimonial guardian

Except in Tunisia, a woman does not have the right to enter into marriage herself even though she is of legal age: her guardian arranges for it in her place. Accordingly, article 11 of the Algerian Family Code provides that: "The conclusion of a marriage for a woman shall be incumbent upon her matrimonial guardian, who is either her father or one of her close relatives. The judge shall be the matrimonial guardian for a person who has no father or close relatives".

All guardians must be males, have good judgement and be of legal age. These same rules were reproduced in article 7 of the Libyan Marriage Code.

Although the situation in Morocco was similar to those in Algeria and the Libyan Arab Jamahiriya, the Moudawana reform introduced through the Act of September 1993 requires real consent on the part of the woman to marriage and prohibits any constraint on the part of the wali (legal guardian). Furthermore, article 12 reads as follows: "A woman of legal age who is fatherless shall have the right to conclude marriage herself or to delegate the task to a wali (guardian) of her choice". Several associations have felt that the distinction between a female orphan of legal age and a female non-orphan should be avoided on ethical grounds.

In Tunisia, article 6 (the new text) provides that marriages of minors (girls and boys) shall be subject to the consent of their guardians — the father or his representative — and the mother, whereas girls who have attained legal age are free to marry without a matrimonial guardian.

Thus, mediation by the woman's guardian for the purpose of contracting marriage is contrary to the basic principles of equality of rights between men and women and of their complete freedom when the marriage is entered into.

Polygamy

With the exception of Tunisia, which has prohibited polygamy since 1956, the legislation of the other Maghreb countries allows men to enter into marriage with a second, third or fourth woman, although this possibility is linked to certain conditions.

In Tunisia, the enactment of the Personal Status Code abolished polygamy in 1956, and article 18 provides penal sanctions for anyone who violates the law.

In Morocco, under the reform introduced, polygamy is subject to monitoring by a judge, and there is a requirement to inform the two wives. Article 30 of the Moudawana thus requires that the first wife must be informed of the intention of her husband to take another wife. Likewise, the latter must be informed that her future husband is already married. A woman has the right to ask her future husband to undertake a commitment not to take another wife and to grant her the right to dissolve the marriage if this commitment is broken. If the woman has not reserved the right of this option and her husband enters into another marriage, she may bring the matter before a judge in order to determine the damage caused to her by the additional union. In all cases, if there are grounds to fear that an injustice will be caused to the wife, the judge concerned will deny polygamy.

In Algeria, article 8 of the Family Code stipulates that it is permitted to contract marriage with more than one wife within the limits of the Shariah (religious law) if the reason for doing so is justified and if the conditions guaranteeing fairness and the intention to ensure it are present and after the current and future wives have been informed in advance. Either woman may institute legal proceedings against the husband in case of fraud or seek a divorce in case of lack of consent.

Under article 3 of the Libyan Code, polygamy is subject to authorization by the competent court after it has considered the social situation of the husband and his material and physical possibilities.

The right to polygamy disturbs the balance in the family and among the children, affects the dignity of the wife and is contrary to the principle of equality under the Convention.

Married life

With regard to relations between the spouses, in all the Maghreb countries, the husband is still the head of the family, and the wife must obey him in accordance with practices and customs. This results in a situation of inequality between the spouses.

The 1993 reforms introduced in article 23 of the Tunisian Personal Status Code abolished the requirement that the wife must obey her husband and enshrined a new concept of relations between the spouses marked by greater respect for the rights of the individual person and based on the partnership and shared responsibility of the husband and wife in managing and taking decisions on matters relating to the family and children, including education, travel and financial transactions. These new provisions are more in conformity with the spirit and letter of the two international conventions on the rights of women and the rights of children.

Dissolution of marriage

With the exception of the Tunisian Personal Status Code, most Maghreb legislation does not permit complete equality between men and women with regard to the right to divorce. The power of men is very broad in this area, compared to that of women, who have the right to seek a divorce only in certain limited cases.

In Tunisia, the law establishes judicial divorce and complete equality concerning recourse to divorce. In order to help women and children claim their rights to alimony and divorce payments, Tunisian legislators are establishing the post of family judge, who will seek to bring about reconciliation, take urgent measures and ensure the smooth operation of legal procedures. In order to guarantee the effective protection of minor children and their mothers from the negative effects of a divorce, the family judge is to make three attempts to reconcile the couple before pronouncing the divorce decision. He also sees to it that the children are not deprived of food following the divorce or as a result of non-payment of alimony by the father. Through the fund to guarantee alimony payments established under the Act of July 1993, the judge ensures that the children and their mother are able to continue to lead a dignified life.

In Morocco, the Moudawana gives the man the possibility of repudiating his wife at any time. Admittedly, the changes introduced in 1993 have made this possibility subject to authorization by a judge; nevertheless, such authorization may be granted when the husband continues his efforts to obtain a divorce even if the wife does not consent. A wife may seek a divorce only when this power has been given to her by virtue of the "right of option" (article 44) or in the cases established by law. Nevertheless, article 52, paragraph 2, provides for the payment to a wife who has been repudiated of a consolation donation (moutaa), which is determined by the judge.

The same rules govern divorce in Algeria and the Libyan Arab Jamahiriya. In addition, the legislation of these two countries provides that a wife has a right to damages for the loss that she has incurred through a divorce, a situation which makes it possible to avoid breaking up the family as a result of a possible lack of income caused by the divorce.

The right to custody of the children

The wife has the priority right to custody of children under Maghreb legislation, which recognizes traditional Muslim law in this area.

In judicial practice, the right of custody may be accorded to the father in the following cases: if the mother is a non-Muslim, the children risk being brought up in a religion other than that of their father; if the mother is a Muslim, the father may be deprived of his authority if the mother chooses a residence which is far from that of the father. These rules are governed by the provisions of articles 107 and 108 of the Moudawana of Morocco and are very similar to the rules laid down in the Libyan and Algerian codes.

In Tunisia, new article 67 provides that, if the marriage is dissolved during the lifetime of the spouses, custody of the children is granted either to one of them or to a third person. The judge decides in this regard by taking into consideration the higher interests of the children. Except in specific cases, the right to custody of children is essentially based on their interests in all the Maghreb countries.

Legal representation of children

In most of the Maghreb countries, the legal representation of a minor is the sole responsibility of the father, who carries out this task throughout his life.

The role of the mother in this area does not exist in the Libyan Arab Jamahiriya, is limited in Algeria since the mother can assume it only after the father's death, and is regulated in Morocco since the law gives precedence to the father and a secondary place is held by the mother, who can assume this role only if the father dies or loses the capacity to represent the children under the 1993 reforms.

Only Tunisia, particularly after the July 1993 reforms, has allowed the mother to have the same rank as the father in administering the personal affairs and property of minors. Furthermore, if custody of the child is granted to the mother, she enjoys guardianship prerogatives with regard to travel by the child, his education and the management of financial accounts. The judge may grant the powers of guardianship to a mother who has custody of a child if the guardian is prevented from carrying out this task or for any other cause which is detrimental to the interests of the child (problems of an unknown residence or a difficult situation on the part of the guardian).

45

In the cases we have cited, when the spouses are Moroccan, Algerian or Libyan nationals, the law is more favourable to the men than the women. What is the situation when one of the partners, either the man or the woman, is an alien? What is the situation with regard to families resulting from mixed marriages and what legal norm is applied in cases where there is a conflict between laws?

The rule for settling conflicts favours the national law of the husband in force when the marriage was performed and this rule applies in the same way throughout the countries of the Maghreb, including Tunisia, except when there are specific bilateral conventions which provide otherwise. This situation has been changing in Tunisia owing to the enactment of the Private International Law Code in November 1998.

The Code will introduce numerous changes and strengthen the two basic pillars of Tunisia's legislative policy: equality of men and women and the necessary protection of children.

For example, when one of the prospective spouses is a national of a country which authorizes polygamy, the civil registry officer may conclude the marriage only if an official certificate states that the future husband has no other marital attachment. Preference is no longer given to the national law of the husband. Henceforth, the marital relationship is based on a neutral element: the home.

With regard to the children, Tunisian legislators will confirm the international competence of Tunisian jurisdictions in respect of provisional measures. The Private International Law Code will apply the law that is most favourable for the child with regard to custody, maintenance obligations and affiliation.

In terms of custody of the children, a choice is made between:

- the law under which the divorce was granted,

- the national law of the child, or

- the law of the child's residence.

It thus appears that domestic laws cannot, in spite of changing sociocultural circumstances, be in complete harmony with international conventions, particularly, in this case, those on the rights of women and of the child.

Ownership and succession

In the economic field, there is no discrimination between men and women with regard to the acquisition, management or transfer of property. The rule is the separation of property, and women manage and dispose of their property during the marriage under the same conditions as their husbands, which is a consistent principle in Muslim law.

With regard to inheritance, Maghreb legislation is based on the rules of traditional Muslim law. Accordingly, a woman inherits half of what is inherited by a man who has the same rank in relation to the deceased.

Tunisia has introduced a number of changes and innovations in this area:

- The institution of the mandatory bequest for the children of a daughter who predeceases her father and the restitution mechanism, which enables a single daughter to inherit all the property of her parents;

- The Act of November 1998 on the joint ownership of property by the spouses provides for an optional arrangement under which real estate and property are held jointly by the husband and the wife. This arrangement is applied without prejudice to the rules on succession and introduces a new legal and social norm on access to ownership, thereby reducing the inequalities the traditional right to inheritance gives rise to.

Marriage and family relations and international human rights law

In most of the countries in the region, the various provisions governing family relations are based much more on cultural practices and custom than on concepts of equality. Private life is still governed by patriarchal principles which prevent women from exercising their public rights satisfactorily and from having the necessary power to combat the resulting sociocultural behaviour and violence. Equality in private life and equality in public life are closely linked. How, for example, can women be said to have the same economic and political rights as men if they are not free to work and come and go without the permission of their husbands? Indeed, the emancipation of women in general necessarily depends on the emancipation of wives and mothers.

While equality between men and women is still incomplete within the family, it is interesting to underscore the consistent political will of those who govern in the Maghreb to develop and promote the rights of women through an interpretive and evolving approach to religious texts in order to develop their domestic legislation and gradually change attitudes. They are assisted in this task by a very active and influential associative movement.

The Committee on the Elimination of Discrimination against Women (CEDAW) has strongly encouraged these States, during the presentation of their reports, to continue their efforts to eliminate measures that still discriminate against women and to withdraw, gradually, reservations that have been made, particularly on article 16 of the Convention. The positive interpretation provided by the Committee in its general recommendation on article 16, which concerns family relations within marriage, has done much to give the Convention a dynamic force enabling it to adapt to all social variations and to provide non-governmental organizations with a useful tool for change.

Through the dynamic interest it generates, its capacity and its ability to mobilize Governments during the presentation of reports or through periodic world meetings to evaluate the emancipation of women, such as the conferences in Nairobi (1985) and Beijing (1995), the Convention is a lasting and powerful mechanism for progress towards achieving equality for women. It is interesting to note that most of the reforms in the legislation of various countries, particularly those of the Maghreb, have come about either following one of the United Nations world conferences on women or in connection with the submission of reports to CEDAW.

In fact, progress in the legal status of women depends basically on the political will to give it its rightful place in society and on society's acceptance of that new situation. The role of judicial institutions is crucial because they can inhibit an evolutionary process in the legal texts since they are able to anticipate the future, egalitarian development of the rights of women. Judicial structures and judges are aware of their important role under the law in interpretive decisions which make it possible, through their implications, to promote adaptation and harmony between the rights of women and the reality of the laws that they apply.

As of October 1999, none of the countries of the Maghreb has withdrawn its reservations to article 16 of the Convention.

A new stage has just been reached with the Optional Protocol to the Convention, which enables women and women's groups to use the petition procedure when they have suffered injury or when a violation of women's rights has been committed.

In reality, international institutions are not going to set themselves up as judicial institutions, but they will be constantly monitoring claims and the real situation with regard to the application of the domestic laws in the countries that have ratified and accepted the Optional Protocol. It is this constant attention focused on the issue of women which makes the new protocol interesting. Governments and political and judicial authorities are thus continuously concerned about the implementation of the principles of universal equality.

The principle of non-discrimination is a basic rule of international law. It protects women and girls against any violation of their human rights. The two conventions, whose twentieth and tenth anniversaries we are celebrating together, namely the Convention on the Elimination of All Forms of Discrimination against Women and the Convention on the Rights of the Child, complement each other in their spirit and through their provisions and condemn any violation of the basic rights of women and girls. Thus, any inequality or abuse that has been experienced in childhood remains a handicap for life. The rights of the girl child are the first milestones in the status of the women of tomorrow. The 1993 Vienna Conference on Human Rights marked a turning point in people's awareness; and henceforth the cause of children and the cause of women are the cause of human rights. The international community has committed itself to defending their basic rights against all forms of discrimination and violence, assisted in this regard by the entire United Nations system, particularly the Division for the Advancement of Women, which integrates a gender-specific approach into all its programmes and policies at all levels in order to ensure the advancement of women. The achievements are many, and the challenges are ever-present since a legal text in itself is nothing if States and their political and judicial structures do not take action to protect women and children and further develop the law with regard to them.

Violence against women

Domestic Violence in International Law and the Inter-American System[*]
Claudio Grossman

Introduction

Family violence is one of the most insidious forms of violence against women. It is prevalent in all societies, regardless of ethnic and economic differences. Within family relationships women of all ages are subjected to violence of all kinds, including battering, rape, other forms of sexual assault, mental and verbal abuse and other forms of violence. These crimes of violence are perpetuated by traditional attitudes regarding the role of women in society and in the family. In addition to these societal restrictions, lack of economic independence forces many women to stay in violent relationships.

Reliable data on the prevalence of violence against women by their partners are scarce, especially in developing countries. The growing body of research confirms the pervasiveness of violence against women in the home. Scientists have completed approximately 40 valid population-based quantitative studies, conducted in 24 countries on four continents. These studies revealed a range of 20 to 50 percent of women being victims of physical abuse by their partners at some time in their lives. Studies in the Americas in particular have shown a high rate of domestic violence. Almost half of the women surveyed in a Latin American study reported being victims of psychological abuse, while one or two out of every five women reported that they experience physical violence from their family members.

One country that has amassed a large amount of research on domestic violence against women is the United States of America. Its statistics report that an estimated 30 percent of women suffer from domestic violence at some point during their lives. On average, these

---

[*] Dean Grossman would like to thank Lisa Trojner, Special Assistant to the Dean, for her assistance in preparing these remarks.

same studies found that 50 to 60 percent of women who are abused by their partners are raped by them as well.

Studies conducted around the world show shockingly similar realities about the nature of violence against women. These studies show that the perpetrators of violence against women are almost exclusively men. Women are at greatest risk of violence from men whom they know. Women and girls are the most frequent victims of violence within the family and between intimate partners.

In addition to facts regarding the percentage of abusers and victims, various studies have also given insight into the nature of the abuse itself. Physical abuse against women in intimate relationships is almost always accompanied by severe psychological and verbal abuse. Sadly, the response of many professionals and social institutions has been to either blame or ignore the victims.

Violence against women comes in numerous forms, from psychological manipulations to murder. Studies show that violence against women in families may be one of the most important precipitating factors of female suicide, and is closely associated with homicide. Global evidence suggests that most homicides of women are committed by a male partner or ex-partner.

The effect of such violence on the physical and mental well-being of women is to deprive them of the equal enjoyment, exercise and knowledge of human rights and fundamental freedoms, such as the right to life, the right to physical integrity, and the right to health. An underlying consequence of these forms of gender-based violence is to undermine women's exercise of their civil and political rights as well—perpetuating conditions that keep women in subordinate roles, impedes their political participation and leads to lower levels of education, skills, and work opportunities for them.

International human rights law can and should be used to combat domestic violence against women, in both domestic and international tribunals. It should also be used to encourage the development of domestic legal systems that prevent this type of violence.

I will first give an overview of the international legal framework as it pertains to domestic violence and discuss the effect this is having worldwide. I will then move into a discussion of the regional system that exists within the Americas.

International legal framework

The Convention on the Elimination of All Forms of Discrimination against Women.

The Convention on the Elimination of All Forms of Discrimination against Women, which was adopted by the United Nations General Assembly in December 1979, is in essence the international bill of rights for women. 165 countries have ratified it so far, including all countries of the Latin American and Caribbean region. Several more States have signed the Convention, including the United States of America (17 July 1980), thereby indicating their commitment to do nothing in contravention of its terms.

The Convention requires States to eliminate discrimination against women in the enjoyment of all civil, political, economic, social and cultural rights. While it does not explicitly address the question of violence against women, this matter has been dealt with comprehensively by the Committee on the Elimination of Discrimination against Women, the expert body established to monitor implementation of the Convention. In its General Recommendation 19 (eleventh session, 1992), the Committee stated that the definition of discrimination given by article 1 of the Convention included "gender-based violence, that is, violence that is directed against a woman because she is a woman or violence that affects women disproportionately. It includes acts that inflict physical, mental or sexual harm or suffering, threats of such acts, coercion and other deprivations of liberty. Gender-based violence may breach specific provisions of the Convention, regardless of whether those provisions expressly mention violence. Gender-based violence, which impairs or nullifies the enjoyment by women of human rights and fundamental freedoms under general international law or under human rights conventions, is discrimination within the meaning of article 1 of the Convention" (General Recommendation 19, paras. 6 and 7).

Discrimination under the Convention is not restricted to action by or on behalf of the State (see articles 2(e), 2(f), and 5). For example, under article 2(e) the Convention calls on States parties to take all appropriate measures to eliminate discrimination against women by any person, organization, or enterprise. Therefore, under general international law and specific human rights instruments, States may also be responsible for private acts if they fail to act with due diligence to prevent violations of rights or fail to investigate and punish acts of violence, and they may be required to provide victims with compensation.

Articles 2 and 3 of the Convention also seek the elimination of traditional attitudes by which women are regarded as subordinate to men or as having stereotyped roles. These attitudes perpetuate widespread practices involving violence or coercion, such as family violence and abuse, forced marriage, dowry deaths, acid attacks, and female circumcision. Such prejudices and practices may be used to justify gender-based violence as a form of protection or control of women.

The full implementation of the Convention requires States to take positive measures to eliminate all forms of violence against women. The Committee on the Elimination of Discrimination against Women regularly raises the issue of violence against women with reporting States, and addresses specific recommendations to them on further steps to prevent and eliminate violence against women. In its General Recommendation 19, the Committee put forward a series of measures to overcome all forms of gender-based violence, whether by public or private act. States are invited to ensure that laws against family violence and abuse, rape, sexual assault, and other gender-based violence give adequate protection to all women, and respect their integrity and dignity. Appropriate protective and support services should be provided for victims by each country, regardless of the nature of the offense or the relationship between the victim and the assailant.

It is not enough for States simply to adopt legal measures to handle violence against women after it has been perpetrated. In order to change the societal attitude towards domestic violence, the Committee, in its General Recommendation 19 called on States parties to provide gender-sensitive training of judicial and law enforcement officers and other public officials. Additionally, effective measures are called for to overcome discriminatory attitudes and practices that lead to domestic violence. Finally, States should introduce education and public information programmes to help eliminate prejudices that hinder women's equality.

Declaration on the Elimination of Violence against Women

Recognizing that violence against women is a violation of their rights and constitutes discrimination, the United Nations General Assembly adopted the Declaration on the Elimination of Violence against Women in 1993 (GA res. 48/104 of 20 December 1993). The Declaration highlights that violence against women constitutes a violation of the rights and fundamental freedoms of women and impairs and nullifies their enjoyment of those rights and freedoms.

In its article 1, the Declaration sets out a definition of "violence against women," stating that "the term 'violence against women' means any act of gender-based violence that results in, or is likely to result in, physical, sexual or psychological harm or suffering to women, including threats of such acts, coercion or arbitrary deprivation of liberty, whether occurring in public or in private life". Furthermore, article 2 elaborates that violence against women shall be understood to encompass, but not be limited to, various types of violence occurring in the family, within the general community, and violence perpetrated or condoned by the State.

The Declaration thus clearly encompasses domestic violence. It is of primary importance in the fight for gender equality in the human rights arena. The Declaration is the first international human rights instrument to address expressly the issue of violence against women.

Implementation of these instruments

Implementation of the Convention on the Elimination of All Forms of Discrimination against Women and the Declaration on the Elimination of Violence against Women must be twofold, with efforts taking place at both the international and domestic levels. The international implementation system is already in place through the Convention and its monitoring mechanism, the Committee on the Elimination of Discrimination against Women. The CEDAW Committee holds a constructive dialogue with the States Parties reporting to it under article 18 of the Convention. Reporting States are expected to describe steps taken to adhere to the Convention, or point out obstacles encountered. Following the exchange with representatives of States parties, the Committee adopts concluding comments addressed to the State party, and contained in the Committee's annual reports. These concluding comments identify positive aspects, factors and difficulties encountered by that State in implementing the Convention, and principal areas of concern. In order to overcome the concerns, the Committee makes specific recommendations for further action by that State. The Committee also prepares General Recommendations on specific articles or issues covered by the Convention to assist States parties in its implementation. As of its twenty-first session in June 1999, the Committee had adopted 24 such General Recommendations, including the above-mentioned General Recommendation 19 on violence against women.

Domestic implementation is more difficult, depending upon the nature of national politics and individual country resources. States that have ratified the Convention are under an international legal obligation to take all necessary measures towards its implementation, including incorporation in their domestic legal systems.

CEDAW principles have been integrated into new constitutions and added to more established constitutions through amendments. They can also gain "constitutional" status in a less direct fashion, when courts are convinced to use the Women's Convention to help give existing constitutional guarantees of women's equality more detailed and concrete meaning. If a State has ratified the Convention, judges in its domestic courts generally have the authority to consider it, either as part of national law or as an aid to interpreting national law, but many judges are unfamiliar and uncomfortable with the idea of doing so.

Some of the most interesting and significant decisions are produced when a domestic court decides to combine a vague or inadequate domestic constitutional guarantee of women's equality with the principles of gender equality articulated in CEDAW. For example, the Constitutional Court in Colombia, which was instituted under the new Colombian Constitution, has made a number of important decisions involving women's human rights. The Constitution created an enforcement mechanism that individual women can use. A Constitutional Court was set up to hear petitions brought by citizens about violations of their rights. It has the power to make an "order of protection" if the petitioner shows that her rights are jeopardized by government action or inaction. This court made a groundbreaking decision in 1992 in response to a petition brought by a female victim of domestic violence. Her husband's actions were not criminal, according to the Colombian penal code, as domestic violence was seen as a private matter that did not concern the State. The court found that the absence of legal recourse violated her rights to life and to integrity and security of the person. Even more important, the court established the principle that the State has a positive obligation to secure protection for women and prevent husbands from continuing to subject them to violence. The police and the Institute of Family Welfare were ordered to take immediate steps to protect the petitioner.

The Inter-American Region[1]

The Inter-American system's norms and procedures provide a framework that is complementary to the international framework I have just described. It allows for the adjudication of individual cases in the Inter-American Commission on Human Rights. For those countries that have accepted the compulsory jurisdiction of the Inter-American Court of Human Rights, there is a second level of review.

In addition to the case system, there are other important regional mechanisms for dealing with the problem of violence against women. The Inter-American Court on Human Rights can also issue advisory opinions on a State's compliance with any regional instrument. The Inter-American Commission has the authority to make visits *in loco* to countries in the region and report on the level of compliance with regional and international human rights instruments.

Emphasizing the importance of resolving the problem of violence against women in Latin America, the Commission has appointed a Special Rapporteur on Women's Rights, with the authority to investigate the status of women's rights in the Americas and produce reports on this issue. The Inter-American Commission on Women is charged with ensuring the civil and political rights of women. It plays an active role in the establishment of norms on the rights of women. It was instrumental in the drafting and presenting of the Inter-American Convention on the Prevention, Punishment, and Eradication of Violence Against Women and helps to monitor compliance with this and other instruments.

Inter-American Convention on the Prevention, Punishment, and Eradication of Violence Against Women ("Convention of Belém do Pará")

Adopted by the General Assembly of the Organization of American States (OAS) on 9 June, 1994, the Inter-American Convention on the Prevention, Punishment, and Eradication of Violence Against Women has been ratified by 29 countries: Argentina, Antigua and Barbuda, Ba-

---

[1] For additional information on the process of bringing cases before the Inter-American Commission on Human Rights, the mechanisms available to protect women from domestic violence in the Inter-American system, and the records of individual States on this issue, see *Report of the Inter-American Commission on Human Rights on the Status of Women in the Americas* [Washington, D.C., Organization of American States, 1998].

hamas, Barbados, Belize, Bolivia, Brazil, Colombia, Costa Rica, Chile, Dominica, Dominican Republic, Ecuador, El Salvador, Guatemala, Guyana, Haiti, Honduras, Mexico, Nicaragua, Panama, Paraguay, Peru, Saint Kitts Nevis, Saint Vincent and the Grenadines, Saint Lucia, Trinidad and Tobago, Uruguay, and Venezuela. It is the strongest international or regional instrument to address domestic violence.

The Inter-American Convention represents a re-envisaging of the inter-American human rights system in a gender-specific way. Its adoption represents a powerful consensus among both state and non-state actors that the struggle to eradicate gender violence requires concrete action and effective guarantees. Article 1 defines "violence against women" as "any act or conduct, based on gender, which causes death or physical, sexual, or psychological harm or suffering to women, whether in the public or *private* sphere" (emphasis added). Article 7 requires that States parties must "apply due diligence" to prevent, investigate, and punish violence against women wherever it occurs. States parties must take the measures necessary to give effect to the objectives of the Convention. Women who have been subjected to violence must have access to available and effective recourse to obtain protective measures and to seek restitution or reparation.

The Convention requires certain implementation measures on behalf of States parties as well. Article 8 sets forth multiple requirements dealing with States' duties to implement progressive measures such as promoting awareness and observance of the right of women to be free from violence; implementing measures to modify the social and cultural patterns of conduct that lead to prejudice and gender stereotypes; training for police and other law enforcement officers; developing programmes for women who are victims of domestic violence, such as shelters and counselling services.

Articles 10 through 12 set forth the protection mechanisms for victims of violence against women. States parties must report to the Inter-American Commission on Women regarding the measures they have adopted and obstacles to be confronted in addressing gender violence.

Additionally, a case system has been established. Any person, group, or non-governmental organization legally recognized in a member State can file a case in the Inter-American Court of Human Rights (IACHR) against a State party, complaining of a violation of its principal undertakings. It is usually necessary to identify the victim, but this may be kept in confidence if necessary. The petition must be in writing, and set forth facts which tend to show the violation of a protected right.

Once the petition is reviewed and requirements to initiate proceedings are met, there is an information gathering process: a request for a response is given to the Government. The petitioner can respond to this response. The Government must also submit its own information. The petitioner has to show exhaustion of domestic remedies, or show that this would have been futile.

The Commission may utilize several options in addressing cases brought before it on the issue of violence against women. It can seek to broker a friendly settlement or it may hold a hearing to allow parties to express their arguments. Additionally, the Commission can issue a report and make recommendations, generally aimed at securing a full investigation of the facts, prosecution and punishment of those determined responsible, and action to repair damage suffered by the victim. The initial report is confidential and gives the State an opportunity to comply. If compliance is insufficient, the Commission can publish the report. The Commission can also request that a State take protective action on an urgent basis if it is necessary to avoid irreparable damage to persons. The Commission can also advise that the Inter-American Court take provisional measures.

Finally, the Inter-American Commission can refer a case to the Inter-American Court if the State in question has accepted its jurisdiction as have Argentina, Bolivia, Brazil, Chile, Colombia, Costa Rica, Dominican Republic, Ecuador, El Salvador, Guatemala, Haiti, Honduras, Mexico, Nicaragua, Panama, Paraguay, Peru (which recently withdrew from jurisdiction of the Court, but the Court has not accepted this), Suriname, Uruguay, and Venezuela. If needed, States parties or any organ of the OAS, including the Inter-American Commission on Women, can request an advisory opinion from the Inter-American Court on the interpretation of the Convention.

Other instruments that confer rights on women

Women in those States that have not ratified the Convention of Belém do Pará are still protected under the American Convention on Human Rights and the American Declaration of the Rights and Duties of Man. Both recognize the right of equality before the law and the right to be free from discrimination on the basis of sex. The American Convention on Human Rights has been ratified by Argentina, Barbados, Bolivia, Brazil, Chile, Colombia, Costa Rica, Dominica, Dominican Republic, Ecuador, El Salvador, Grenada, Guatemala, Haiti, Honduras, Jamaica, Mexico, Nicaragua, Panama, Paraguay, Peru, Suriname, Uruguay, and Venezuela. Trinidad and Tobago ratified the Convention and accepted the jurisdiction of the Court, but later withdrew its ratification.

Compliance with the Convention of Belém do Pará and other regional instruments

Many countries in the region have created institutions to promote gender equality and many of these have specific mandates to prevent domestic violence. These institutions are also responsible for presenting legal initiatives with a view towards achieving full equality for women. In Argentina, Brazil, Colombia, and the United States of America, institutions have been established at different levels to assist and provide guidance to women victims of domestic violence. Bolivia and Guatemala have adopted national plans for the elaboration of standards on the situation of women.

Despite the advances these institutions have been able to offer women in their respective nations, many problems still exist. There are still numerous technical problems that underlie their struggle against violence against women. Many countries report an absence of appropriate personnel or a failure to train personnel adequately to process claims of violence. Others countries report that there is no mechanism to follow up cases after they have been filed. Still others report that there is no adequate training for police, judicial authorities, and health care professionals in treating women who are victims of domestic violence.

In addition to these technical problems, there are legal limitations that have restricted the advancement of women's rights. In some countries, domestic violence is seen as a crime that must be prosecuted as a private action. Sometimes victims of domestic violence do not have access to civil remedies for damages because the dignity of the individual is seen as a juridical interest not susceptible to inclusion as a pecuniary interest. In still other countries, domestic violence is seen as a health problem rather than as a crime. In many countries, the concept of "honour" is still incorporated into laws on violence against women, so that only "decent women" can be victims and rape by one's spouse is not a crime. Until these issues have been resolved, violence against women will go on.

Recommendations within the Commission

The Inter-American Commission on Human Rights has formulated several recommendations on how to end violence against women in Latin America, and how to overcome some of the current obstacles.

First, the Commission has suggested establishing a Voluntary Fund to support the Commission in performing functions such as training on the case system and human rights, conducting studies, and preparing materials. Next, the Commission should give coverage to women's rights in its reports on *in loco* visits to member nations. The Inter-American system should encourage Governments and NGOs to participate as *amicus curiae* in specific cases before the Inter-American Commission and Court.

In the context of its activities of supervision and its case system, the Inter-American Commission should cooperate with international agencies and bodies involved in promoting and protecting women's rights and within the OAS with other entities concerned with the progress of women's rights.

Recommendations for the Inter-American States

The first recommendation for members of the OAS is for States that have not ratified the Convention of Belém do Pará to do so as soon as possible. Next, States should undertake a broad review of their legislation to identify provisions establishing distinctions, exclusions, or restrictions on the basis of sex, that have the purpose or effect of preventing recognition or exercise by women of human rights, and to amend such laws or abolish them. States need to adopt legislation on domestic violence to ensure that it is not tolerated by the State, and that it is duly investigated, tried before a court, and punished.

Countries should look at the response capacity of the public and private sectors in training law enforcement and judicial personnel. Such capacity needs to be strengthened in order to provide proper treatment for the causes and effects of violence. States need to fully implement existing programmes and laws, which for lack of sufficient resources frequently have yet to be initiated or are only partially implemented.

Conclusion

Women's low status everywhere has been encoded in law, and women continue to face injustice—including being subjected to domestic violence—solely on the basis of their sex. This injustice still exists in virtually every country in the world. Where legal reform has been won, reality generally lags far behind. Even where gender equality has been constitutionally mandated, legal remedies for discrimination are typically non-existent or exasperatingly slow to work.

CEDAW and the Convention of Belém do Pará are rooted in the conviction that law—both international and national—is a powerful tool in the struggle for social and economic justice. In affirming that a single standard of gender equality must prevail beyond considerations of family, culture, or nation, these instruments provide a working agenda for moving toward gender equality. Promoting women's legal capacity in law as well as in practice means infusing a gender perspective into every aspect of daily life.

These instruments are also rooted in the realization that, if they are to be effective, a gender perspective needs to exist in the courtroom as well as in the Constitution. Ensuring legal personhood means not only revising laws that are discriminatory, and enforcing laws that bar discrimination, but also launching programmes in gender equality, including training, for judges and other court personnel. After all, the institutions that enact and enforce laws are not neutral; they have been constructed by societies dominated by men, and they reflect their interests and bias.

We should also recognize the important connection between the struggle for equality and the struggle for democracy. A true democracy cannot exist when half of a population is effectively without a voice. I am grateful to see that there is growing recognition of the principles set forth in these instruments: that equality before and under the law is a fundamental human right and that situations that allow or perpetuate domestic violence are violations of that right. This recognition is a recent development, and a very positive one. In spite of the formidable challenges that remain in the elimination of domestic violence, I believe that we, as a community of nations, have already made strides simply by recognizing this critical problem. As a community of nations, we must continue to strive to eradicate the universal scourge of domestic violence.

Violence Against Women: State-Sponsored Violence
Navanethem Pillay

Introduction

This presentation will give an overview of international law, its development and justification, strengths and weaknesses as it pertains to violence against women: State–sponsored violence, and the relationship between international human rights law on this issue and domestic law.

Violence against women

Several features strike us when we look at the issue of violence against women:

1. Violence against women in its many forms is no longer suffered in silence but has become part of public debate. The United Nations Special Rapporteur on violence against women observed: "A revolution has taken place in the last decade. Women's rights have been catapulted into the human rights agenda with a speed and determination that has rarely been matched in international law. There are two aspects to this process: first, the attempt to make mainstream human rights responsive to women's concerns; and second, the conceptualization of certain gender-specific violations as human rights violations. These developments may have far-reaching implications for the theory and practice of human rights in the UN system." [1]

2. Violence against women has escalated worldwide. The United Nations Division for the Advancement of Women, upon a review of 86 country reports on measures taken to realize the goals of the 12 critical areas of concern of the Beijing Platform for Action noted: "Ethnic, communal and other forms of violent conflicts were a reality everywhere, with women and children suffering most. Women and children constituted 80 per cent of the world's refugees and displaced persons. Civilian fatalities had climbed from 5 per cent of war-related deaths at the beginning of the century to more than 90 per cent in the wars of the 1990s; once again most of the casualties were women and children. They were victims of massive violations of human rights in armed conflicts, and they faced the particular risk of rape and sexual violence, including systematic rape. Better communications technology – including the Internet – as well as ease of travel, had led to an increase in trafficking in women and children, mainly for sexual exploitation..." [2]

---

[1] Radhika Coomaraswamy, Reinventing International Law: Women's Rights as Human Rights in the International Community. Human Rights Program, Harvard Law School, 1996, p. 9.

[2] Angela King, Assistant Secretary-General, Special Adviser on Gender Issues and Advancement of Women, United Nations Division for the Advancement of Women, in her statement to the Third Committee of the General Assembly. Press release GA/SHC/3473, 12th meeting, 14 October 1998.

3. Significant progress has been made toward the criminalization of gender-based violations against women in wartime. The conclusions of the United Nations Diplomatic Conference of Plenipotentiaries on the Establishment of the International Criminal Court in Rome, in July 1998, marked a significant step in the quest to hold perpetrators of gender-based crimes accountable. Ms. King highlighted "the historic conviction of the former Mayor of the Rwandan town of Taba, Jean Paul Akayesu, by the International Criminal Tribunal for Rwanda (ICTR). In making rape part of the perpetrator's conviction for genocide, the tribunal had advanced the world treatment of rape and sexual violence and begun the long process of reversing the climate of impunity that sexual crimes in war had enjoyed."[3]

4. State-sponsored or -authorized violence encompasses acts or omissions perpetrated by state actors such as the government, its institutions, officials and agents, as well as where the state is under legal obligation to protect the individuals within its jurisdiction and has not been diligent in doing so. State responsibility may arise in situations of war and armed conflict both international and internal; violence by agents or employees of the State, such as police, military, prison guards and other officials; custodial violence in hospitals; prisons and other institutions where there is a special relationship to provide security; government-sanctioned cultural and other practices such as female genital mutilation, honour killings, marital rape and domestic violence.

State responsibility

State responsibility flows from the sovereign's national duty to protect its citizens, as well as from the observance of international obligations and commitments to international customary laws; treaties; instruments and resolutions of the United Nations.

"Under international law, state responsibility is generated when state conduct constitutes a breach of its international obligations such as the obligations contained in customary or treaty-based human rights law."[4]

---

[3] *Ibid.* Citation of the Prosecutor vs. Jean Paul Akayesu, ICTR-96-4-T.

[4] See Thomas Meron. Human Rights and Humanist Norms as Customary Law 155 (1989).

Major international and regional treaties all contain provisions that impose duties on States parties to "respect and ensure" the rights of all individuals within their states as well as to take steps to adopt legislative and other measures as may be necessary to give effect to the rights recognized.[5]

Academic and judicial interpretation of state responsibility to "respect and ensure" the rights is that States are expected to do more than incorporate the rights in legislation to ensure observance of the rights embodied in conventions. "The obligation to respect rights and prevent violations is not confined to a restriction of governmental action, but must to some degree extend to positive governmental action to overcome violations of rights by private actors."[6]

The Inter-American Court of Human Rights interpreted State obligations to ensure the free and full exercise of the rights recognized by article 1(I) of the American Convention on Human Rights as implying the duty "to organize the governmental apparatus" to ensure the achievement of the right.[7]

Evolution of human rights norms

Until recently, the subject of violence against women was absent in international human rights discourse. The norm evolved over the past three decades:

a) 1970s: The key issue was discrimination against women in the public arena and the need to ensure equitable participation of women with men in the development process.

---

[5] The International Covenant on Civil and Political Rights, adopted by the United Nations General Assembly on 16 December 1966, entered into force 23 March 1976; European Convention for the Protection of Human Rights and Fundamental Freedoms, opened for signature 4 November 1950, entered into force 3 September 1953; American Convention on Human Rights, opened 22 November 1969, entered into force 18 July 1978; African Charter on Human and Peoples' Rights, adopted by African Heads of State 27 June 1981, entered into force 21 October 1986.

[6] See Rebecca Cook "State Accountability under CEDAW in Human Rights Law", 237 (1994).

[7] Inter-American Court of Human Rights: Judgment in *Velasquez Rodriquez* case, 29 July 1988. 35 OAS DOC-OEA/SER. L/V/III.19 doc.13 (1988), case No.7920, Ser.C, No.4.

b) 1979-1981: The Convention on the Elimination of all Forms of Discrimination against Women[8] (the CEDAW Convention) sought to promote equality of rights of men and women by elimination of discrimination against women. Article 1 defines the term "discrimination against women" as "any distinction, exclusion or restriction made on the basis of sex which has the effect or purpose of impairing or nullifying the recognition, enjoyment or exercise by women, irrespective of their marital status, on a basis of equality of men and women of human rights and fundamental freedoms in the political, economic, social, cultural, civil or any other field." There is no explicit prohibition of violence against women in the CEDAW Convention. It was given the silent treatment, with little appreciation that violence against women restricted the assertion by them of fundamental rights and enjoyment of economic and social rights; and that women's economic dependence was a major reason why they were targeted for violence.

c) July 1985: The Third United Nations World Conference on Women at Nairobi, Kenya, focused on the three themes of equality, development and peace. The Nairobi Forward–looking Strategies for the Advancement of Women, agreed upon by States, relegated violence against women under the headings of discrimination and development.

d) 1990: By then, violence against women had found a place on international agendas – but as aspects of women's rights and crime prevention.

e) 1992: The Committee on the Elimination of Discrimination against Women issued General Recommendation 19 which stated that gender-based violence was an issue of gender discrimination and required States to discuss it in their reports. Paragraph 7 of General Recommendation 19 contains a general prohibition against gender-based violence that is directed at women because they are women or that affects women disproportionately. The document established the principle of state responsibility for acts of state agents and citizens.

f) 1993-1994: The Commission on the Status of Women drafted the Declaration on the Elimination of Violence against Women

---

[8] A/RES/34/180, 18 December 1979.

(DEVAW).[9] Article 1 states: "Violence against women means any act of gender-based violence that results in or is likely to result in physical, sexual or psychological harm or suffering to women, including threats of such acts, coercion or arbitrary deprivation of liberty, whether occurring in public or private life."

As a General Assembly resolution, the Declaration does not have the status of a legally binding instrument, but has persuasive authority and sets important standards for States. It covers violence in the family, within the general community, and violence perpetrated or condoned by the State. It sets out preventative and protective measures that States can take to achieve the objective of eliminating violence against women.

g) 1993: The World Conference on Human Rights in Vienna represented a defining moment in the history of human rights protection. Women's rights were accorded the status of human rights.[10]

Paragraph 18 (Part I) of the Vienna Declaration: "The human rights of women and of the girl-child are an inalienable, integral and indivisible part of universal human rights. The full and equal participation of women in political, civil, economic, social and cultural life, at the national, regional and international levels, and the eradication of all forms of discrimination on grounds of sex, are priority objectives of the international community.

"Gender-based violence and all forms of sexual harassment and exploitation, including those resulting from cultural prejudice and international trafficking, are incompatible with the dignity and worth of the human person, and must be eliminated. This can be achieved by legal measures and through national action and international cooperation..."

h) 1994: The Cairo United Nations Conference on Population and Development reached an understanding that a holistic multidisciplinary approach was needed to combat violence against women.

i) February 1995: A Special Rapporteur on violence against women was appointed, based on a resolution adopted by the United Nations Commission on Human Rights in 1994.

---

[9]   A/RES/48/104 (1994).

[10]   Vienna Declaration and Programme of Action adopted at the World Conference on Human Rights, A/CONF.157/24, 25 June 1993.

j)   1995: The Fourth World Conference on Women of the United Nations took place at Beijing.

The Beijing Platform for Action, adopted by 189 States, has no legally binding status but is an indicator of universally acceptable norms of international custom. It highlights critical areas of concern and strategic objectives for national policy and plans. The implementation of the Platform by States comes under review at the Beijing + 5 Conference in June, 2000.

The Beijing Platform for Action expanded the content of violence against women to include violations of women's human rights in situations of armed conflict, in particular murder, systematic rape, sexual slavery, forced pregnancy, forced sterilization, enforced abortion, enforced use of contraceptives; and recognized that violence can be sponsored by States by perpetrating, as well as condoning, it. It urged that rape during armed conflict be treated as a war crime with survivors having a right to compensation.

k)   1998: The Statute of the International Criminal Court, articles 7 and 8, designates rape, sexual slavery, enforced prostitution, forced pregnancy, enforced sterilization or any other form of sexual violence of comparable gravity, as crimes against humanity and war crimes.

Regional instruments and activities

The European Convention for the Protection of Human Rights and Fundamental Freedoms of 4 November 1950 has no specific provision relating to violence against women. Article 5 provides for liberty and security of person in the context of freedom from arbitrary arrest. By way of progressive judicial pronouncements, the European Court on Human Rights has kept pace with evolving norms of human rights.

The African Charter on Human and Peoples' Rights, adopted by African Heads of State in June 1981, also contains no explicit prohibition on violence against women. Article 6 provides for liberty and security of person in the context of freedom from arbitrary arrest.

Article 29.7 provides for the preservation and strengthening of positive African cultural values with other members of society in a spirit of tolerance.

It is not clear which right trumps which, when culture conflicts with women's human rights.

At the tenth Anniversary Workshop on the African Charter in 1996, it was noted that the Charter had not prevented genocide, torture, extra-judicial executions, and impunity. But the Charter is there and it is an asset. The workshop passed resolutions on the human rights situations in Tunisia and Nigeria, the rights of women, support for the ICTR and other matters.

Regional human rights conventions complement the human rights regime of the United Nations as they both serve to protect the rights of individuals and seek accountability of Governments.

The Inter-American Convention on the Prevention, Punishment and Eradication of Violence against Women adopted in June 1994 has pro-visions similar to the United Nations Declaration on the Elimination of Violence against Women. Article 3 explicitly provides for the distinct right that "every woman has the right to be free from violence in both public and private spheres."

Apart from CEDAW, which is legally binding on ratifying States, the remaining instruments including the Violence Declaration, the Bei-jing Platform for Action and the regional conventions lack legal status and act through persuasive authority. They set norms and generate a consensual body of international customary law.

States make a political commitment to implement the norms and subject themselves to scrutiny through reporting procedures.

International humanitarian law

History

The law of war dates back to the fifth century B.C. in writings from China on the treatment of prisoners.

Traditionally, international law concerned itself exclusively with governing the relationship between States and with the rights and duties owed by States to one another. It observed the basic principle of respect for state sovereignty, i.e. that States had exclusive jurisdiction over their internal affairs and over their citizens. Citizens and individuals within the jurisdiction of state territories were not rights-holders or subject to the protection of international law. As international law regulated ac-tions of sovereign States, it refrained from judging criminality of indi-viduals.

Justification

As a result of the atrocities and Holocaust of World War II, the victorious nations set up the International Military Tribunal at Nuremberg with jurisdiction over crimes against peace and crimes against humanity.

The basic principle underlying the regime of crimes against humanity was that they constituted violation of human rights and offended all of humankind, not States alone. This provided the legal justification for overriding State sovereignty and asserting international criminal jurisdiction.

As we see in subsequent developments, it was understood that the essence of human rights protection required machinery that moved away from traditional barriers between internal order and international order. Human rights should be viewed in the spirit of cooperation and coordination between States and international organizations. While States are the ultimate depositories of human rights, where they are unable or unwilling to protect human rights; or where authoritarian regimes in abuse of sovereign power commit large-scale violations of human rights, such circumstances provide the legal and institutional construction for intervention.

International Military Tribunal at Nuremberg

The Nuremberg Charter

It defined crimes against humanity as murder, extermination, enslavement, deportation and other inhumane acts committed against any civilian population before or during the war or persecution on political, racial or religious grounds in execution of or in connection with (crimes against peace or war crimes) within the jurisdiction of the Tribunal, whether or not in violation of the domestic law of the country where perpetrated.

Principle of individual criminal responsibility

The International Military Tribunal was challenged on two grounds:

1) That international law was concerned with actions of States and had no jurisdiction over individuals.

2) That individuals acting under state authority cannot be held personally liable but were protected by the doctrine of state sovereignty.

The Court rejected the challenge and ruled: "International law imposes duties and liabilities upon individuals as upon States.... The very essence of the Charter is that individuals have international duties which transcend the national obligations of obedience imposed by the individual State. He who violates the law of war cannot obtain immunity while acting in pursuance of the authority of the State, if the State in authorizing action moves outside its competence under international law."

Strengths and weaknesses of Nuremberg

Its weaknesses lay in the fact that prosecution was confined to major Nazi war crimes under the jurisdiction of the International Military Tribunal. This selective criminalization of one party to the conflict made it known as "victors' justice". Crimes of violence against women were not prosecuted. Fair trial and due process, as we understand it, were lacking.

The strength lay in the expeditious dispensation of justice against major perpetrators. It created legal precedent that was followed in the International Military Tribunal for the Far East with jurisdiction over Japanese war criminals.

These two World War II tribunals set out principles of international humanitarian law that were subsequently affirmed by the United Nations in the following:

a) United Nations Charter and Statute of the International Court of Justice. Article 1 of the Charter sets out the purpose of the United Nations, including to maintain peace and security, take collective measures to prevent threats to peace and settle disputes, in conformity with the principles of justice and international law. Article 24 of the Charter gives primary responsibility to the Security Council for the maintenance of international peace. Article 39 establishes that the Security Council shall determine the existence of any threat to the peace and decide what measures shall be taken to maintain or restore international peace and security.

b) Economic and Social Council resolution establishing the Commission on Human Rights (E/RES/9 (11), 21 June 1946)

c) General Assembly resolution on the crime of genocide (A/RES/96(1) of 11 December 1946) affirmed that genocide is a crime under international law.

Nuremberg set the precedent for the establishment of the ad hoc United Nations international criminal tribunals for former Yugoslavia and Rwanda in 1993 and 1994.

The International Criminal Tribunals for the former Yugoslavia (ICTY) and for Rwanda (ICTR)

The ad hoc tribunals were established by resolutions of the Security Council under Chapter VII, rather than by treaty signed by Member States, as a more expeditious route. The Security Council made a determination that the situation in former Yugoslavia and Rwanda constituted threats to international peace and concluded that prosecution of serious violations of international humanitarian law would achieve justice, peace and reconciliation.

The ICTY resolution was adopted unanimously. The ICTR resolution was opposed by Rwanda, even though Rwanda had requested the tribunal, and China abstained. The Security Council decided that all States were to cooperate fully with the international tribunal and take measures under their domestic law to implement the Statute, including the obligation of States to comply with requests for assistance or orders issued by the tribunal's trial chambers.

The Statute is neutral and does not selectively target for prosecution any particular ethnic group or side in the conflict.

The Statutes place temporal and territorial as well as subject matter limitations over the jurisdiction of the Tribunals. Accordingly, the jurisdiction of the ICTY goes from 1991 onwards, with no cut off date (hence the current investigations in Kosovo fall within the mandate) within the territory of the former Yugoslavia and applying the laws of existing international humanitarian law. The ICTR has jurisdiction for events from January to December 1994 in Rwanda and neighbouring territories.

Subject matter jurisdiction

Historically, international humanitarian law regulated affairs in international war. In recent times, internal conflicts within States, civil wars, rebellions and state-sponsored violence have created imperatives for extension to internal conflicts, inasmuch as the needs of civilians for

71

protection are as valid when sovereign States are in battle as they are in conflicts within borders.

The ICTY Appeal Chamber in the *Tadic* case (appeal decisions) recognized that the dichotomy between international and internal conflict must be narrowed as the focus of international law moves from safeguarding the legitimate interests of States to the protection of human beings.

The ICTY Statute covers both international and internal conflict in former Yugoslavia. The ICTR Statute applies to internal conflict in Rwanda.

The Security Council acknowledged that it had no legislative powers and lacked competence to order retroactive prosecution when it respected the principle of legality inherent in the principle *nullum crimen sine lege*. Accordingly, a person cannot be prosecuted for conduct that did not constitute crimes at the time of commission.

The Security Council did not create new law but incorporated in the Statutes of the tribunals well recognized and universally practiced norms of both international humanitarian law and human rights law. It incorporated genocide, crimes against humanity and grave breaches of the Geneva Conventions and violations of article 3 common to the Geneva Conventions and Additional Protocol II.

Individual criminal responsibility

Only individuals, and not entities, are subject to prosecution. The tribunals have no jurisdiction to hold trials *in absentia*. Article 7 of ICTY and article 6 of ICTR Statutes provide:

1) A person who planned, instigated, ordered, committed or otherwise aided and abetted in the planning, preparation or execution of a crime referred to in articles 2 to 4 of the present Statute shall be individually responsible for the crime.

2) The official position of any accused person, whether as Head of State or Government or as a responsible government official, shall not relieve such person of criminal responsibility nor mitigate punishment.

3) The fact that any of the acts referred to in articles 2 to 4 of the present Statute was committed by a subordinate does not relieve his or her superior of criminal responsibility if he or she knew or had reason to know that the subordinate was about to commit such acts or

had done so and the superior failed to take the necessary and reasonable measures to prevent such acts or to punish the perpetrators thereof.

4)   The fact that an accused person acted pursuant to an order of a Government or of a superior shall not relieve him or her of criminal responsibility, but may be considered in mitigation of punishment if the International Tribunal for Rwanda determines that justice so requires.

This lays the basis for "command responsibility", and liability of state actors for state-sponsored violence.

Gender-related violations

The Statutes and rules of procedure and evidence made by the judges are gender-neutral. Indictments issued to date allege rape and sexual violence committed on both women and men. It is noteworthy that in determining threats to peace in the former Yugoslavia and in Rwanda, the Security Council accepted reports of massive and systematic rape of women.

There is a noticeable dearth of sexual assault prohibitions within international conventions and human rights treaties. This is understandable as the laws were written by men, and militarists, whose preoccupation was to win wars, not to protect human rights.

Article 27 of the Fourth Geneva Convention has a specific prohibition against rape, enforced prostitution and indecent assault. The three remaining Geneva Conventions call for "due consideration to women" and prohibit violation of bodily integrity without explicitly mentioning sexual assault. The "grave breaches" provision common to all of the Geneva Conventions do not enumerate rape and sexual assault. These crimes have been interpreted as falling under the prohibition of torture or causing great suffering or serious injury to body and health.

Rape and sexual assaults are not enumerated acts under *genocide* in the Statutes. They may, as we shall see later, call for consideration as "causing serious bodily or mental harm to members of the group" provided that the act was perpetrated with the intent to destroy in whole or in part, a national ethnical, racial or religious group. Note that the list of groups does not include a gendered group.

Rape is explicitly specified as a prohibited act under crimes against humanity in both statutes, albeit with some differences. In article 5 of the ICTY Statute, rape is specified as a crime against humanity when committed in connection with armed conflict, whether international or national in character, and directed against any civilian population.

In article 3 of the ICTR Statute, rape is specified as a crime against humanity when committed as part of a widespread or systematic attack against any civilian population on national, political, ethnic, racial or religious grounds. The implication is that, if the attack was not on any one of those grounds but on the ground that the victims were women and raped because they were women, the rape will not constitute a crime against humanity.

Evidence that rape was part of a widespread and systematic attack is an additional requirement for proof of commission of the offence.

Article 4 of the ICTR Statute - Violations of article 3 common to the Geneva Conventions and Additional Protocol II

For the first time in history, grave breaches of international humanitarian law committed in an internal conflict are subject to international criminal jurisdiction. Article 4 of the ICTR Statute does not contain an exhaustive list of serious violations but goes further than the crimes prohibited in article 3 common to the Geneva Conventions, and explicitly mentions rape.

(i) Sexual violence and rape as crimes against humanity and genocide: The case of *Prosecutor vs. Jean Paul Akayesu* (ICTR-96-4-T)

Jean Paul Akayesu, the mayor of Taba Commune in Rwanda was charged, *inter alia*, with three counts of rape and sexual violence involving displaced Tutsi women.

The Prosecutor suggested the following definition of sexual violence: "In this indictment acts of sexual violence include forcible sexual penetration of the vagina, anus or oral cavity by a penis and/or of the vagina or anus by some other object, and sexual abuse such as forced nudity."

Count 13 of the indictment charged Akayesu with rape as a crime against humanity punishable under ICTR Statute article 3(g).

The Chamber noted that "there is no commonly accepted definition of the terms of rape and sexual violence in international law." The Chamber regarded rape as a form of aggression and looked to the Convention against Torture and other Cruel, Inhuman or Degrading Treatment or Punishment for guidelines in its formulation of a definition. The Chamber observed that that Convention "does not catalogue specific acts in its definition of torture" but rather focuses on the conceptual framework of state-sanctioned violence. The Chamber reasoned that rape, like torture, is used for such purposes as "intimidation, degradation, humiliation, discrimination, punishment, control or destruction of a person" and that "like torture, rape is a violation of personal dignity and rape constitutes torture… when inflicted by, or at the instigation of, or with the consent or acquiescence of, a public official or other person acting in an official capacity."

The Chamber defined rape and sexual violence as "a physical invasion of a sexual nature, committed on a person under circumstances which are coercive. Sexual violence, which includes rape, is considered to be any act of a sexual nature which is committed on a person under circumstances which are coercive".

The Chamber observed that coercion need not be physical force alone but includes threats and intimidation. It stated that sexual violence was not limited to physical invasion of the human body and may include acts which do not involve penetration or even physical contact. The Chamber noted as an example of sexual violence the incident described by witness KK in which Akayesu ordered the Interahamwe to undress a student and force her to do gymnastics naked before a crowd in the public courtyard of the Bureau Communal before she was killed.

The Chamber did not limit sexual violence to bodily penetration, as suggested by the Prosecutor.

The Chamber found that there was sufficient credible evidence to establish beyond a reasonable doubt that Tutsi girls and women who had taken refuge at the Bureau Communal were subjected to sexual violence, beaten and killed. The Chamber found that Akayesu knew or had reason to know that sexual violence was being inflicted on these women; that he ordered, instigated, aided and abetted sexual violence, and failed to prevent it.

The Chamber found evidence establishing the elements of crimes against humanity, namely:

1) as part of a widespread or systematic attack;

2) on a civilian population;

3) on ethnic grounds against Tutsis.

It found Akayesu guilty of rape as a crime against humanity.

Akayesu faced the charge of genocide under article 2 of the Statute which defined genocide as any of five listed acts, including "causing serious bodily or mental harm to members of the group, with the intent to destroy, in whole or in part, a national, ethnical, racial or religious group as such".

The Chamber concluded that rape and sexual violence constitute infliction of serious bodily and mental harm on victims. In light of all the evidence before it, the Chamber was satisfied that the acts of rape and sexual violence were perpetrated solely against Tutsi women, many of whom were subjected to the worst public humiliation, being mutilated and raped several times, often in public, on the premises of the Bureau Communal and in other public places and frequently by more than one assistant. The Chamber concluded that these rapes "resulted in physical and psychological destruction of Tutsi women, their families and their communities. Sexual violence was an integral part of the process of destruction, specifically targeting Tutsi women and specifically contributing to their destruction and to the destruction of the Tutsi group as a whole."

The Chamber decided that Akayesu "aided and abetted" the acts of sexual violence, was "verbally encouraging" by allowing them to take place in his presence at the premises of the Bureau Communal. The Chamber reasoned that because of his position of authority, his open encouragement was a clear signal of official tolerance for sexual violence which would not have occurred if he had not done so.

The Chamber decided that the acts of rape and sexual violence constitute the crime of genocide and found Akayesu individually criminally liable.

Akayesu has appealed his conviction on all counts and his sentence of life imprisonment and a decision is awaited.

Relationship between international humanitarian law and domestic law

The evolving norms set in human rights instruments and progress made under international humanitarian law impact incremental change in domestic law provided the political will exists. One case in point is South Africa. Post-apartheid South Africa has one of the most enlightened constitutions in the world with an entrenched Bill of Rights. The Government comprising almost one-third female Members of Parliament has progressively enacted laws such as the Prevention of Family Violence Act which also criminalizes conjugal rape, the Right of

Choice Act, and the Traditional Marriages Act which recognizes the property rights of women in non-civil law marriages.

The Constitutional Court recently declared as unconstitutional the so-called "cautionary rule" whereby the evidence of complainants in sexual offence cases was treated with caution.

The 1993 Interim Constitution of South Africa had guaranteed the right to freedom and security but did not specify protection against violence as a component of the right to security. In 1996, the year following the adoption of the Beijing Platform for Action, the Interim Constitution in South Africa ended and the country adopted its present Constitution. It also ratified the CEDAW Convention.

Section 12(1) c of the Constitution of South Africa specifically entrenches the right to be free from all forms of violence, including from private sources.

Women are the principal targets of violence in South Africa where it is reported that a woman is raped every 30 seconds. These constitutional changes offer scope to hold government accountable for preventative and protective action. Article 7 of the Constitution provides that "the State must respect, protect, promote and fulfill the right in the Bill of Rights."

Strengths and weaknesses of the ICTY and the ICTR

The strengths and weaknesses of these two tribunals are evident from their experience. On the one hand, they give us all hope for justice, which I believe is an integral component of peace. They give us a new avenue of recourse, in a world that desperately needs the rule of law as an alternative to the use of force.

On the other hand, as creations of a political process without independent enforcement mechanisms, these tribunals are to a great degree dependent on political will for their success. While NATO forces have made several arrests in the former Yugoslavia, at the highest level of political accountability the military and political leaders of the Bosnian Serb forces responsible for ethnic cleansing in the former Yugoslavia remain at large four years after their indictment. We have to question whether this reluctance to bring such leaders to trial has fuelled the fire of further campaigns of aggression in the region. The rule of international law has tremendous, largely untapped, potential to deter violations of human rights as well as to hold perpetrators of these violations accountable. But in order to do so, it must be seen as impartial and unbending to political considerations.

Another weakness of the ad hoc tribunals, which has been addressed by the creation of the International Criminal Court (ICC), are the geographical and temporal limits of their jurisdiction. There is no inherently compelling logic to the selection of the former Yugoslavia and Rwanda in the creation of ad hoc tribunals. These were essentially political decisions made at certain moments in time, and I think it is fair to say that the creation of the first tribunal in some way politically compelled the creation of the second one. It is also of note that the jurisdiction of the ICTY runs forward in time indefinitely, so that this tribunal is able to investigate and prosecute war crimes, crimes against humanity and genocidal acts which are taking place today or which might take place in future.

In contrast, the jurisdiction of the ICTR is limited to events which took place in 1994. The ICTR is therefore not positioned to investigate and prosecute crimes which might take place in the future. There has been some discussion of establishing an international tribunal with jurisdiction over Burundi, or expanding the jurisdiction of the ICTR accordingly. These discussions highlight the need for an International Criminal Court which has universal jurisdiction and is therefore somewhat insulated from sudden and potentially arbitrary or biased waves of concern.

Many people have told me how glad they are that there is a woman judge in the ICTR, and have asked why there are not more women judges, as the gender imbalance of the tribunals makes them less than fully representative of humanity. The fact that I am the only woman out of nine judges on the Rwanda Tribunal must perpetuate the perception of inequality in the hall of justice itself.

The lack of representation for another group, victims and witnesses, has been criticized as a weakness of the ad hoc tribunals. This has been addressed in the ICC Statute. Article 68(c) provides not only for protection of, but participation by, victims and witnesses in trial proceedings. Their participation may contribute towards raising awareness of the work of the tribunals in local regions.

We have a long way to go in establishing the rule of international law, to effectively safeguard women against violence and the principles of peace and justice which are so fundamental and yet seem so elusive at times. Nevertheless, I am excited to be entering the new millennium with so much promise which gives us all hope in the face of so many violent conflicts and fundamental human rights violations which daily claim so many lives. I would summarize this moment in the history of human rights as a watershed. Institutional protections such as sovereign immunity are finally coming under serious question, and institutional mechanisms are finally becoming available to hold accountable, even at the highest level, the perpetrators of human rights violations.

Work and work-related rights of women and girls

Work and Work-related Rights of Women and Girls
Krisztina Morvai

Introduction

This presentation will discuss why, and how, judges should use international human rights instruments at the domestic level in gender-specific labour law cases. I will first review certain parallels between the institution of the family and the institution of the workplace (as an element of the larger context of the market) and point out the challenges for using the international human rights framework in women's cases in these two fields. As part of the analysis of the similarities I would like to challenge the private/public dichotomy and introduce a slightly new approach to the related traditional dilemma, which is so central to the redefinition of human rights as well as to the redefinition of women's lives. I shall then move on to ask: were international human rights instruments meant to be used by domestic courts? My answer will be longer than a brief "yes" but it will be affirmative. Later I shall try to explore the relationship between the application of relevant domestic law and relevant international human rights law, focusing on interpretation. I shall conclude that the relevant domestic laws should be interpreted in the light of the relevant international human rights norms, but emphasize that the letters of the treaties and convention must be interpreted, too. Finally I would like to use a couple of examples for finding the normative meaning behind some of the articles of the Convention on the Elimination of All Forms of Discrimination against Women (CEDAW) in conjunction with other international norms, in particular certain elements of ILO Conventions.

79

Women in the "private family" and in the "free market"

In order to demonstrate that there are certain quite obvious parallels between women's rights issues in the workplace and women's rights issues in the family (in particular violence against women in the family), let me ask the following question: what are the two strongest pillars on which modern (patriarchal) society is based? I am sure that most of us would answer: the market and the family. Unbelievable investments have been made into these two during human history. "Disturbing" the "private" family or the "free" market, interventions into any or both of these elements of the "world order" are serious threats to the *status quo*.

The family is characterized as a sphere of intimacy and love which should be protected from outside interventions, in particular by the State and by the law. The market is characterized as free and rational and its spontaneity should not be disturbed by external interventions such as laws which threaten spontaneity or restrict efficiency. The maintenance of the status quo would require both of these spheres to be left intact, undisturbed, be driven by love (as opposed to justice) in the case of the family, and by business rationality (as opposed to justice) in the case of the workplace. Such thinking has obvious consequences for women: isolation, exploitation and violence in the family, limited opportunities and the wide variety of forms of discrimination in the workplace.

It follows from the common roots of these two elements of the "world order" that attitudes towards women's rights in the family and women's rights in the workplace have certain fundamental similarities. Most importantly from the point of view of the present colloquium, there is enormous resistance to seeing these issues as rights issues to be approached by the means and procedures of the law, let alone by the means of human rights law, such as international human rights instruments.

What is so specially threatening in dealing with "issues" or "problems" of women in the family or "issues" and "problems" of women in the workplace within the framework of international human rights law? The most threatening is the message: these "issues" and "problems" are nothing less than matters of *universal* human rights. In other words, the fact that a husband rapes *his* wife or that a private employer, manager of a private company dismisses *his* female employee because she does not smile enough are dealt with not as "private issues", not even as issues of domestic law alone but as issues of concern for the whole civilized world.

The individual judge in the Philippines, in Chile, in Finland or in Canada, by referring to these international instruments and by applying norms which are shared by the whole community of nations creates a link between an isolated, individual woman and the rest of the world.

The private/public dichotomy: a slightly new approach

This is especially shocking if we consider that "the woman" and "privacy/the private sphere" are traditionally and deeply interrelated.

It is a truism that women's lives are defined and determined by their traditional belonging to the "private sphere", most eminently the family. It is also known to most lawyers that human rights in the traditional sense were not meant to be applied in the private sphere in cases of (human rights) violations by private actors, such as husbands or lovers, but only in the public sphere in cases of state action, i.e. human rights violations committed by the State or by its agents, such as police officers or censors of political speech. We are aware of the harsh consequences for women of this traditional understanding of human rights.

Much less thought is given to the question of how we define the so-called private sphere, and where we draw the line between that and the so-called public sphere. Women's experiences in the workplace and women's labor law-related cases often show a phenomenon which I would call the privatization of the public, and the publication of the private. What do I mean by this?

Perhaps most people think that the borderline of the private sphere is at the door of the family home. It follows that women are traditionally - quasi "biologically" - linked to the family and therefore they are identified with the private sphere. It also follows that, by leaving the family home behind, "the woman" can leave "the private sphere" and is no longer identified with it once on the street, much less when she is in the workplace which is the stereotypical symbol of "the public sphere". Based on experience and on the reading of many labor law cases of women I would say that the latter presumption is incorrect. The relationship between the private sphere and "the woman" is not a one-way relationship. Not only does the private sphere define and determine women's lives, it also works the other way around. The presence of the woman creates a private sphere around her even within the space which is considered to be the most public of spheres, the workplace. Let me explain using the example of the phenomenon of sexual harassment.

The workplace, which is a traditional public sphere, can turn into a private sphere once a woman is present who is attacked, harassed as a woman because she is a woman.

It seems that her body magically transforms the space around her. The workplace, which just minutes ago was considered to be part of the public sphere, a place to work, driven by business rationality or by formal regulations, suddenly becomes a private sphere. What happens to her is "her business", she should sort it out, probably she asked for it. Public norms of the public sphere no longer apply. Another example has recently happened to me. I returned to work after the birth of my twin babies. I had been asked earlier to prepare for the special course on law as a second degree which I was going to teach. A week before the beginning of the semester we had a faculty-department meeting. About a dozen of my colleagues, all male except another female professor and the secretary, were sitting around a long table.

Everybody looked a bit embarrassed. The head of the department said: "We do not think you should teach that course. It is a priority for the law school, also because students pay a lot of money for it. It requires high quality work. What would you do in case any of your kids becomes ill?"

I do not think my boss would have ever thought of asking one of our male colleagues sitting there in jacket and tie what he would do should his child fall ill. Interestingly enough it was me who felt embarrassed. I thought it was me who changed the atmosphere of a hardworking community of scholars. I felt very bad, because I thought I should not talk about my private things, and that particular space and situation had to do with work and scholarship and not with me as a person, who happens to be a mother of three children and has to organize her life accordingly. I felt that I was privatizing the workplace by my mere presence in it as a woman who happens to be a worker. I felt that I was there only to complicate things and to interfere with the affairs of "real workers". In my opinion this is exactly the effect women are meant to feel. Women are still considered by many to be in employment either due to a pressing economic necessity - in case the "real bread-winner" does not make enough money for the family or, alternatively, as a luxury. I often feel that behind many of women's workplace discrimination cases is the view that women's work outside the home is an essentially private matter of the woman. In exchange for accepting an individual woman or women as a group in the public sphere of work, those in real power, "the real workers" feel that they have control over the woman's privacy.

How can domestic courts apply the CEDAW Convention?

Were international human rights instruments meant to be applied by domestic courts? In my opinion the answer is, clearly, yes. The most important characteristic of a human right is that it has a legal character and that it is enforceable. Institutionally, in democracies operating under the rule of law, the characteristic of enforceable legal rights is that their enforcement can be claimed - at least ultimately - from the courts. If a State undertakes the duty to enforce a certain element of an international human rights instrument, its domestic courts are under the duty to apply the international human rights instrument. As I shall soon explain, they can use the instrument either directly as law, or indirectly as a source of interpretation of existing domestic laws in the form of statutes or the constitution.

Let us consider the CEDAW Convention, which clearly demonstrates this. Under article 2, "States Parties......undertake: ...(c) to ensure through *competent national tribunals*...the effective protection of women against any act of discrimination..." (emphasis added).

In the context of the Convention, the term - competent tribunals - does not only mean that the tribunals must be competent in general terms. In other words, it cannot mean that judges are generally wise, knowledgeable and use domestic laws appropriately. In the given context the term must mean that the tribunals - the judges - are aware of the content of the Convention, that they fully understand its meaning and purpose, and that they can apply its elements competently.

Obviously the domestic courts' direct use of the Convention as a primary source of law is not the only way for a State to enforce the norms of the Convention. Another way of enforcing the rights embodied in the international instrument is the transformation of all its elements into domestic, i.e. written, codified law. Making the Convention itself directly enforceable is only one way of doing this. The other (theoretically also appropriate and even more effective) way is to build every single normative element of the international document into every single domestic law, from the constitution to statutes to administrative regulations of legal character, in every single area in which these norms can be relevant. The problem is that even in the latter case, these international norms are far more principles to be interpreted than technical regulations which can be applied without any interpretation.

In reality, the most likely way for domestic judges to apply international human rights instruments such as the CEDAW Convention is to filter the interpretation of domestic statutes that are relevant to a given case through the normative meanings of the relevant elements of the international instrument. In other words, the interpretation of domestic statutes should be done in the light of the norms contained in the international document.

The knowledge of any judge in any jurisdiction is far deeper and wider than the mere knowledge of written laws relevant to her caseload. Judges learn, read, compare and create principles, policies and theories in order to be able to apply the law. In fact, the individual law itself is far more than its letters, the words of the statute. This is the case in the context of both domestic law and international human rights law. Written laws were created on the basis of principles, policies, theories. On the other hand, theories, principles and policies grow out of the written laws as they are applied. This is the same with international human rights law in general and with particular fields of international human rights law, such as, say, the international human rights law of equal protection in the field of labour relations.

The way to be competent in international human rights law and to apply for example the CEDAW Convention competently is essentially the same process that makes a judge competent in domestic law and in its competent application.

The judge should be familiar with the roots, the history of the relevant law, theory or theories of relevance to the given field of the law, the aim/ purposes of the law, etc. In my view the main obstacle for the application of international women's human rights law at this stage, apart from those I outlined in the introduction is that there is very limited theory and systematically compiled applicable knowledge collected in the different fields. I do not want to be misunderstood: this is not a shortcoming which I want to criticize but a natural consequence of the fact that international women's human rights law as a discipline or quasi-discipline is extremely young. While a labour court judge can find hundreds of books on labour law in general, dozens on theories and applied norms of different areas of labour law, she can hardly find a single book on applied labour law of women's international human rights.

International human rights is a relatively new concept in the history of the law. The prohibition of discrimination on the basis of sex is also a new norm. The idea that women's rights are human rights is perhaps the latest, still widely contested development and concept in the law.

In order to be able to use women's international human rights law and its instruments competently within the meaning offered above, theoretical scholarship and theoretical as well as applied jurisprudence need to be developed and compiled in all the specific fields of women's human rights. A special part needs to be added to international women's human rights law's existing general part.

By general part, I mean the existing norms and principles concerning the responsibility of the State under international women's human rights law; the challenge to the public/private distinction; the rejection of the traditional approach which argues that in the context of human rights States are responsible only and explicitly for state action, that is violations carried out directly by the State and its actors; the principle of positive state duties, as opposed to the negative duty of non-action alone. These are questions which have been dealt with by excellent scholars in the last several years. Outstanding books and articles have been published in the field of what I call the general part of women's international human rights law. The next step should be an equally deep, analytic special part which should deal with the specific issues of e.g. labour law, family law, or criminal law within international women's human rights law.

I am not suggesting that domestic judges should wait for these developments and not apply and refer to international women's human rights instruments until the special part will be available. On the contrary. I think that domestic judges should familiarize themselves with international women's human rights instruments such as the CEDAW Convention as well as with general human rights instruments, apply them and refer to them in gender-specific cases. The more cases become available and accessible around the world, the earlier we shall have an applied women's human rights law, and special part(s) of international women's human rights law.

But how can you apply these instruments at this stage? In particular, how can you apply them in labour law cases? The task is undoubtedly more complex and more difficult than to apply domestic labour law. As lawyers we all studied our domestic labour law in law school. We had textbooks and later on we read lots of further books, law review articles, cases and reports and we have learned our labour law. We had very limited opportunities to do the same in the context of international human rights law as applied to gender-specific labour law cases. Many of us probably had limited opportunities to deal with gender-specific cases in our courts with the means of either domestic or international human rights law.

More precisely, many of us probably have not considered cases involving women as gender-specific cases that raise gender-specific issues, discrimination issues in the wider sense. Many of us are probably in a learning process of developing gender sensitivity. Familiarizing ourselves with the gender aspects of labour law could happen in parallel with, or through familiarizing ourselves with, the instruments of international women's human rights law or general instruments of human rights law as applied to women.

Given the lack, or shortage of readily available commentaries, textbooks and case-books on the applicability of women's human rights law in labour cases, the actual content and meaning of the norms contained in international human rights instruments relevant to the given case should be discovered by original research. Some of the sources of interpretation of the letters of these documents are common to all international treaties and are summarized in the Vienna Convention on the Law of Treaties. According to article 31 (1): "A treaty shall be interpreted in good faith in accordance with the ordinary meaning to be given to the terms of the treaty in their context and in the light of its

86

object and purpose." The preamble and annexes of a treaty should be taken into account in the course of the interpretation. If there are still uncertainties "any subsequent agreement between the parties regarding the interpretation of the treaty or the application of its provisions" and /or "any subsequent practice in the application of the treaty which establishes the agreement of the parties regarding its interpretation" can be taken into account.

In the case of the CEDAW Convention, a useful tool for interpretation is the work of the monitoring body, the Committee on the Elimination of Discrimination against Women, which monitors implementation through consideration of the periodic reports submitted by States parties. The Committee's questions and issues raised with a reporting State, and its concluding comments, can be very helpful in understanding how the Committee, as an authentic source of interpretation, understands specific elements of the Convention.

Under article 22 of the CEDAW Convention, "the Committee may invite the specialized agencies [of the United Nations] to submit reports on the implementation of the Convention in areas falling within the scope of their activities." In the context of labour law, an extremely useful source of information about and interpretation of the Convention is found in the ILO's reports on work issues in the country reports.

Normative meanings and possible useful interpretations of certain CEDAW Convention articles relevant to women's and girls' work-related rights

The following are examples for interpreting women's and girls' work-related rights in the light of the CEDAW Convention and other international human rights instruments.

Can the CEDAW Convention be applied in the context of work-related legal disputes?

CEDAW article 1. "…discrimination against women shall mean any distinction, exclusion or restriction made on the basis of sex which has the effect or purpose of impairing or nullifying the recognition, enjoyment or exercise by women irrespective of their marital status, on a basis of equality of men and women, of *human rights…*" (emphasis added).

Question/problem: Does this article refer to the right to work, too? Can it be applied by judges in the context of labour law-related debates?

The answer depends on whether the right to work is to be considered a human right. Article 23 of the Universal Declaration of Human Rights states that "1. Everyone has the right to work, to free choice of employment, to just and favourable conditions of work and to protection against unemployment."

In answer to the question whether the right to work is a human right, it follows that article 1 of the CEDAW Convention can be applied in the context of work-related debates.

Equal pay for equal work

The preamble of the CEDAW Convention states: "Considering the international conventions concluded under the auspices of the United Nations and the specialized agencies promoting equality of rights of men and women…"

Interpreting this statement one can conclude that the norms of the CEDAW Convention can be applied in conjunction with the norms of other United Nations conventions, for example the norms of relevant ILO conventions.

CEDAW article 11 (d) states: "The right to equal remuneration, including benefits, and to equal treatment in respect of work of equal value…"

Interpreting this article one can conclude that women have the right, under the CEDAW Convention, to equal pay for work of equal value.

Question/problem: What is "equal pay for work of equal value"? What is the meaning of "work of equal value"?

In order to answer this question, reference can be made to ILO Convention No. 100 (1951), article 3 (1) and 3(3): "3.1. Where such action will assist in giving effect to the provisions of this Convention measures shall be taken to promote *objective appraisal of jobs on the basis of the work to be performed*"… . "3.3 Differential rates between workers which correspond, *without regard to sex, to differences, as determined by such objective appraisal, in the work to be performed* shall not be considered as being contrary to the principle of equal remuneration for men and women workers for work of equal value" (emphasis added).

For purposes of interpretation, reference can also be made to CEDAW General Recommendation 13 (1989) on equal remuneration for work of equal value, stating in paragraph 2: "[States parties] should consider the study, development, and adoption of job evaluation systems based on gender-neutral criteria that would facilitate the comparison of the value of those jobs of a different nature in which women presently predominate".

From the above, the following conclusion can be drawn: If domestic law refers to "equal pay for equal work", it should be interpreted as equal pay for work of equal value. In the context of "equal value of work", the value of work should be evaluated on the basis of the work actually performed; on the basis of objective criteria; and without regard to sex. Jobs do not need to be the very same, the value of jobs of different nature can be also compared.

The normative meaning of "discrimination against" women (with children), e.g. in hiring, promotion, training

The preamble of the CEDAW Convention states: "Bearing in mind … that the role of women in procreation should not be a basis for discrimination…"

It follows that job vacancies which are "not open for women with children/mothers/pregnant women/women under 30", etc., are contrary to the provisions of the CEDAW Convention. Similarly "Vacancy not open for parents who have the duty to care for small children" (similar effect test: even though not discriminating on the basis of sex - on its face - its effect is discriminatory for women); or "We could not hire/promote/train Mrs. X because she has children" are in violation of the CEDAW Convention.

In order to assess further the normative meaning of certain elements of discrimination in the context of work-related rights and disputes, reference can be made to article 1 of the CEDAW Convention: "…discrimination against women shall mean *any distinction, exclusion or restriction made on the basis of sex which has the effect or purpose*

89

of impairing or nullifying the recognition, enjoyment or exercise by women irrespective of their marital status, on a basis of equality of men and women, of human rights..." (emphasis added).

- "any" (distinction, exclusion, restriction) - Meaning: business rationale is not a justification for discriminatory treatment. The text does not say "any irrational" distinction or "any unreasonable" exclusion, but uses the word "any".

- "which has the effect or purpose of impairing or nullifying the recognition...of human rights" - Meaning: effect OR purpose are used disjunctively, not conjunctively, i.e. either discriminative effect or discriminative purpose is covered by the Convention. Effect is an objective element, purpose is a subjective element. Examples of discriminatory purpose: "We do not (want to) train women". "We pay less per hour for women". Examples of discriminatory effect: "We do not train part time workers". "We pay less per hour for part-time workers".

Given that women are highly overrepresented among part-time workers, any specific (negative) measure against part time workers in effect discriminates against women.

*Interpretations relevant to the right to standing (*locus standi*) in women's work-related disputes*

Article 2 (b) of the CEDAW Convention states: "States Parties ...undertake... to adopt appropriate legislative *and other* measures, including *sanctions* where appropriate, prohibiting all discrimination against women" (emphasis added).

Interpretation of this paragraph can be relevant to making decisions concerning standing.

Article 2 (c) of the CEDAW Convention states: "States Parties undertake ... to ensure through competent national tribunals ... the *effective* protection of women against *any* act of discrimination" (emphasis added).

- "effective" (actual meaning varies by case, the employer might have applied some way to protect the woman against discrimina-

tion but it is possible that it was not effective and only court proceedings can ensure effective protection).

- "any" act of discrimination: this word can also be relevant to decisions on standing.

State action and private action in the interpretation and application of
the CEDAW Convention

Article 2 (d) of the CEDAW Convention states: "States Parties undertake…to refrain from engaging in any act or practice of discrimination against women and to ensure that public authorities and institutions
shall act in conformity with this obligation". Meaning: protection from
discriminatory state action.

Article 2 (e) of the CEDAW Convention states: "[States Parties
undertake] to take all appropriate measures to eliminate discrimination
against women by any person, organization or enterprise". Meaning:
protection from discrimination by private actors (employers). All the
norms apply to private action as well as to state action.

Interpretation of norms relevant to cases concerning stereotypical,
gender-based roles for women

Article 5 of the CEDAW Convention states: "States Parties shall
take all appropriate measures: (a) To modify the social and cultural
patterns of conduct of men and women, with a view to achieving the
elimination of prejudices and customary and all other practices which
are based on the idea of the inferiority or the superiority of either of the
sexes or on the stereotyped roles for men and women…".

In concrete cases before domestic courts the above article can be
interpreted in conjunction with other relevant articles, e.g. article 11 (b)
and (d) which states: "11. (b) [States Parties shall take all appropriate
measures… in order to ensure, on a basis of equality of men and
women, the same rights, in particular:] The right to the same employment opportunities, including the application of the same criteria for
selection in matters of employment". "(d) …The right to equality of
treatment in the evaluation of quality of work".

Comparative cases can also be used, e.g. *Price Waterhouse* (United
States Supreme Court case, in which a female employee who did not
have a "feminine enough" behaviour was not promoted to partner).

Stereotyped roles for women in similar cases: a woman should smile, be kind, wear make up, be pleasant for the eyes, etc.; not the same selection criteria as for men; evaluation is based on non-equal criteria.

The interpretation of the right to free choice of profession and employment versus protective legislation for women

Question/problem: To what extent can the right to free choice of profession/employment be exercised by women who choose "hazardous" work?

Articles relevant to this issue include article 11 (c) of the CEDAW Convention on the right to free choice of profession and employment, in conjunction with 11 (b) on the right to the application of the same criteria, and the general non-discrimination clauses within the Convention (e.g. article 1).

With regard to the second part of the problem, attention is drawn to article 11(f) on the right to protection of health and to safety in working conditions, including the safeguarding of the function of reproduction.

This article should be interpreted in conjunction with the free choice of employment-clause and with article 11.3 which states: "11.3. Protective legislation relating to matters covered in this article shall be reviewed periodically in the light of scientific and technological knowledge...".

It follows that restrictions on the free choice of employment for the protection of women cannot be arbitrary.

Conclusion

The CEDAW Convention was meant to be used by domestic courts, in cases of work-related disputes of women appearing before them, too. Domestic labour laws should be interpreted in line with the norms of the Convention and with other related human right norms, including ILO Conventions. The main obstacle appears to be the lack of compiled knowledge in the field, especially textbooks and casebooks on a special part of women's human rights law - applied women's labour law. This gap can be filled effectively by professional meetings such as the 1999 United Nations Judicial Colloquium in Vienna.

Prohibition of Discrimination and the Concept of Affirmative Action
Marc Bossuyt

The principle of equality and the prohibition of discrimination are concepts frequently invoked in political debate, sometimes arousing strong feelings. However, these concepts are, first and foremost, legal ones, which, moreover, are deeply rooted in the consciousness of every one of us. For all that, they are concepts that are difficult to delimit and still more difficult to apply, with respect both to legal norms, which are inevitably general, and to individual cases. The debate surrounding these concepts has become no less problematic for the growing number of references to the concept of "affirmative action", or "positive discrimination". There is a need, first of all, to review the concepts of equality and prohibition of discrimination.

Prohibition of discrimination

The prohibition of discrimination (or the principle of equality, which amounts to the same thing) is laid down in the European Convention for the Protection of Human Rights and Fundamental Freedoms, the International Covenant on Civil and Political Rights and the Belgian Constitution, all of which have precedence over legal norms.

In article 14 of the European Convention ("The enjoyment of the rights and freedoms *set forth in this Convention* shall be secured *without discrimination on any ground* such as sex, race, colour, language, religion, political or other opinion, national or social origin, association with a national minority, property, birth or other status"), discrimination is prohibited solely with respect to the rights and freedoms set forth in the Convention.

Clearly, this does not mean that States parties to the European Convention can discriminate with respect to rights and freedoms not set forth in the Convention. This limitation is only of institutional significance (in terms of the competence of the monitoring bodies and, in particular, of the European Court of Human Rights) and is of no normative value.

Both of the international human rights covenants contain clauses in their article 2 guaranteeing, in the case of the International Covenant on Economic, Social and Cultural Rights (para. 2), "that the rights *enunciated* ... will be exercised without *discrimination* of any kind", and in the case of the International Covenant on Civil and Political Rights (para. 1), "the rights *recognized* ... without *distinction* of any kind". It emerges from consideration of the preparatory work that by using the term "distinction", the International Covenant on Civil and Political Rights does not in fact extend the prohibition referred to in the International Covenant on Economic, Social and Cultural Rights, which uses the (more appropriate) term of "discrimination".

In both cases, article 2, just like article 14 of the European Convention, forbids discrimination only with respect to the rights "enunciated" or "recognized" in the Covenants. In other words, the prohibition is limited to the rights guaranteed by the instrument concerned.

Article 26 of the International Covenant on Civil and Political Rights does, however, also contain a general prohibition of discrimination, as follows: "All persons are equal before the law and are entitled without any discrimination to the equal protection of the law. In this respect, the law shall prohibit any discrimination and guarantee to all persons equal and effective protection against discrimination on any ground [...]."

In order to illustrate the scope of the general prohibition of discrimination contained in article 26, mention must be made of two cases brought by Dutch women, Ms. *S. W. M. Broeks* (UN document A/42/40, pp. 139-150) and Ms. *F. H. Zwaan-de Vries* (ibid., pp. 160-169), who made complaints to the Human Rights Committee established by the International Covenant on Civil and Political Rights that they were receiving a lesser benefit because they were married. In these cases, the Human Rights Committee, on 9 April 1987, found a violation of article 26 of the International Covenant on Civil and Political Rights, as applied to the field of social security.

The Netherlands Government, however, took the view that that article could only be invoked under the Optional Protocol to the Covenant in the sphere of civil and political rights, rights not necessarily limited to those civil and political rights embodied in the Covenant. The complaints, however, concerned the enjoyment of economic, social and cultural rights, which fall under the International Covenant on Economic, Social and Cultural Rights, which deliberately does not provide for an individual complaints procedure.

In the Committee's view, on the other hand, the International Covenant on Civil and Political Rights applies even if any of the matters referred to therein is mentioned or incorporated in the provisions of other international instruments. Notwithstanding the interrelatedness of the two Covenants, it is necessary for the Committee to apply fully the terms of the International Covenant on Civil and Political Rights. The provisions of article 2 of the International Covenant on Economic, Social and Cultural Rights do not detract from the full application of article 26 of the other Covenant. Article 26 is thus concerned with the obligations imposed on States in regard to their legislation and its application.

The fact that a married woman had to prove that she was a "breadwinner", a condition that did not apply to married men, constituted, according to the Committee, a differentiation that was in fact one of sex, placing married women at a disadvantage compared with married men. The Committee was of the view that such a differentiation was not reasonable.

It is questionable whether the drafters of article 26 of the International Covenant on Civil and Political Rights really intended to entrust the Human Rights Committee with monitoring its application in the sphere of economic, social and cultural rights. However, the text adopted clearly encompasses all the various rights and freedoms, without making any exception in the case of economic, social and cultural rights. The Committee therefore had no choice but to recognize the general character of the prohibition on discrimination. In States parties in which the covenants are incorporated in the internal legal order, another consequence of the broad scope of article 26 is the considerable expansion of the supervisory power of judges.

If there were any doubt, the first sentence of article 26 guarantees both "equality before the law" (stating that "all persons are equal before the law") and "equality in law" (adding that they are entitled to "the equal protection of the law"). According to a classic distinction made by Kelsen, it is in fact necessary to distinguish between "equality before the law", which concerns the application of legal rules and is the province of judges, and "equality in law", which concerns the creation of law and is the province of legislators.

But, whatever the terminology, there is no doubt that the prohibition on discrimination in the international instruments covers all the powers of the States parties and thus both legislators and judges. This is also true of the prohibition on discrimination (or the principle of equality) laid down in national constitutions. Constitutional norms are therefore as much an obligation on legislatures as on the judiciary.

The differences that exist between constitutional systems with respect to supervision of the constitutionality of laws do not relate to the lawfulness, or otherwise, of the adoption by legislators of discriminatory norms, but to the competence (or lack of competence) of the judiciary to verify that laws are in conformity with the prohibition on discrimination or, in other words, the power (or lack of power) of judges to make their interpretation of the prohibition of discrimination prevail over that of legislators. In a break with long-standing tradition, the Belgian Constitution, by empowering the Court of Arbitration, in 1989, to verify the compliance of legal norms with articles 10 and 11 of the Constitution, gave the interpretation of constitutional judges precedence over that of federal, district and regional legislators.

With regard, once again, to the European Convention, it is worth noting that, whereas the French version of article 14 appears to prohibit any "distinction", the European Court of Human Rights had occasion to comment in the *Belgian use of languages* case (Series A, p. 34) that "in spite of the very general wording of the French version (*'sans distinction aucune'*), [...] this version must be read in the light of the more restrictive text of the English version ('without discrimination')".

Indeed, it is clear that what is prohibited is not "any distinction", but only "discrimination", that is, arbitrary distinctions. It is true that, following the — rather unfortunate — use of the term "distinction" in the Charter of the United Nations, it took some time, particularly in French, for the term "discrimination" to become generally accepted as the appropriate term for designating unjustified, unfounded or arbitrary differences of treatment.

For some time now, the term "discrimination", which has a definitely pejorative connotation, has been reserved solely for unjustified differences of treatment, whereas the term "distinction" is completely neutral. The term "differentiation", by contrast, designates a difference of treatment for which there are legitimate reasons. In order to determine whether a difference of treatment amounts to discrimination, the various constituent elements of discrimination must be analyzed.

One of these elements is the ground for the difference of treatment at issue. It is very important to realize that the list of these grounds is indicative, not restrictive. This is clear from the increase in the number of grounds cited from four in the Charter of the United Nations (race, sex, language, religion) to 12 in the Universal Declaration of Human Rights (and the international human rights covenants) and 13 in the European Convention, as well as the use of the words "such as" before the list of these grounds.

Since the list of the grounds for distinction is not restrictive, the grounds do not constitute in themselves the decisive element in determining whether a distinction is arbitrary. A difference of treatment based on grounds other than those listed in the instrument concerned may nevertheless be discriminatory, just as a difference of treatment on one of these grounds will not necessarily constitute discrimination.

In order to determine whether or not a difference of treatment is discriminatory, it is necessary to look at both the grounds for the difference of treatment and the right or freedom in relation to which it is practised. In particular, the matter in which the difference of treatment is practised must be a right or freedom, that is an entitlement protected by law. If the difference of treatment is practised in matters that are not protected by law, or, in other words, matters that are not yet regulated by law, it cannot constitute prohibited discrimination.

In the area of private life, for example, that is the domain reserved for the private actions of any individual in which the law cannot interfere without violating the right to privacy, distinctions, even arbitrary ones, cannot be penalized. However, it is the law that delimits the scope of private life, and it may, if the need becomes apparent, subject some aspects of what is normally part of the private sphere to regulation by law. This may be the case, for example, with respect to certain aspects of the functioning and, more particularly, the membership policies of private clubs.

Once a matter is regulated by law, it is no longer permissible to practise discrimination, that is to make arbitrary distinctions, in relation to it, because law and arbitrariness are irreconcilable, contradictory concepts.

A difference of treatment is arbitrary when there is no valid connection between the right or freedom in relation to which it is practised and the grounds on which it is based. Thus, some grounds may, because they are relevant, justify a difference of treatment in relation to one right, but not another, and, likewise it may be acceptable to base a difference of treatment in relation to a particular right on some grounds, but not on others.

In its judgement of 23 July 1968 in the *Belgian use of languages* case (Series A, p. 34), the European Court of Human Rights held that "the principle of equality of treatment is violated if the distinction has no *objective and reasonable justification*. The existence of such a justification must be assessed in relation to the aim and effects of the measure under consideration, regard being had to the principles which normally prevail in democratic societies. A difference of treatment in the exercise of a right laid down in the Convention must not only pursue a *legitimate aim*: article 14 is likewise violated when it is clearly established that there is no *reasonable relationship of proportionality between the means employed and the aim sought to be realized*" (emphasis added).

Since its first judgements, in 1989, on the application of articles 10 and 11 of the Constitution, the Court of Arbitration has drawn extensively on the jurisprudence of the European Court of Human Rights concerning article 14 of the European Convention. The Court of Arbitration observed, for example, in its judgement 21/89, B.4.5.b of 13 July 1989 that "the constitutional provisions on equality of Belgians and non-discrimination do not preclude differences of treatment established according to certain categories of persons, provided that there is an objective and reasonable justification for the criterion on which the differentiation is based. The existence of such a justification must be assessed in relation to the aim and effects of the measure under consideration; the principle of equality is violated when it is clearly established that there is no reasonable relationship of proportionality between the means employed and the aim sought to be realized".

The Court of Arbitration has also recognized that the constitutional prohibition is not restricted to the rights and freedoms set forth in the Belgian Constitution itself but is applicable "in regard to all the rights and freedoms to which Belgians are entitled" (judgement 23/89, B.1.2 of 13 October 1989), including "the rights and freedoms resulting from provisions of the international instruments to which Belgium is a party and which have come into effect by virtue of an act of assent" (judgement 39/91, B.11.3 of 19 December 1991).

The Court of Arbitration concluded on the basis of article 191 of the Constitution ("Every alien who is in Belgian territory shall enjoy the same protection granted to persons and property, save in exceptional cases established by the law.") that aliens may invoke the principles of equality and non-discrimination enshrined in articles 10 and 11 of the Constitution "provided that two conditions are met: that they are in Belgian territory and the law does not provide otherwise" (judgement 20/93, B.2.2 of 4 March 1993).

However, in judgement 61/94 (B.2) of 14 July 1994 the Court of Arbitration took the view that "article 191 [does not detract] in any way from the obligation on legislators, when they establish a difference of treatment to the detriment of aliens, to ensure that that difference is not discriminatory, whatever the nature of the principles in question".

Article 191 of the Constitution does not therefore legitimate all legislative distinctions between Belgians and aliens. Nor does it mean that all distinctions between Belgians and aliens are *ipso facto* contrary to the Constitution. This is also true of distinctions established among aliens.

It emerges from judgement 51/94 of 29 June 1994 that the Court of Arbitration considered that, in the field of social assistance, legally resident aliens should be accorded the same treatment as Belgians, unlike those aliens who were not in the same situation as Belgians because they were residing illegally in the territory: "It is not unreasonable that the State should not assume the same duties in respect of those who, on the one hand, are residing legally in its territory (its nationals and certain categories of aliens) and aliens, on the other hand, who remain there after being ordered to leave it."

As to the universal right to an adequate standard of living, recognized in article 11 (1) of the International Covenant on Economic, Social and Cultural Rights, the Court held, in the same judgement, that "for each State, this can apply only to the persons for which it is responsible. Such persons cannot include, although they are in the territory of the State, aliens who have been ordered to leave it after it has been established that the conditions for their stay have not been or are no longer being complied with" (B.5.5).

The concept of "affirmative action"

"Affirmative action", a concept of American origin, is best translated into French by the term "action positive". The term "discrimination positive" (positive discrimination), on the other hand, is to be avoided at all costs. Indeed, it is a contradiction in terms: either what is under consideration is a "positive" difference in treatment and thus cannot be termed "discrimination", or it is "discrimination" and the difference of treatment cannot therefore be qualified as "positive".

It must be recognized, however, that there have been situations in the past where specific groups of individuals, who may be identified by reference to the grounds mentioned in the instruments prohibiting discrimination, have been subjected to systematic discrimination. It may be justified or even necessary in such situations to take affirmative measures in order to help such groups to overcome the unfavourable situations in which they are placed.

However, the fact that a measure is taken in pursuit of a legitimate aim does not in itself justify the measure. The aim, moreover, is not a constituent element of a discriminatory action. Indeed, it is difficult to see how a legitimate aim could suffice to legitimate any difference of treatment based on any grounds and practised in relation to any right or freedom. Conversely, even a measure taken in pursuit of an illegitimate aim would not constitute discrimination if, contrary to the intention of the perpetrator, the measure did not achieve the desired effect.

There is no way of considering the question of "affirmative action" without referring to the jurisprudence of the United States Supreme Court in the matter of discrimination and more particularly racial discrimination.

100

The first example of such jurisprudence is the judgement passed in 1896 in the famous *Plessy v. Ferguson* case (163 U.S. 537), in which the United States Supreme Court legitimated the "separate but equal" doctrine. Almost 60 years were to pass before that doctrine was reversed by the judgement delivered in 1954 in the equally famous case of *Brown v. Board of Education* (374 U.S. 483), in which the Supreme Court held that separate schools inevitably created a feeling of inferiority.

Even before that case arose, the Supreme Court had held in its 1944 judgement in *Korematsu v. United States* (323 U.S. 214) that any legal restrictions limiting the civil rights of a single racial group were immediately suspect and had to be submitted to "strict scrutiny". On the other hand, with respect to distinctions on the ground of sex, the Supreme Court subsequently considered only "intermediate scrutiny" to be necessary.

In American law, the expression "affirmative action" appears for the first time in Executive Order 10925, signed by President Kennedy in 1961, requiring federal employers to hire more employees belonging to minorities. Two major Civil Rights Acts were signed, one in 1964 by President Johnson and one in 1972 by President Nixon.

In 1974, the Supreme Court considered that it did not have to rule on affirmative action measures in the matter of admission to university in the *DeFunis v. Odegaard* case (416 U.S. 312), on the grounds that the Jewish white student, who had been denied access to the Law School of the University of Washington, had meanwhile been admitted.

In the *Regents of the University of California v. Bakke* case (438 U.S. 265), the Supreme Court was very divided. Judge Lewis F. Powell, who agreed partly with the four judges in favour and partly with the four judges against the affirmative action programme of the School of Medicine of the University of California in Davis, issued a judgement in 1978 in which he held that such a programme had to be subject to very strict scrutiny, but that one of the arguments mentioned in favour of the programme, namely the wish to obtain the benefits derived from an ethnically diversified body of students, was sufficiently compelling for the university to apply it as one of the factors to be taken into consideration in the selection of students.

In the years that followed, the Supreme Court issued many judgements, some accepting and some rejecting the affirmative action programmes that came before it. The judgements in favour of affirmative action programmes which had been challenged included the following:

Steelworkers v. Weber, 443 U.S. 193 (1979),

Fullilove v. Klutznick, 448 U.S. 149 (1980),

Sheet Metal Workers v. EEOC (Equal Employment Opportunity Commission), 478 U.S. 421 (1986),

United States v. Paradise, 480 U.S. 149 (1987),

Johnson v. Santa Clara County, 480 U.S. 1442 (1987),

Metro Broadcasting Inc. v. FCC (Federal Communications Commission), 497 U.S. 547 (1990).

In the *Steelworkers* case (1979), the Supreme Court accepted the affirmative action programme reserving training places for black workers, on the grounds that the programme had been set up by a private employer and was intended to apply to job categories traditionally affected by segregation.

In the *Sheet Metal Workers* (1986), *Paradise* (1987) and *Johnson* (1987) cases, affirmative action programmes were accepted because they were intended to remedy cases of intentional discrimination practised in the past to the detriment of Blacks in the metal workers' union of the City of New York and in the Alabama police corps and to the detriment of women belonging to the skilled craft category in Santa Clara County (California).

In other judgements, the Supreme Court turned down action programmes which were brought before it. The cases were:

Firefighters v. Stotts, 467 U.S. 561 (1984),

Wygant v. Jackson Board of Education, 476 U.S. 267 (1986),

City of Richmond v. Croson, 488 U.S. 469 (1989).

In the *Firefighters* (1984) and *Wygant* (1986) cases, the affirmative action programmes called respectively for the dismissal of firefighters of the township of Memphis and of teachers in a school in Michigan, all whites and senior to their black colleagues. In the *Croson* (1989) case, the programme reserved 30 per cent of the contracts issued by the township of Richmond (Virginia) to companies belonging to minorities, namely "Blacks, Hispanics, Orientals, Indians, Eskimos and Aleuts". The Court held that such a measure was not "narrowly tailored" to the objective pursued and that it was unconnected with any past discrimination against Eskimos in Virginia.

In 1995, the Supreme Court passed judgement in the important case *Adarand Constructors v. Pena* (115 St. Ct. 2097). The Adarand company was complaining that it had lost a public works contract to a company belonging to a Hispanic on account of a federal law whereby 10 per cent of all public works contracts had to be attributed to minorities.

Writing on behalf of a majority of six, Judge Sandra Day O'Connor held three propositions derived from earlier Court judgements concerning race-based programmes:

a) Scepticism: preferences based on racial or ethnic criteria needed to be subjected to the closest scrutiny;

b) Consistency: the control standard should not depend on the race of those who benefit or suffer from the plan concerned;

c) Coherence: equal protection should be the same regardless of the level of government (federal or otherwise) involved.

Thus, it is now established that even federal programmes instituting affirmative action in favour of persons belonging to a single racial group must be subjected to very strict scrutiny.

In Belgium, the Court of Arbitration, in judgement 9/94 (B.6.2) of 27 January 1994, held in regard to the minimum income guaranteed to older persons that unequal treatment of men and women was discriminatory. However, the Court acknowledged that "in certain circumstances, unequal treatment is not irreconcilable with the principle of equality and the prohibition of discrimination, when it is intended precisely *to remove an existing inequality*. It is also necessary in order for such *corrective inequalities* to be compatible with the principle of equality and the prohibition of discrimination:

> "- That they should be applied only in cases in which there is an obvious inequality;

> "- That the elimination of this inequality should be identified by the legislators as the aim pursued;

> "- That the measures taken should be of a temporary character, the intention being that they will be discontinued as soon as the aim identified by the legislators is achieved; and

> "- That they should not needlessly restrict the rights of others".

As far as the jurisprudence of the Court of Justice of the European Communities is concerned, the Luxembourg Court, passing judgement in the *Kalanke v. Freie Hansestadt Bremen* case on 17 October 1995, held that: "national rules which guarantee women *absolute and unconditional priority* for appointment or promotion go beyond promoting equal opportunities and overstep the limits of the exception in article 2 (4) of the Directive".

According to article 2, paragraph 4, of Directive 76/207 of 9 February 1976, the latter shall be "without prejudice to measures to promote equal opportunity for men and women, in particular by removing existing inequalities which affect women's opportunities" in the areas of access to employment, promotion and vocational training.

However, the law under challenge, which concerned equal treatment of men and women in public services, *automatically* gave priority "where candidates of different sexes short-listed for promotion are equally qualified [...] to women in sectors where they [were] under-represented, under-representation being deemed to exist when women do not make up at least half of the staff in the individual pay brackets in the relevant personnel group or in the function levels provided for in the organization chart".

However, in the *Marschall v. Land Nordrhein-Westfalen* case, the Court of Justice of the European Communities issued a judgement on 11 November 1997 in which it ruled that the above-mentioned Directive did not preclude "a national rule which, in a case where there are fewer women than men at the level of the relevant post in a sector of the public service and both female and male candidates for the post are equally qualified in terms of their suitability, competence and professional performance, requires that priority be given to the promotion of female candidates *unless reasons specific to an individual male candidate tilt the balance in his favour* [...] provided that:

> "- In each individual case the rule provides for male candidates who are equally as qualified as the female candidates a guarantee that the candidatures will be the subject of an objective assessment which will take account of all criteria specific to the candidates and will override the priority accorded to female candidates where one or more of those criteria tilts the balance in favour of the male candidate, and

> "- Such criteria are not such as to discriminate against the female candidates".

In the Court's view, unlike in the *Kalanke* case, owing to the "saving clause" ("Öffnungsklausel"), the automatic preference given to women may be waived "if reasons specific to an individual male candidate tilt the balance in his favour".

It should be noted that several Governments made representations to the Court concerning their views in this case. The law of the *Land* of *Nordrhein-Westfalen* was strongly supported by the Austrian, Finnish, Norwegian, Spanish and Swedish Governments, as well as by the European Commission.

Conclusion

Nevertheless, the fact that a particular category of people suffered, in the past, from inferior economic or social conditions does not in itself mean that any difference of treatment based on a characteristic identifying this category must be considered legitimate, even where this characteristic has no relevance as a basis for a difference of treatment in relation to the right concerned. There would be no justification, for example, for providing special social assistance to persons who did not need it but belonged to a category that had, in the past, been placed in an inferior position and refusing such assistance to persons who did need it but belonged to a category that had, in the past, enjoyed better conditions in society.

Affirmative action must focus on taking measures that can be expected primarily to meet the needs of persons belonging to a group that requires special protection. It is by choosing the measures, as well as when and where they will be put into effect, that Governments can assist the categories concerned, without depriving those who do not belong to these categories of the benefits of such measures. Under no circumstances can someone be deprived of one of his or her rights, including the entitlement "without any discrimination to the equal protection of the law", on the pretext that this might help disadvantaged groups overcome more effectively the consequences of past discrimination.

Good intentions cannot justify differences of treatment based on grounds that, in the past, served as criteria for discrimination but are no more relevant as a basis for preferential treatment today than discrimination then. Affirmative action is not an exception to the principle of prohibiting discrimination. On the contrary, it is the principle of prohibiting discrimination that sets the limits of all affirmative action. In other words, affirmative action is permissible, even desirable, provided that it does not violate the prohibition of discrimination, that is so long as it does not result in differences of treatment, in relation to certain rights or freedoms, based on grounds that are not relevant to the right or freedom concerned..

Working group presentations

The relationship of international law and domestic law

Section 39(1) of the Constitution of South Africa: The Gateway for Application of the Convention on the Elimination of All Forms of Discrimination against Women and the Convention on the Rights of the Child in South Africa
Kate O'Regan

Introduction

Section 39(1) of the South African Constitution provides:

> "When interpreting the Bill of Rights, a court, tribunal or forum

> a)   must promote the values that underlie an open and democratic society based on human dignity, equality and freedom;

> b)   must consider international law; and

> c)   may consider foreign law".

The South African judiciary is made up of magistrates' and regional courts, high courts, the Supreme Court of Appeal (SCA) and the Constitutional Court. The high courts, Supreme Court of Appeal and Constitutional Court all have significant constitutional jurisdiction. The constitutional jurisdiction of magistrates' and regional courts has yet to be determined.

Reliance on conventions by South African judges

South Africa ratified CEDAW in December 1995, and CRC in June 1995. They are accordingly international law which is binding in South Africa. A survey of high court, SCA and Constitutional Court judgements suggests that in light of section 39(1) and the ratification of the treaties, courts are beginning to refer to international conventions.

Examples include:

1. *Brink v Kitshoff NO* 1996 (4) SA 197 (CC); 1996 (6) BCLR 752 (CC).

2. *In re School Education Bill, Gauteng* 1996 (3) SA 165 (CC); 1996 (4) BCLR 537 (CC).

3. *S v Howells* 1999 (1) SACR 675 (C)

Van Heerden AJ concerning the sentencing of an accused guilty of fraud. She had defrauded her employer of approximately R100,000. A divorcee with three minor children, she had used the money for gambling. She was sentenced in a regional court to four years' imprisonment plus two years suspended for five. On appeal, the Court held that the 'best interests of the child principle', part of the Constitution and the Convention on the Rights of Child should inform sentencing process. If the mother were imprisoned, the children would be put into care, had to be weighed in balance. On balance, it was held that she still deserved prison sentence. Thus, the sentence was upheld amended slightly.

In addition to direct reliance on the conventions, recent cases also show a clear trend to observe their spirit:

*   *Amod and Another v Multilateral Motor Vehicle Accidents Fund* (Case No 444/98, judgement delivered by Mahomed CJ on 29 September 1999).

This case concerned a dependant's action for damages against the Motor Vehicle Accidents Fund arising out of the death of her husband in a motor collision on 25 July 1993, six months after South Africa had ratified CEDAW and nearly a year before the 1994 Constitution came into operation. The plaintiff was a Muslim woman married to her husband according to Muslim personal law. This marriage was not recognized as a marriage for purposes of South African common law and, therefore, she was not entitled to claim damages against Fund.

Mahomed CJ traced the historical origins and evolution of the dependant's action in common law and found that the exclusion of the applicant from the class of persons entitled to benefit from the dependant's action "is inconsistent with the new ethos of tolerance, pluralism and religious freedom which had consolidated itself in the community even before the formal adoption of the interim Constitution on 22 December 1993".

* *S v J* 1998 (4) BCLR 424 (SCA).

After looking at case-law (both South African and foreign), various academic writings and statutory developments in numerous countries, Olivier JA dismissed an appeal against both a conviction and sentence for rape in which it was argued that "the trial court [had] misdirected itself in not truly applying the cautionary rule in respect of the evidence of complainants in sexual cases".[1] As in the *Amod* case, CEDAW was not mentioned, but the concerns of CEDAW clearly motivated the judgement.

Recent legislation

Our lawmakers have fared better. Take, for example, the Domestic Violence Act.[2] Its preamble reads in part as follows:

"AND HAVING REGARD to the Constitution of South Africa, and in particular, the right to equality and to freedom and security of the person; and the *international commitments and obligations of the State towards ending violence against women and children, including obligations under the United Nations Conventions on the Elimination of all Forms of Discrimination Against Women and the Rights of the Child...*" (emphasis added).

The South African Law Commission

In numerous issue and discussion papers - particularly in relation to violence against women and children - the South African Law Commission (SALC) has set an exemplary lead. Take the recent discussion paper (and annexed draft bill) on sexual offences, issued by the SALC on

---

[1]   At 428C.

[2]   Act 116 of 1998.

12 August 1999,[3] as well as its issue paper of 18 April 1998 on a review of the Child Care Act.[4]

Conclusion

Section 39 of the Constitution is a very important provision which should open the way to consideration of our international law obligations under both CEDAW and the CRC. This has not happened yet as extensively as one would have hoped but it may well happen in the future.

Nationality issues

National Implementation of International Law: The Dow Case
Unity Dow

Introduction

I take the position that women in many African countries are second class citizens, with limited rights as compared to their male counterparts. In some countries, this second class citizenship status has translated into situations where women have limited rights to pass on their citizenship to their children. In some cases, women have lost their citizenship upon marriage to a foreigner, on the reasoning that a woman who gets married transfers her loyalty to her husband and thus to his country. This makes sense if one accepts that the woman was never a full citizen to start with and when it is considered that her access to the public sphere is traditionally through a male, who would be the full

---

[3]   Discussion paper 85 of project 107 titled "Sexual offences: the substantive law".

[4]   Issue paper 13 of project 110.

citizen. This was the reasoning advanced in support of the Botswana Citizenship Act of 1984.

Thus, although the Constitutions of countries such as Botswana (section 15), Swaziland (section 15), Zambia (section 25), Mauritius (section 16), and Lesotho (section 17) guarantee to everyone protection against discrimination, their language is problematic. The equality guarantees are subject to exceptions making it lawful, it has been argued, to discriminate in the area of personal law. That area is of course very broad and the seat of some of the most discriminatory provisions against women in many countries.

The question poses itself how can women, with limited access to the public sphere and enjoying limited protections within the private sphere, participate on an equal basis with men in taking Africa to democracy and good governance? I use below what has come to be called the *Citizenship case* as an illustration of how local activism, in partnership with global action, can contribute to the implementation of international human rights law at the national level (*Attorney-General of Botswana v Unity Dow* [1991] LRC (Const) 574 (High Court of Botswana); [1992] LRC (Const) 623 (Court of Appeal of Botswana)).

The *Citizenship case*

In mid-1990, I instituted court action seeking declarations to the effect that certain sections of the Citizenship Act of Botswana were *ultra vires* the Constitution for the reasons that they discriminated against women. I drew up the papers for the case and then had an advocate argue it in court. I was then an attorney in private practice married to a non-citizen of Botswana. We had three children, one born to me before our marriage and adopted by my husband after our marriage. The two children from our marriage were born after the 1984 amendment of the nationality laws, which had abolished citizenship of Botswana by birth in the country. Under this amendment, citizens of Botswana were children whose fathers were Botswana citizens, if such children were born in marriage, and children whose mothers were Botswana citizens if the children were born out of marriage. The effect was that our two children born after the amendment were not, by operation of that law, Botswana citizens. The fact that they were born in Botswana to a Botswana

citizen mother made no difference. They were aliens in the land of their
own mother. Thus the constitutional challenge.

A constitutional challenge assumes that you have the Constitution
on your side. The truth however is that many of the constitutions of the
ex-British colonies are framed in either vague language or specifically
allow discrimination against women in areas of personal law. The Botswana Constitution for example defines discrimination as "affording
different treatment to different persons, attributable wholly or mainly to
their respective descriptions by race, tribe, place of origin". The word
"sex" is conspicuously missing from that definition. In addition, there is
specific language that allows discrimination "with respect to adoption,
marriage, divorce, burial, devolution of property on death or other
matters of personal law". With this sort of language, arguments had to
be ingenious and that is where international human rights law played a
key part.

First, we claimed that nationality was not a matter of personal law,
but rather of public law. We argued that, by operation of that law, I was
precluded from passing my citizenship to my children whilst a man in
my position would not have been so precluded. We argued that I was
denied equal protection of the law. We also suggested that my freedom
of movement, a right under the Constitution, was limited by the fact that
my children were not citizens. A man in that position, we argued, would
not be so restrained. We noted that the law amounted to inhuman and
degrading treatment.

The counterarguments included that the heartbeat of Botswana was
not the Constitution but its culture and traditional practices. In support
of this point it was argued that "[t]he whole fabric of the customary law
in Botswana, without reference to tribe, is based upon patrilineal society, which is gender discriminatory in its nature. It is not unfair to say
that if gender discrimination were outlawed in customary law, very little
of customary law would be left at all" (Respondent's Heads of Argument, B.11.5).

The relevance of the *Citizenship case* for today is that it provides
an example of how local action can draw support from the international
arena. The case used the international arena in two main ways. It util-
ized international human rights law in support of interpreting the equal-

ity provisions in the Botswana Constitution; and partnerships were formed with international groups.

National application of international human rights norms

In my view, one of the major contributions of the *Citizenship case* was its reinforcement of the principle that international human rights norms have a place in domestic law. National judges are often reluctant to incorporate international human rights norms into their decisions. And even if they do, they are reluctant to refer specifically to international treaties and conventions. In the *Citizenship case*, the Court of Appeal judges who found in my favour relied extensively on international treaties and conventions, including the Convention on the Elimination of All Forms of Discrimination against Women (CEDAW), the Convention on the Rights of the Child (CRC), the Universal Declaration of Human Rights, and the African Charter on Human and Peoples' Rights.

In the words of Justice Aguda, "[t]he domestic application of human rights norms is now regarded as the basis for implementing constitutional values beyond minimum requirements of the Constitution. The international human rights norms are in fact part of the constitutional expression of liberties guaranteed at national level. The domestic courts can assume the task of expanding these liberties" (Justice Aguda, p.167: The *Citizenship case*).

It is noteworthy that at the time of the decision in the *Citizenship case*, Botswana had not yet ratified CEDAW or CRC. In fact, many believe that the decision led to Botswana's ratification of CEDAW. The Court of Appeal judges also sought guidance from decisions of many different courts. This is happening more and more in national courts as judges recognize that no nation can stand alone, even in the area of law. This is not to say that there is no resistance to this development.

International collaboration

Very early in the *Citizenship case*, a foreign journalist took up the story and syndicated it around the world. This was valuable as it pushed the story out of the confines of the national and gave it international visibility. The Urban Morgan Institute of Human Rights in the United States got involved early in the case and filed an a*micus* brief. The stu-

115

dents at that Institute provided research and much needed cases and materials, which were not available in local libraries. The International Women's Rights Action Watch (IWRAW) also provided support with cases and materials. After the second judgement, when the Government made no move to implement the Court of Appeal decision, IWRAW helped in organizing petitions pressing for implementation of the decision.

International intervention was not limited to United States-based groups. Regional organizations, for example Women in Law and Development in Africa (WiLDAF) and Women and Law in Southern Africa (WLSA), both Southern African networks on women and law, organized petitions urging the Botswana Government to implement the Court's decision.

International support helped in many ways. It gave the case prominence, both internationally and nationally. At the national level, all actors were very much aware that the world's eyes were on them. This created some pressure, especially after the final judgement. But the negative effects of international attention can not be ignored. Governments often resent international involvement in what they consider to be a national sovereign affair, and international involvement can harden views. This did happen in the *Citizenship case*, with the result that some traditionalists saw some international plot to destroy their culture. Attacks in the press, of a very personal nature were directed at my husband and me. But, it is my view that no human rights abuse can be too local for international involvement. The nature of the involvement must depend on the nature of the issue and the circumstances of the particular nation. That is, strategies for involvement must be drawn up with local or national actors.

The Effect of the Deportation of Alien Husbands upon the Constitutionally Protected Mobility Rights of Citizen Wives in Zimbabwe
Anthony Gubbay

The inequities of the practices of immigration officers in Zimbabwe to deny permanent residence permits to alien husbands married to Zimbabwean citizens and to deport them from the country, was exposed and remedied by the decision in *Rattigan and Others v Chief Immigration Officer and Others* 1994 (2) ZLR 54 (S).

The facts of the *Rattigan* case

Three women married to foreign husbands brought a joint application direct to the Supreme Court under section 24(1) of the Constitution of Zimbabwe. The first applicant was married to a Scot. He had come to Zimbabwe in June 1991 for a three month holiday. During that visit he met and fell in love with the first applicant. They married in January 1992. Consequent upon being served with a notice to leave Zimbabwe, he and the first applicant left to reside in the United Kingdom. Both, however, were anxious to return and set up their matrimonial home in Zimbabwe.

The second applicant married an Irishman in January 1992. He first entered Zimbabwe in June 1993 and thereafter made numerous visits to the country. He too was denied a permit to work and reside in Zimbabwe as he possessed no scarce skills. At the date of the application he was on an extended visitor's permit and was living with the second applicant who was pregnant with his child. Both were anxious to establish the matrimonial home permanently in Zimbabwe.

The third applicant married an Irishman in 1972. Since the latter part of 1988 the third applicant, her husband and their children had resided in Zimbabwe. The husband was granted a two year residence permit which was extended from time to time. It was due to expire in September 1993. His application for a permanent residence permit was refused. Fearing deportation he obtained an order from the High Court interdicting the immigration authorities from deporting him pending the determination of his wife's application.

The applicants founded their claims for relief on section 22(1) of the Constitution. This provision mandates that "no person shall be deprived of his freedom of movement". Embodied in such protection are (i) the right to move freely throughout Zimbabwe; (ii) the right to reside in any part of Zimbabwe; (iii) the right to enter and leave Zimbabwe; and (iv) immunity from expulsion from Zimbabwe. Under subsection (2) any restriction on the person's freedom of movement that is involved in his/her lawful detention shall not be held to be a contravention of subsection (1). Subsection (3)(a) only permits the imposition of restrictions on the movement or residence within Zimbabwe, or the expulsion from Zimbabwe, of persons who are neither citizens of Zimbabwe nor regarded by virtue of a written law as permanently resident in Zimbabwe.

The case made by the applicant wives was that the refusal of the Chief Immigration Officer to issue a residence permit to each husband and the consequent requirement that they leave the country, circumscribed their fundamental and unqualified right as citizens to freedom of movement. In essence the freedom of movement of the wives determined what happened to their husbands, for in order to secure and maintain the marital relationship they would have to accompany them out of the country.

The Court's decision and reasoning

In upholding the contention the Court emphasized that the predicament of each wife had not been caused by the decision of the husband, as head of the family, to establish a common household in a country other than Zimbabwe. To the contrary, the husbands shared the desire of the wives that the matrimonial abode be located in Zimbabwe. It was said:

"Marriages are almost invariably entered into by parties who have a deep affection for one another and who intend to devote the remainder of their lives together. Although the condition of matrimony does not, as a concept of law, make the spouses one flesh, it nevertheless embodies the obligation to found a home, to cohabit, to have children and to live together as a family unit."

Accordingly it was held that: "to prohibit the husbands from residing in Zimbabwe and so disable them from living with their wives in the country of which they are citizens and to which they owe allegiance, is in effect to undermine and devalue the protection of freedom of movement accorded to each of the wives as a member of a family unit."

In coming to its conclusion the Court applied the reasoning in *Dow v Attorney-General* and also referred to decisions of the European Court of Human Rights which stressed the protection afforded by article 8(1) of the Convention upon the importance of preserving well established family ties.

The *Rattigan* decision was confined to the fundamental right of a citizen wife to have her alien husband living with her in Zimbabwe. It did not expressly extend within the wife's own mobility rights the right of her spouse to lawfully engage in employment or other gainful activity in Zimbabwe. That issue was dealt with a few months later in *Salem v Chief Immigration Officer and Another* 1994 (2) ZLR 287 (S).

The Salem case

In *Salem v Chief Immigration Officer and Another* 1994 (2) ZLR 287 (S), it was there held that:

"unless the protection guaranteed under section 22(1) of the Constitution embraced the entitlement of a citizen wife, residing permanently with her alien husband in Zimbabwe, to look to him for partial or total support, depending upon her circumstances, the exercise of her unqualified right to remain residing in this country, as a member of a family unit, is put in jeopardy".

The basis for this conclusion was that the right of the citizen wife under section 22(1) of the Constitution, "to reside in any part of Zimbabwe", would be nullified where, through inability adequately to support her alien husband and children, she was compelled by necessity to forego her right to remain living in the country and accompany her husband to a land where he was not prohibited from earning a livelihood. To impart a narrow meaning to the words "the right to reside in any part of Zimbabwe" would be to differentiate between the affluent wife, not dependent upon the support of her husband for herself and children, and the wife who was impoverished or destitute, and partly or wholly dependent upon him.

The constitutional amendment of 1996

The aftermath of these two decisions was an amendment passed by Parliament, on 6 December 1996, to section 22 of the Constitution. This provided in material part that:

"Nothing contained in or done under the authority of any law shall be held to be in contravention of subsection (1) to the extent that the law in question makes provision for the imposition of restrictions on the movement or residence within Zimbabwe of any person who is neither a citizen of Zimbabwe nor regarded by virtue of a written law as permanently resident in Zimbabwe, whether or not he is married or related to another person who is a citizen of or permanently resident in Zimbabwe."

The impact of this amendment was considered in *Kohlhaas v Chief Immigration Officer and Another* 1997 (2) RLR 441 (S). It was pointed out that the limitation to the freedom of movement was not directed at a citizen of Zimbabwe. Therefore the expulsion from Zimbabwe of a non-citizen under the authority of any law did not contravene his fundamental right to freedom of movement, no matter that he was married or related to a person who is a citizen of, or permanently resident in, Zimbabwe. Thus if Mr. Kohlhaas, who was the alien husband, had brought an application protesting that his right of freedom of movement had been infringed by the refusal of the immigration authorities to permit him to remain in the country, he would have been met by the unassailable answer that the decision was justified under the provisions of the Immigration Act. But it was the wife of Mr. Kohlhaas who was the applicant. It was her right of freedom of movement as a citizen of Zimbabwe that was affected by the declaration that her husband was a prohibited person and was to be removed. Ultimately accepting that the amendment to section 22 did not assist him - for it merely restated the law in relation to the rights of non-citizens and left untouched the rights of the citizen spouse - the Chief Immigration Officer sought to avoid the effect of the judgements in *Rattigan* and *Salem* by arguing that the marriage was one of convenience. In dismissing the argument the Court held that the *onus* of proving the marriage to be one of convenience rested upon the party making the assertion - the Chief Immigration Officer - and what he had to prove was that the applicant and Mr. Kohlhaas had entered into the marriage in order (i) to allow Mr. Kohlhaas to continue to reside in the country in evasion of the immigration laws; and (ii) without any intention of living together permanently as man and wife. Each ingredient being of equal importance. Proof of the first alone would not suffice to defeat the application; there had to be an absence of an intention to establish a true marriage relationship. On the facts the submission of the respondent that the marriage was stage-managed in an attempt to escape the tentacles of the immigration laws was found to be totally far-fetched. Neither ingredient of a marriage of convenience was established.

Recent developments

Only the other week in the matter of *Anthony v Chief Immigration Officer* the Supreme Court was faced with the situation that notwithstanding the existence of his genuine marriage to the applicant, Mr. Anthony was deported from the country as a prohibited person. In purporting to justify such action the respondent raised the preliminary point that Mr. Anthony had not exhausted his remedies under the Immigration Act. He had not appealed against the deportation order. The Court held that of concern was the violation, by the removal of her husband from the country, of Mrs. Anthony's right to freedom of movement. Consequently the Chief Immigration Officer was ordered to issue Mr. Anthony with written authority to enable him to enter and remain in Zimbabwe on the same standing as any other alien married to a citizen.

Customary law practices concerning marriage and family relations

Application of Customary Law Rules in Fiji and the Pacific Region: Dual Systems
Gwen Phillips

Introduction

The Pacific Islands have two legal systems operating at the same time – a formal legal system inherited from their colonizers and the customary laws inherited from their ancestors.[1] In the Pacific (excluding New Zealand and Australia), the establishment of state governments and the creation of state legal systems have not done away with customary law and processes. Customary law still operates and in many countries is still strong, both at the village level and as part of their national state law.

---

[1] Jalal, Patricia Imrana, *Law for Pacific Women: A Legal Rights Handbook.* P. Imrana Jalal, Suva, Fiji. Fiji Women's Rights Movement, 1998.

In much of Melanesia for example, where numerous traditional cultural groups each have their own customary rules and processes, one could say that in addition to state law, there are many customary legal systems. In Fiji, there are at least three legal systems in operation - state law, the customary law of indigenous Fijians and the customary law of Indians. The issue for most Pacific States and territories is not so much whether to recognize customary rights and rules, but in what way and to what extent.[2]

Customary law is recognized by state agencies and integrated into state law by constitutional provisions, statutes and court decisions. Within the region there is much diversity pertaining to definitional provisions of custom as a source of law and in the ranking and priority of custom in the hierarchy of laws.

Conflict between constitutions and custom

Each Pacific constitution provides that it is the supreme law. Individual rights contained in today's constitutions can conflict with customary law, and with customary values and beliefs, in a number of ways.

First, most bills of rights focus on protecting the individual. They do not focus on protecting the community or on promoting a sense of responsibility to the community, which is the focus of many customary governmental systems.

Second, bills of rights grant individual rights, they do not establish individual responsibilities. Customary law places more emphasis on the responsibilities that individuals owe to their kin group or society than on the rights that the kin group or society owes to them.

Third, certain rights granted in constitutions that are derived from the western model may especially conflict with particular aspects of customary law. For example, the assumption that all people are equal under the law and the guarantees of equal protection and due process

---

[2]   Jean Zorn, *Sec. 16 Customs and Customary Law Course Book One*. Rev. ed. Suva, University Extension USP 1994.

may run counter to traditional values, such as the higher status of chiefs or unequal relations between genders.

Finally, the equal protection provisions, as well as other constitutionally guaranteed rights, may conflict with legislation that is intended to protect customary ways. For example, it may be a denial of equal protection to enact legislation containing special rules favouring customary land tenure or prohibiting anyone other than indigenous inhabitants from acquiring or owning land.[3]

Examples where the application of customary law is discriminatory

Melanesia marriage custom of bride price

The Solomon Islands, Vanuatu, New Caledonia and Papua New Guinea all share the Melanesian marriage custom of bride price. In this custom, a man's family gives gifts to the family of the woman he marries. The gifts now may include money, cloth and clothes as well as custom valuables, and may involve housing and feedings the wife's family during the ceremonies, and paying their transport costs if they come from another area. In general, bride price represents the recognition of the social and economic value of women. It is also a way of compensating the woman's family for the loss of her work and of connecting the two families, especially as the children of that union are regarded as belonging to the father's clan. Under the formal legal system, custody decisions are made on the principle of "the best interests of the children". This often directly conflicts with the customary practices.[4]

The bride price custom has had good and bad aspects. In the Solomon Islands it is considered as a token of appreciation. In Vanuatu it is considered as compensation to the family for the loss of the bride's labour. Others feel it helps bring wealth into the family and enhances the status of the girl child. For instance, the birth of girls will be a cause of

---

[3]   Ibid.

[4]   Ibid.

joy, not the dismay felt by poor families who expect to have to provide dowries for their daughters.

Those against the practice argue that the effects of bride price include valuing women in material terms, their virginity, chastity or sexual purity, capacity to reproduce, educational qualifications and labour. Bride price may be affected and devalued by things outside the woman's control. If bride price encourages competition between women and applies only to women, not to men, that should alert women to the discriminatory nature of the practice. Finally, as stated by the learned writer Imrana Jalal, the practice means that women are treated as a commodity with a price tag. Placing a material value on human beings is a violation of human rights and a breach of article 5(a) of the Convention on the Elimination of All Forms of Discrimination against Women.

Traditional reconciliation process ("Bulubulu" in Fiji)

In all Pacific countries, traditional methods of reconciliation are still widely promoted and although this may be advantageous in some instances, in most cases the "victim" and more importantly the offender, play hardly or no significant role at all. The reconciliation is carried out between the families of the two concerned parties and the victim who in most cases is a woman, has no say in whether she accepts the reconciliation or not.

Formal courts appear to accept and apply customary law when it favours the interests of men. There are few examples of customary law used in favour of women. We see this in decisions on whether or not to accept "bulubulu", the practice whereby a family apologizes for the behaviour of a relative who has harmed someone and dishonoured the family. The underlying intent is to preserve good relations between the families despite the wrong done to the injured family. For example if a man fathers an illegitimate child, his family may present "bulubulu" to the child's mother's family. In this way, the father's family apologizes to the mother's family and recognizes the child's parentage. In an affiliation case, an offer of "bulubulu" could provide the required proof of paternity. However, courts often do not accept "bulubulu" as proof of paternity. They have argued that unless the alleged father participates in the "bulubulu", he cannot be taken to have approved of it, and therefore does not recognize the child as his.

However in a rape case, if the victim's family accepts "bulubulu" for the rape, the rapist often successfully uses the acceptance to reduce his sentence.[5]

Balancing dual systems

John Noel & Others v Obed Toto, case No.18 (1994), Supreme Court of Vanuatu, Luganville Santo. The Supreme Court held that notwithstanding the fact that customary law is the basis of land ownership in Vanuatu, it is subject to the Constitution and cannot be applied if it discriminates against women. The principle established by this decision is that, in Vanuatu, the Constitution takes precedence over customary law if the two systems conflict.

The position is the same in Western Samoa. In *Tariu Tuivati v F Fila & Others* [1980 - 1993] WSLR 17- 21, the Supreme Court held that the Constitution was paramount despite its recognition of custom law.

Emily Waiwo v Willie Waiwo, case No.324195, Supreme Court of Vanuatu, reaffirmed application customary law in divorce/custody proceedings.

Inheritance Rights of Women under Customary Law *vis-à-vis* International Human Rights Instruments: The Case of Zimbabwe
Elizabeth Gwaunza

Introduction

---

[5] Ibid.

125

Inheritance in Zimbabwe is governed by both customary and general law, a reflection of the system of legal dualism, which has existed since the advent of colonial rule. The intestate estates of Africans married according to African law and custom, and those of unmarried Africans whose parents were married according to customary rites are governed by one law[1] while non-Africans estates and those of Africans married according to civil rites and their unmarried offspring are governed by another.[2] The fact that the inheritance system favoured males over females did not mean the latter were not protected. Young widows were expected to, and generally did, choose a new husband from within the ranks of their deceased husband's brothers, cousins or nephews. The chosen husband was also expected to see to the widow's welfare and that of her children and to administer the estate on behalf of the heir. Older widows and those who chose not be "inherited" became the responsibility of the heir. In every respect the widow's position within the family was assured. So was that of the daughters who were unmarried. They also became the responsibility of the heir.

Statutory provisions vs. customary law

Between the colonial and the present post-colonial era, many laws have been passed in an effort to balance the need to preserve the customs and laws of the indigenous people of Zimbabwe, and the need not to stifle the natural dynamism of customary law that is necessitated by the changing social, economic and political environment. This has proved to be a difficult balance for both the legislature and the courts to maintain, particularly in light of constitutional provisions and international human rights instruments like the Convention on the Elimination of All Forms of Discrimination against Women, which the Government has ratified.

Although the relevant provision of the law does not specifically provide that only one heir, and that a son, should inherit - leaving the issue rather to be determined on the basis of the relevant customs and

---

[1] See 68 (I) of the Administration of Estates Act as amended by the Administration of Estates Amendment Act 6/97.

[2] Deceased Estates Succession Act and Common Law.

usages of the tribe or people to which the deceased belonged - it became standard practice for the courts at all levels to appoint the deceased's eldest son as the sole heir to all the movable assets. Legislative provisions reinforced the heir's position by providing that such heir inherited immovable property, ownership of which is a concept unknown to customary law, in his individual capacity. There was, however a rider, at the theoretical level, that such an heir inherited the movable assets in a representative capacity (to be used for the good of all the deceased's dependents) and the immovable property in his individual capacity but with the responsibility to ensure the deceased's other dependents had a roof over their heads - in the same or other property.[3] At the practical level, and given the suffering to which widows, daughters and other dependants of the deceased were subjected after being denied any of the benefits from the estate, this rider might as well not have existed.

To get around this problem and ensure the essence or underlying value of customary law was upheld, some families put forward the name of the widow, or a daughter of the deceased, as the heir. Research established that lower courts dealing with the appointment of heirs generally honoured such wishes of the deceased's family. In the cases that went to the higher courts on appeal, a lack of uniformity became apparent, over the manner in which these cases were determined. While these judgements were passed in 1990, before the Government ratified the CEDAW Convention in April 1991, there is very little likelihood, as discussed below, that such ratification could have averted the gender discriminatory essence of the judgement. Nor is it likely that the amendment to the Zimbabwe Constitution, effected in 1998, which had the effect of outlawing discrimination based on gender, could have had any positive influence, had it been passed after the amendment. This is because subsection (3) of section 33 of the Constitution provides clearly that as long as any sex discriminatory practice or ruling of the court could be said to relate to inheritance under customary law, the constitutional provision barring gender-based discrimination was not infringed.

---

[3] See *Masango vs. Masango, SC 66/86.*

The case of *Magaya and Magaya*

This was the context in which the widely publicized and criticized case of *Magaya and Magaya*[4] was determined. In it, the deceased was survived by his eldest daughter from his first wife, and several sons from his second wife, who were younger than the daughter. The Supreme Court upheld a decision of the magistrates' court which had appointed one of the sons as heir to the estate.

The judgement sparked not only national but international controversy, particularly from women's rights advocates who asserted it was retrogressive and enshrined, within customary law, discrimination against women on the basis of gender. Although the judgement was passed after the promulgation of what has been termed the revolutionary Administration of Estates Amendment Act,[5] which amended customary law in order to allow widows and children of a deceased person, regardless of sex, direct inheritance rights from the estate, the non-retroactive nature of the law meant that the new law could not apply in the *Magaya* case. Hence its gender discriminatory essence. The harshest condemnation of the judgment was premised on the apparent denial of the country's obligations in terms of the CEDAW Convention, other related human rights instruments, the 1997 Declaration on Gender and Development of the Southern African Development Community (SADC), and the Bangalore (1988) and Harare (1989) Principles, adopted at judicial colloquia administered by the Commonwealth Secretariat.

It is important to note that the ratification of international conventions and instruments does not, in Zimbabwe, make them part of domestic law. Under section 111B of the Constitution this can only happen through an Act of Parliament. The CEDAW Convention, despite having been ratified in April 1991, has not been incorporated into the domestic law of Zimbabwe. What this means effectively is that the courts are not obliged to apply the provisions in the CEDAW Convention that advocate the disregard of customary laws and practices that discriminate against women. This is, however, not to say that the courts

---

[4]   S 210/98.

[5]   Act No 6/97.

cannot be influenced by any of the provisions of the CEDAW Convention in their determination of matters that relate to gender discrimination. Indeed the courts in Zimbabwe have been clearly influenced in a number of cases, as indicated by reference to the CEDAW provisions in the relevant judgements. None of these cases, however, relate to inheritance under customary law. In the same vein, the Harare and Bangalore Principles, formulated and adopted at meetings of judges from Commonwealth countries, have no more than a persuasive influence on the courts.

Conclusion

What seems to be evident is that as long as the human rights instruments, protocols, and declarations that Zimbabwe has aligned itself with, continue to have no more than persuasive force and are to be taken into consideration at the discretion of individual judicial officers, any positive impact they may have been meant to have is seriously compromised.

It therefore need not be emphasized that the sooner international human rights instruments that provide equality between men and women in matters of personal law – customary or otherwise – are incorporated into domestic law, the easier it would be for the courts to play a more meaningful role in interpreting and applying laws that promote the development of women in particular, and family relations in general.

Inheritance Rights or Women's Role in Succession in the Customary Law of Benin
Conceptia Ouinsou

Benin remains one of the few countries of French-speaking Africa where a legal incompatibility persists regarding personal status and property, characterized by the coexistence of traditional law and modern law inherited from colonialism. Traditional law derives from oral customs marked by a desire to uphold models of behaviour handed down by the ancestors, which extol male dominance. The main examples of these customs are recorded in *The Customary Law of Dahomey*, made applicable by circular AP 128 of 19 March 1931. This text is still in force in our country because we have failed to adopt a family code containing a unified system of laws for all citizens. Clearly, these ancestral traditions do not meet international legal standards and attack the dignity of women by perpetuating a status based on discrimination and exclusion, particularly with regard to succession.

Content of the customary law of succession

The principle

Virtually all customs exclude women from the line of succession. This exclusion only applies to inheritance from the father, husband or brother. The surviving spouse, whether man or woman, is excluded from the inheritance of the deceased spouse.

The reasons for unequal treatment lie in the method of partition of personal property. Under article 256 of the Customary Law, the general rule is that only the male descendants of the deceased receive an inheritance. Indeed, in the words of article 15 of the Customary Law "the family includes all the descendants in the male line of a common male ancestor, including unmarried women ... Married women follow their husbands but remain a part of their family of origin as far as ritual ceremonies are concerned ...".

An unmarried daughter cannot inherit in order to prevent her from transmitting the property from her family line to another line, and the surviving spouse, in particular the wife, is excluded from the family of the deceased spouse.

The exclusion of the wife of the deceased from his estate can easily be understood from reading article 127 *in fine* of the Customary Law, under which "a woman is part of the property of a man and of his estate". How can she inherit when she herself is the property of the estate? The practice of widowhood and especially of the levirate amply demonstrates it.

On the death of the head of the family, the family property is administered by the eldest son. His mother is required to submit to him. She therefore loses her authority because she is a woman.

Mitigation of the principle

Nevertheless, certain customs grant women the right to inherit cloths and household utensils, since the women's place is in the home (article 256 of the Customary Law). That same idea is involved in the liquidation of the matrimonial regime under common law, which is the separation of property. But since all property is considered to be the husband's exclusively, when the wife fails to provide proof of her contribution to its acquisition, the courts have no choice but to rule in favour of the husband.

Goun, Mina and Nagot customs allow women to inherit cola trees and coconut palms both from their mother's and their father's estate. The Adja and the Pila Pila grant inheritance rights to women even if the deceased had sons, but only to movable property. In the absence of sons or brothers, the inheritance goes to the sisters of the deceased among the Baribas and the Peulhs.

However, since inequality is at the core of partition in traditional law, women allowed to inherit receive less in comparison with male heirs. Even among male heirs, unequal partition is the rule, either favouring the eldest or the youngest heir.

The exclusion of daughters from inheritance is a form of gender discrimination that is incompatible with changing values, unconstitutional and contrary to all international legal instruments in their provisions concerning the prevention of all forms of discrimination based on grounds such as sex, religion, or race. Those provisions "are an integral part of the Constitution of Benin of 2 December 1990 and of the law of Benin, and consequently prevail over internal law".

Evolution of jurisprudence concerning implementation of the principle of exclusion from succession

Implementation of the principle of exclusion

In general, judges have strictly applied the customary provisions excluding women from succession.

• The Supreme Court, in decision No. 23 of 15 July 1964, reversed a decision of a local court which had granted inheritance rights to women in competition with male heirs for a building belonging to their father because "by allowing daughters to inherit and freely dispose of land, the local court violated a fundamental rule of customary law".

- The court of first instance of Porto-Novo, by decision No. 213 of 23 September 1970, ruled that Goun custom, the customary law of the deceased, denied any inheritance rights to women, in a case pitting the daughter of the deceased against his brothers.

- In a decision of 4 August 1988, the court of first instance of Cotonou granted the daughters of the deceased inheritance rights based on the evolution of jurisprudence on the matter and on the constitutional principle of equality as stipulated in article 124 of the "Basic Law of 9 August 1977".

That decision was overturned by the Court of Appeal of Cotonou, which in its judgement No. 23 of 6 March 1991 ruled that "the three daughters of the deceased, in the case against third parties," had no standing on which to claim land which, according to customary law, had never belonged to them. The courts have tried not to stray very far from customary law for fear of censure, which has given rise to disparate jurisprudence lacking in uniformity. Nevertheless, for several years judges hearing cases on the merits, taking into account the changes in society and the Constitution, have been attempting to interpret these backward and anachronistic customary laws in a way that does some justice to women.

Judicial relief

Pursuing an approach of judicial relief, judges in Benin ruling on traditional matters have recognized that the daughter of the deceased:

- Has the right of usufruct, by stating that, "while Goun custom, followed by the parties, excludes women from the estate of a parent, it does so only if there are male children in competition with her; the sole purpose of such an exclusion is to prevent daughters from transferring family property to another family, and it is not in opposition to the simple right of a child, even a daughter, of use or enjoyment" (court of first instance of Porto-Novo), decision No. 213 of 25 September 1970);

- Has full inheritance rights, even for immovable property, where exclusion is the rule. The Cotonou court ruled that "... the attempt by X to take possession of the building in dispute, the only property comprising the estate left by the deceased, can be explained solely by the fact that he is the only male heir; this possible explanation cannot be accepted, since it has no basis in law" (court of first instance of Cotonou, decision No. 1656/87 of 19 June 1987).

The position of the courts varies in cases of competition between male heirs and women. For some, inequality is at the heart of partition, but others adopt a principle of modern law, equality.

In referring to equality between men and women, the court of Cotonou, in its decision No. 27/90 of 30 October 1990, ruled that, in accordance with tradition, women could not inherit more than half of what men could inherit. Taking into account the close relationship, the courts give preference in inheritance to the daughter of the deceased over collateral descendants.

Improvements can also be seen regarding the rights of widows, on condition that a legal marriage had been contracted and no divorce decree or legal separation had been pronounced. Nowadays, widows benefit from a right of usufruct to the extent that the courts grant them the right to raise their children and even to administer their husband's property within the framework of decisions of the family council. The courts also attempt to explain to such councils the reasoning behind their decisions. A living allowance can be granted to the widow from the estate of her deceased husband.

Many women deep in the countryside of Benin however, remain unaware of their rights, fear magic spells and esoteric forces, and continue to suffer inequality in silence.

Moreover, no woman in Benin has had enough courage to file a complaint of gender discrimination with the Constitutional Court.

Conclusion

A true paradox exists between customs and law. Therefore, whether they arise from the customs themselves or are of judicial origin, mitigations of the principle of the exclusion of women are the lesser of two evils. These derogations do not fundamentally change traditional succession law, nor are they uniform for all. Furthermore, judicial interpretation has its limits. Judge are not bound by precedents, and, out of fear of censure, can reverse such decisions.

In order to improve women's inheritance rights, it is imperative to adopt a code on the family and civil status that takes into account evolving practice. Change is still very slow in rural areas.

But over and above this code, which in draft form has already taken into account such existing legal mechanisms as wills, gifts and matrimonial regimes, the most important task that lies ahead for women themselves, through their child-rearing role, is to help men view such matters in a new light, by ceasing to pass on in particular to their sons, and thus perpetuate, these negative cultural values.

Unmarried Women's Right to Inheritance
Krishna Jung Rayamajhi

Introduction

Nepal ratified the Convention on the Elimination of All Forms of Discrimination against Women (CEDAW) on 22 April 1991, and the Convention on the Rights of the Child (CRC) on 14 September 1990. The 1990 Constitution of the Kingdom of Nepal, in its preamble, makes a commitment to guarantee basic human rights. Article 1 proclaims the fundamental law of the country, and states that all laws inconsistent with it are, to the extent of such inconsistency, void. This provision further guarantees the fundamental rights conferred in the Constitution. If any law imposes an unreasonable restriction on the enjoyment of the fundamental rights conferred in the Constitution or on any ground, the Supreme Court, by exercising its extraordinary jurisdiction of judicial review under article 88 (1) of the Constitution may, upon the petition of any Nepali citizen, declare a law as void either *ab initio* or from the date of its decision. Part 3 of the Constitution codifies all rights and freedoms recognized by the international community through various international as well as regional instruments to which Nepal is a party as fundamental rights of citizens.

Article 11 of the Constitution provides that all citizens shall be equal before the law, and no person shall be denied the equal protection of the laws. It prohibits discrimination based on religion, race, sex, caste, tribe or ideological conviction.

Supreme Court cases on women's equality

The Supreme Court of Nepal has decided several cases involving women's property rights and right to equality guaranteed by the Constitution of Nepal.

In a writ petition, writ no. 3392 of the year 2050 B.S. (1993), lodged by pleader Meera Kumari Dhungana, the main issue to be decided before the Special Bench of the Supreme Court was whether the provision contained in No 16 of the chapter on partition of the General Law was to be declared invalid or not. That law provided that, while a son was entitled to a partition share of his father's property at birth, a daughter was only entitled to obtain a share when she reached the age of 35 and was still unmarried. The petitioner contended that it should be declared invalid because it was inconsistent with Article 11 of the Constitution of the Kingdom of Nepal 2047 (1990), and contrary to article 15 of the CEDAW Convention providing that women had all property rights on an equal footing with men. The affidavits presented on behalf of the respondent claimed that an unmarried daughter gets her partition share from her father after the age of 35 years, and after marriage she gets it from her husband. Thus the daughter had not been discriminated in the right to get her partition share, and the provision of No 16 of the chapter on partition was not subject to be invalidated under Art 11 of the Constitution.

The provision set forth in article 11(1) (2) (3) and (4) of the Constitution absolutely incorporates the provision of article 15 of the Convention. No. 16 of the chapter on Partition of the General Law (Muluki Ain) 2020 B.S. (1963) provides that an unmarried daughter having attained the age of 35 is entitled to obtain a partition share equal to that of a son, and if she marries after obtaining the partition share, the property obtained by her shall, after deducting therefrom the marriage expenditure pursuant to law, devolve to the legal heirs.

In its judgement the Court observed that the Nepalese law provided for certain differences as to how women and men obtain their partition

135

share, taking into consideration the social condition of men and women. It considered that the negative implications on society of a daughter's entitlement at birth to a share equal to that of a son needed to be taken into account. Such implications included the impact on the structure of the patriarchal society like Nepal's which had been handed down from ancient time. Furthermore, such an entitlement was considered as creating a daughter's right to a larger partition share than a son's, a situation that would be discriminatory against a son, and would affect all property rights legislation. Therefore, declaring No. 16 of the chapter on partition void and enacting a provision entitling a daughter to get a partition share equal to that of a son was not considered a solution to the problem.

The Supreme Court agreed that rather than voiding the law, extensive consultations and deliberations were needed on the family law relating to property in its entirety, and taking also into account the constitutional provision on equality. Consequently, the Supreme Court issued a directive order to His Majesty's Government to introduce an appropriate bill in Parliament within one year of receipt of the order, following necessary consultations on this matter with recognized women's organizations, sociologists, the concerned social organizations and lawyers as well as by studying and considering the legal provisions made in other countries in this regard. In pursuance of that order, His Majesty's Government has introduced a bill in Parliament which is now under consideration.

In another case, writ No. 2816 of the year 2051 (1994), the constitutionality of No. 12 of the chapter on partition, No. 2 of the chapter on inheritance, No. 5 and 9 (a) of the chapter on adoption, No. 4 of the chapter on adultery, No. 9 of the chapter on marriage, No. 2 of the chapter on husband and wife, No. 2 of the chapter on bestiality of the General Law were challenged claiming that they were discriminatory and contrary to the right to equality conferred by the Constitution. The Supreme Court gave similar directive orders with similar observations as in the case described above. The Court observed in its judgement that the conducts accepted and continuously practised reflected the culture and customs of that society, and that the legal system had been developed by learned people in line with such traditions and customs, and amended as reflected in the present General Law. The Court noted that Nepalese society had its own distinct social structure, culture, traditions, social values and norms. Hindu jurisprudence also influenced the country's legal provisions. Hence in bringing changes to traditions which had been followed by society, their impact on society and whether society could adopt them needed to be considered. The legal provisions regulating familial and social practices and conducts were interwoven, and the relevance and effect of one legal provision depended on other legal provisions.

From the above verdicts, it is clear that the Supreme Court has not declared the contested laws void. The directive orders issued to His Majesty's Government, however, show that the Court is aware that the legal provisions in respect of which the petitioners raised questions, have different connotations for men and for women.

In writ Full Bench No 29 of the year 2049 (1992), the petitioner Meera Gurung raised the question that sub-rules (3) and (4) of rules (14) of the Foreigner's Rules 2032 (1976) were discriminatory and against the right to equality guaranteed by the Constitution. The rules state that if a male Nepali citizen is married to a foreign wife, she may get a visa under sub-rule 3 so that she may stay in the Kingdom of Nepal while marital relations are maintained. For up to 3 months after the end of a marital relationship, the (former) wife does not need to extend the term of her visa. The rules further state that if a female Nepali citizen is married to a foreigner, her foreign husband may obtain a visa only for a term not exceeding four months under sub-rule 4. The Supreme Court said that the above sub-rules provide that visas of different nature and with different terms may be issued to foreign spouses depending on whether the Nepali citizen is a man or a woman. The Court noted that the law provided unequal and discriminatory treatment of Nepali citizens mainly on the basis of sex. The Supreme Court has issued an appropriate order in favour of the petitioner.

Conclusion

In my opinion, in a country like Nepal, continuous effort are necessary to educate and prepare society to accept new perceptions on the elimination of all forms of discriminations against women under the concept of human rights. It seems to me that events like this judicial colloquium will enhance the realization of women's human rights.

Legislative and Judicial Treatment of Family Relations in Cameroon
Florence Rita Arrey

Introduction

Cameroon, a country with two legal systems, has ratified the Convention on the Elimination of All Forms of Discrimination against Women (CEDAW) and the Convention on the Rights of the Child. According to article 45 of the Constitution, international treaties and conventions have superior authority over domestic laws. Based on the Constitution which guarantees the right to life, liberty and security, Cameroon has adopted a catalogue of laws guaranteeing women's rights.

Protection of women's rights under the law

Special consideration is made for pregnant women and mothers in criminal law. Rape is considered a sexual offence under criminal law, and abortion is also dealt with under criminal law.

Article 16 of the Universal Declaration of Human Rights, and article 16 of CEDAW guarantee women, on a basis of equality with men, the right to enter into marriage, including the right not to marry, the right freely to choose a spouse, and to enter into marriage only with their free and full consent. Section 356 of the Penal Code makes forced marriage a criminal offence. Cameroonian law establishes the minimum age of marriage at 16 years. Marriage involving a child bride is void, and the law offers protection from abusive practices related to bride price. Section 70(1) of the Civil Status Ordinance states that bride price has no effect on the validity of the marriage. A married woman has the right to a matrimonial home, financial support, and divorce.

In Cameroon, women's economic rights include the right to undertake gainful employment outside the home. Women are guaranteed equal pay for equal work. Every woman is entitled to 14 weeks of maternity leave with full pay. A woman has a right to operate a separate bank account in her name.

With regard to nationality, a foreign woman is not required to take on Cameroonian nationality upon her marriage to a Cameroonian man.

Factors preventing women from enjoying human rights

Such factors can be found both in statutory law and in customary law and practices.

Poverty and legal illiteracy are also factors that impede women from realizing their rights.

Customary law and practices relating to bride price can be an obstacle. The levirate continues to be practised by some tribes in Cameroon. This is a custom whereby a deceased man's widow is expected to marry one of his brothers. This is linked to the belief that bride price is paid by the husband's family. When he dies, the thinking goes, his family still has a lien on it.

This practice is contrary to the written law and repugnant to natural justice. In *CASWP/42M/98 - David Tchakokam vs. Koeu Madeleine*, among other things the applicant sought an order of the court to force his levirate wife to return to him as part of his late brother's property. The case was dismissed on appeal where it was held that this was a most obnoxious action which was not only repugnant to natural justice, but was contrary to article 16 of the CEDAW Convention (judgement by Arrey, C.J).

The law itself can be a hindrance, where discriminatory elements persist, for example in the area of adultery. Likewise, polygamy reduces the status of women in that the woman has less bargaining powers.

Section 24(2) of the Civil Status Ordinance gives the husband a right to object to his wife's employment in the interest of the marriage or the children. The law also discriminates between men and women by establishing the age of majority for boys at 18 years, while that of girls is 16.

Married women's property rights also need to be reassessed. Under the traditional concept, a woman who gets married gives up her right to landed property. Property rights issues usually are raised in divorce or in succession cases. This was illustrated in *HCK/8/94/28M/94 - Ngoe Theresia Alekeng vs. Besankeng Atemkeng John*. The husband abandoned his wife and six children for another woman. When he got into debt, he pledged the matrimonial home where his wife continued to live with the six children. When he was about to sell the property, the wife obtained a court order restraining the husband from selling the house.

Women's property rights in divorce remain tenuous. In a long line of cases, for example, *Achu vs. Achu & Ade vs. Ade,* the courts have decided against women who attempted to show that they contributed to the accumulation of property, especially the matrimonial home, and should therefore be granted a share upon divorce. Even with the passing of the Matrimonial Property Act 1976 which recognized the value and importance of housework as a contribution to the acquisition of the matrimonial home, the male-dominated courts in Cameroon still refused to give women a share in the matrimonial home. In 1986 a landmark decision was handed down by a woman judge in the case of *Alice Fodje vs. Ndansi Kette, Appeal No. BCA/45/86.* The judge awarded the wife a share in the matrimonial property by giving her some houses even though she was a customary law wife (per Arrey, C.J.).

A widow's right in succession also remain unequal. Such rights should include a widow's right to her share of her deceased husband's property, as well as to a widow's pension. The courts have held that the widow's rights are superior to those of the deceased husband's brother, father and other relatives (*BCA/12/93 - Rev. Jeremiah Toh Mundi & Dr Emmanuel Mundi vs. Regina Mundi).* The Supreme Court decided in the *Florence Zamcho* case that a girl child has a right to inherit her late father's property and that refusing her this right was discrimination. Before this decision the girl child could not inherit.

Conclusion

There has been very little litigation on issues concerning women's rights. This is due to ignorance on the part of women and the conflict between human rights laws and customs. Since women NGOs have been carrying out sensitization campaigns, it is expected that many cases on women's issues will be brought to the courts in the future.

The Right to Marry
Tassaduq Hussain Jilani

The Convention on the Elimination of all Forms of Discrimination against Women (CEDAW) is a Magna Carta of women's rights in various spheres. On issues of marriage, article 16 of CEDAW, *inter alia* mandates:

"1. States parties shall take all appropriate measures to eliminate discrimination against women in all matters relating to marriage and family relations and in particular shall ensure, on a basis of equality of men and women:

a) ....

b) The same right freely to choose a spouse and to enter into marriage only with their free and full consent."

The right of an adult woman to marry a person of her choice is well recognized in the civilized world today. However, in the East this right has been subjected to clogs which are the outcome of pride, prejudice and a myopic conception of faith. Instances are not lacking when parents and elders react to their adult daughters marrying a person of choice and the reaction at times leads to violence which may include killing in the name of "honour".

The right to marry in sociological and historical perspective

The right to marry has been regulated throughout history. Societies laid down parameters within which it was permissible to marry. The first sexual taboos seem to have aimed at preventing the mating of parents and children, then of brothers and sisters and gradually the prohibitions spread to exogamy and endogamy.

Be it the Occident or the Orient, girls were given in marriage by parents whose main concern in choosing a spouse were proprietary interests. However, with the spread of education and economic independence of men and women, women attained greater independence in the West where today, they seem to enjoy complete freedom in choosing a spouse.

Marriages in our part of the world however, in the great majority of cases, are arranged by parents. This may look shocking to an observer from the West but in a socio-economic milieu where many young women do not have primary education and where even among the educated classes discrimination between men and women persists, it appears only logical that the head of the family would take decisions on issues of marriage. Notwithstanding certain grey areas these arranged marriages have several advantages. The merits and disadvantages of the matrimonial proposals are weighed dispassionately and the question of marriage is decided with mature advice. Such decisions are a relief, particularly to those girls who do not enjoy substantive equality in a male dominated society. However, there are situations when the head of the family completely ignores the wish of a girl and decides the question of marriage for considerations which may not necessarily be in accord with a girl's interest. In such situations, some girls rebel to insist on their right to marry a person of their own choice.

The right to marry in Islam

There has been some controversy amongst the jurists in Islam over the right of an adult woman to marry a person of her choice. Some thought that she cannot marry a person without the consent of her *wali*, i.e. father or guardian, whereas some thought that an adult woman does not need her *wali*'s consent and is free to marry a person of her own choice. However, the superior courts in Pakistan have now finally resolved the issue and held that an adult girl can enter into marriage without the consent of a *wali*. The relevant cases are *Muhammad Imtiaz and another vs. The State (PLD 1981 FSC 308), Arif Hussain and Azra Perveen vs. The State (PLD 1982 FSC 42), Muhammad Ramzan vs. The State (PLD 1984 FSC 93), Hafiz Abdul Waheed vs. Miss Asma Jahangir and another (PLD 1997 Lahore 301)* and *Mst. Humaira Mehmood vs. SHO PS North Cantt and others (PLD 1999 Lahore 494, PLJ 1999 Lahore 1474 & 1999 P.Cr.R. 542 Lahore)*.

In the latter, Humaira had married Mahmood against the wishes of her father who forced her to enter into a false matrimonial arrangement with a cousin. At stake in the case was the importance of consent of the two parties entering into a marriage contract, and whether a woman of majority age can marry a man of her own choice and against the wishes of her guardian/father. The court also had to address the question of the legal effect of the second marriage which, according to the woman, was forced upon her by her father but without her joining her second husband. The Lahore High Court upheld the right of a woman of majority age to marry a person of her choice, and the second marriage was held to be void *ab initio*.

Several Muslim countries have codified a woman's right to marry without the consent of the *wali*, including Syria, Tunisia and Morocco. A woman's right to marry has also been recognized in the Cairo Declaration on Human Rights in Islam of 5 August 1990 (Encyclopedia of Human Rights, by Edward Lawson, 2nd edition at page 176) which in its article 5 states:

"(a) The family is the foundation of society, and marriage is the basis of its formation. Men and women have the right to marriage, and no restrictions stemming from race, colour or nationality shall prevent them from enjoying this right."

Constitutional provisions and role of the courts in Pakistan

The Constitution of the Islamic Republic of Pakistan guarantees equal rights to women. Article 25(2) provides that "there shall be no discrimination on the basis of sex alone", article 25(3) reiterates that "nothing in this article shall prevent the State from making any special provision for the protection of women and children", and article 35 provides that "the State shall protect the marriage, the family, the mother and the child".

While upholding a woman's right to marry a person of her choice, the courts in Pakistan have never minimized the importance of the family as an institution. The family is a natural and divine institution which delineates the respective spheres of the father and mother, the husband and wife, and the brother and sister. The Pakistan judiciary endeavours to instill serenity to comprehend the winds of change in those who are jealous of their right as guardians to decide about their ward's marriage on the one hand, and a sense of maturity in the young women to make an informed choice, on the other. Society in our part of the world is undergoing change and is suffering the pangs which are the natural consequence. The courts in Pakistan are conscious of the dynamics of change and have demonstrated a profile through their judgements in consonance with the spirit of our faith, constitutional commitment on gender equality and in accord with the underlying norms of the Convention on the Elimination of All Forms of Discrimination against Women.

Best interests of children

Children's Rights in the Framework of the Canadian Charter of Rights and Freedoms with Reference to Section 15
Michel Bastarache

Introduction

This presentation provides an overview of how Canadian courts have used the United Nations Convention on the Rights of the Child (CRC) in their decision-making, and then to identify new approaches to incorporating the values of the Convention in the work of our judicial system.

Because of the structure of Canadian Parliamentary institutions, an international treaty is not part of Canadian law unless it has been incorporated by domestic legislation. As a result, the Convention on the Rights of the Child is not directly binding on Canadian courts, and cannot be invoked as a direct source of rights and obligations. However, the Convention can serve as a powerful interpretive aid. In the context of the Canadian Charter of Rights and Freedoms, Canadian courts have adopted the approach recommended by former Chief Justice Brian Dickson in *Re Public Service Relations Act.*[1] He argued that, though the judiciary is not bound by the norms of international law in interpreting the Charter, these norms provide a relevant and persuasive source for interpretation of its provisions, especially when those norms arise out of Canada's international obligations under human rights conventions. More recently in *Baker v. Canada* (Minister of Citizenship and Immigration),[2] the Supreme Court of Canada confirmed that the values re-

---

[1] [1987] 1 S.C.R. 313.

[2] [1999] S.C.J. No. 39 (QL).

flected in international human rights law may also be considered in a contextual approach to statutory interpretation and judicial review. This decision has given Canadian courts the opportunity to incorporate the values of the Convention into the work that they do generally.

Use of the Convention by Canadian courts

The Supreme Court of Canada has referred to the Convention primarily in the context of family law decisions. The Court has referred to the Convention to emphasize and support the "best interests of the child" standard which exists in family law statutes. For example, in both *Gordon v. Goertz* [3] and *W. (V.) v. S. (D.)*, [4] the Court examined the implications for custody and access when a custodial parent moves away from the jurisdiction with the child. The Court emphasized that the focus should be on the best interests of the child and not on the interests and rights of parents. Madame Justice L'Heureux-Dubé (in concurring reasons) referred in both cases to the fact that the Convention serves as evidence of the universal recognition that the interests of children must prevail in custody determinations.

The Supreme Court of Canada has also referred to the Convention to uphold the best interests standard in the face of constitutional challenge. In *Young v. Young* [5] and *P.(D.) v. S.(C.)*, [6] two fathers challenged the constitutionality of court orders restricting them from discussing their religion with their children when they had access to them. Both orders had been made in the best interests of the child, and the fathers argued that the orders violated their religious freedom, and that the best interests principle was too vague to withstand constitutional challenge. The Court rejected the vagueness argument and referred to the Convention as evidence of the enduring value of the best interest standard as a legal norm.

---

[3] [1996] 2 S.C.R. 27.

[4] [1996] 2 S.C.R. 108.

[5] [1993] 4 S.C.R. 3.

[6] [1993] 4 S.C.R. 141.

The Supreme Court of Canada's recent decision in *Baker* illustrates that the Convention may also be relevant in the determination of issues where the law does not explicitly require that the interests of children be considered, and where the rights of children are not obviously engaged. In this case a woman with four Canadian-born children was facing deportation. She asked for an exemption for humanitarian and compassionate considerations, citing her children and their emotional dependence on her. The Court found that the Convention could illustrate the values that are central in determining whether the immigration officer had exercised his humanitarian and compassionate discretion reasonably. Here the Convention was used, not as a tool to support an existing legislative pronouncement on the rights of children, but as a tool to incorporate considerations of children's needs and interests into administrative decisions that affect their futures.

As in *Baker*, lower courts in Canada have also invoked the Convention as an interpretive tool outside the context of custody disputes. In *Schafer v. Canada (A.G.)*,[7] the Ontario Court, General Division, referred to the Convention's declaration against discrimination on the basis of birth or other status in determining that a denial of employment insurance benefits to adoptive parents violated adopted children's equality rights. In *Francis (Litigation Guardian) v. Canada (Minister of Citizenship and Immigration)*,[8] a case currently under appeal, the Ontario Court, General Division, found that a child's liberty rights are engaged when his or her parents are subject to a deportation order, and invoked the Convention in determining the principles of fundamental justice. The Court found that these principles require that the rights and interests of children be considered in deportation proceedings.

The Convention has also been used in cases where children are engaged in the criminal justice system. For example, in *R v. B.M.*,[9] the Ontario Court of Justice referred to the Convention's guarantee of legal assistance when children are engaged in the penal justice system in the course of reviewing the practice of denying children legal aid when

---

[7] [1996] 135 D.L.R. 707.

[8] [1998], 40 O.R. (3d) 74.

[9] [1998] O.J. No. 3398 (QL).

their parents met a certain financial level. In *R v. C.J. P.*, [10] the Saskatchewan Youth Court referred to the Convention, along with the Charter in denouncing the abusive practices of prison guards in a youth detention center. In *R v. James*,[11] an Ontario Court Provincial Justice questioned whether section 43 of our Criminal Code, which permits parents and teachers to use reasonable force against children, is consistent with the protections provided by the Convention.

Areas for further consideration

While Canadian courts have successfully implemented the values of the Convention in the context of custody disputes and in cases where children are in conflict with our penal laws, there are still other areas where Convention values could be considered. Section 15 of the Canadian Charter of Rights and Freedoms protects children against discrimination on the basis of age, and is designed to promote and ensure substantive equality. The Convention can play a role in our determination of the content of the Section 15 right for children and in the way that right informs the regulation of other aspects of society. While Convention and Charter values can influence the way courts interpret many aspects of society that affect children, there are some areas where these values may be particularly germane. Should we incorporate the values of the Convention in our regulation of reproductive technology? Should we incorporate the values of the Convention in determining the meaning of a family? Should we incorporate Convention values into the consideration of when children, who are born alive, can seek compensation for their prenatal injuries? These values might also inform our assessments of damages in torts involving children, the legal protections against child labour and other forms of exploitation and our treatment of children as victims of crimes.

---

[10][1999] S.J. No. 237 (QL).

[11] [1998] O.J. No. 1438.

It is the role of courts to be alert to the potential for incorporating the interests of children into their decision-making and to ensure that the values of the Convention are realized in the law affecting children's rights.

Best Interests of the Child
Marta E. Battistella de Salaberry

Introduction

The concept of the "best interests of the child" emerged during the 1960s as an element of doctrine and jurisprudence which was subsequently incorporated in legislation. Guidelines for the content of the concept were drawn up at the Fourth Colloquium on European Law, held in Vienna from 5 to 7 March 1976.

Analysis reveals that the concept is broad in scope and varies depending on the culture and the place where the child is located. The topic is deeply rooted in family law and is related in particular to the questions of guardianship, visiting rights and custody, as well as to the legislation on child offenders.

The judge must have a general idea of the child's family background, of the family's habits and financial situation and of what the child's life has been so far, in order to be able to determine with complete impartiality what are the best interests of the child. Among the factors to be taken into account, the judge will attach importance to the parenting skills of the parents and their ability to take time out from their activities to help the child. The analysis of these factors must not overlook the fact that the child is a legal person and that her/his needs and requirements may differ from those of her/his parents and may even conflict with them. An effort must be made to separate the two positions, so as not to confuse what seems to be right for the child with what in fact is beneficial to one or both of the parents.

Two cases in which the concept was applied in Uruguay

Under a court-approved agreement between the parents, custody of the child was awarded to the mother. Subsequently, invoking new facts, the father appealed the decision granting custody to the mother. The father claimed that the mother's behaviour showed serious signs of social maladjustment making it impossible for the daughter to live with her. A study of the case did not confirm the father's allegations. The child was questioned by the court and she asked to remain with her mother.

The cases brought before the court often involve frequent complaints by fathers about possible misconduct and/or neglect of minor children by the mother, in cases of custody, guardianship and visiting rights, which may often be motivated by financial considerations (exemption from payment of alimony).

As a juridical solution, the applicability of the Convention on the Rights of the Child must be permanently established and, in particular, the child must be heard. In such proceedings, it is most important to have a multidisciplinary team, so as to ensure the least possible traumatization of the child as regards her/his subsequent development, since it is inappropriate to subject the child to repeated interrogations.

In this particular case, after hearing the child and considering the facts alleged by the parties, the court ruled that the mother should retain custody, taking into account principally the "best interests of the child". Thus the appeals process did not reveal factors requiring the revision of the initial ruling, in this case of an eight-year-old girl who had been living with her mother and maternal grandparents for four years.

At the time when the case was brought before the court, the child was pursuing her studies normally. It was the opinion of a psychologist who was consulted that there were no factors requiring any change in the stable situation which undoubtedly existed at the time. It was therefore concluded that, in the best interests of the child, the present arrangements should continue.

As an example of the application of the concept of the best interests of the child, reference may be made to a very interesting decision of the Supreme Court of Justice of Uruguay, which may be summarized as follows: as a precautionary measure, an HDL [sic] test was ordered on a child presumed to be the plaintiffs' son. The courts of first and second instance did not support the request, because the minor stated under questioning that he was not the biological child of the plaintiffs and that he was not interested in undergoing the requested testing. His refusal was reiterated several times and noted in the records.

In Uruguay, the minor's right to an identity has the status of a constitutional law under article 72 of the Constitution. The Supreme Court maintained that there was a conflict between two personal rights: on the one hand, the right of the plaintiff to prove that the minor BB and XX are the same person and therefore her son, with the ensuing consequences, and, on the other hand, the personal and no less valid right to preserve one's identity and not to have any alteration or modification in the social and family circumstances in which one has spent the crucial years of childhood and adolescence.

The Court concluded that the right recognized by article 173 of the Children's Code and article 8 of the Convention on the Rights of the Child is an essential right of the child to know his own identity and that, in exercise of this right to preserve his current identity, the adolescent refused (and reiterated the refusal when he came of age) to submit to tests which might alter the social and family situation in which he had been able to develop his personality in a harmonious and satisfactory manner. The appeal was therefore rejected.

Conclusion

There is a definite trend in both public and private institutions to provide training to all those involved in the administration of justice. The Supreme Court of Justice has organized training courses for officials in order to disseminate the Convention on the Rights of the Child. There are private organizations which have publicized the Convention and encouraged its application by judges.

The Rights of the Child: The Case of Uganda
Stella Arach-Amoko

Upon ratification of the Convention on the Rights of the Child (CRC), States parties assume specific obligations for its full implementation. Article 4 requires them to undertake all appropriate legislative, administrative and other measures for the implementation of the rights recognized in the Convention. Uganda ratified the CRC in September

1990. The following paper provides several examples of how Uganda has used this Convention or its principles to promote the rights of the child.

General measures taken to implement the Convention on the Rights of the Child in Uganda

In Uganda, the 1995 Constitution is the proper starting point to discuss the legal protection of the rights of children. Like all constitutions, it is the supreme law of the land, and its provisions have binding force on all authorities and persons throughout the land. The 1995 Constitution is based on the principles of unity, peace, equality, democracy, freedom, social justice and progress. One of the objectives declared by the Constitution is the protection and promotion of fundamental and other human rights and freedoms in general. Article 34 provides specifically for the rights of children. It states:

"34(1). Subject to the laws enacted in their best interests, children shall have the right to know and be cared for by their parents or those entitled by law to bring them up.

"34(2). A child is entitled to basic education, which shall be the responsibility of the State and the parents of the child.

"34(3). No child shall be deprived by any person of medical treatment, education or any other social or economic benefit by reason of religious or other beliefs.

"34(4). Children are entitled to be protected from social or economic exploitation and shall not be employed in, or required to perform, work that is likely to be hazardous or to interfere with their education or to be harmful to their health or physical, mental, spiritual, moral or social development.

"34(5). For the purposes of clause (4) of this article, children shall be persons under the age of sixteen years.

"34(6). A child offender who is kept in lawful custody or detention shall be kept separately from adult offenders.

"34(7). The law shall accord special protection to orphans and other vulnerable children."

From the above constitutional provisions it is clear that the rights of children in Uganda are protected by the Constitution. All ministries are reviewing their programmes and activities to ensure that they take into account these constitutional provisions.

The Children's Statute of 1996

In Uganda, the law on children has been reformed and consolidated by the Children's Statute of 1996, which makes provisions for their care, protection, adoption and maintenance. It also provides for local authority support for them and the establishment of a family and children's court. It defines a child in its section (3) as "a person below the age of eighteen years", which is in conformity with article (1) of the CRC. The Statute lays down the guiding principles for its implementation in schedules. The first schedule states that, whenever a State, court, legal authority or any person determines any question with respect to the upbringing of a child or the administration of a child's property, the child's welfare shall be the paramount consideration, and time shall be of the essence. It further states that in determining any questions mentioned above regard shall be had to:

a)   the ascertainable wishes and feelings of the child concerned;

b)   the child's physical, emotional and educational needs;

c)   the likely effects of any changes in the child's circumstances;

d)   the child's age, sex, background and any other relevant matter;

e)   any harm that the child has suffered or is at risk of suffering;

f)   where relevant, the capacity of the child's parents or guardians or any person involved in the child's care in meeting the needs of the child.

Apart from rights such as the right to education, adequate care, clothing, shelter, medical attention, parental protection and guidance, the Statute provides in the first schedule that the child "shall have the right to exercise, in addition to all the rights stated in the Statute, *all the rights set out in the United Nations Convention on the Rights of the Child and the OAU Charter on the Rights and Welfare of the African Child* with the appropriate modification to suit the circumstances in

Uganda, that are not specifically mentioned in the Statute" (emphasis added).

Constraints to implementation

As can be seen from the above provision, the CRC has been incorporated into the laws of Uganda. The only problem remains the implementation of the law, with poverty being the major constraint. It is estimated that 61 percent of the Ugandan population is classified as poor. Implementation requires, for example, the setting up of children's and family courts, which unfortunately has not yet been possible due to lack of funds. Instead, the implementation of the Children's Statute has now been assigned to the lowest courts of grade 11 magistrates who are neither trained nor equipped to deal with such intricate matters. With regard to most crimes, e.g. murder, defilement or robbery, they lack jurisdiction to try such cases. Civil strife and violence, particularly in the north of the country, also continue to have a negative impact on children. Children become victims directly when abducted or as a result of destruction and breakdown of essential services.

Under the Uganda Penal Code any person who has unlawful sexual intercourse with a girl under the age of 18 commits the offence of defilement (known as "statutory rape" in most developed countries) and is liable to suffer death on conviction. This law was intended, *inter alia*, to safeguard the girl child from sexual abuse and from endemic diseases, such as AIDS, which is now rampant in Uganda. Although several cases of defilement have gone through the courts, no one has ever been sentenced to death. The highest sentence was recently handed down by one of my brother judges, and it was 21 years imprisonment. This is because the courts, in handing down sentences in cases of defilement, take into account a number of mitigating circumstances such as the age of the accused *vis-à-vis* the victim's. If a boy of 19 for instance defiles a girl of 17 who happens to be his girlfriend, the situation becomes even trickier. The court will have to decide whether to sentence such a young man to death, or to give him a sentence that will eventually enable him to continue with his education and look after the child which usually results from such adventures.

On the question of procedure, the victim of defilement is usually allowed to have her case heard *in camera* to avoid embarrassing her and aggravating her trauma.

The following case illustrates how courts can decide taking into account the best interest of the child. In the case of *Reverend Father Kiwanuka vs. Mayumi Corporation, H.C.C.S. No. 119/96*, Mr. Mutebi, the proprietor of the defendant corporation, entered into a contract to supply a vehicle from Japan to the plaintiff. The plaintiff paid him the full purchase price of $6,000. Mr. Mutebi failed to supply the vehicle and was unable to refund the money. The plaintiff sued him and judgement was entered in favour of the plaintiff for the sum of $6,000 plus interest and costs of the suit. The plaintiff got a warrant of attachment of the residential house. At that point, Mrs. Mutebi applied to court and objected to this attachment on the ground that the house was not only their residential home but she lived there with her six children. If the order of attachment were executed, then her children would have no shelter. The judge deciding the case (Justice Arach-Amoko) took into account the best interest of the children and allowed Mrs. Mutebi's application, who continues to live in her house.

Genocide committed by minors
Odette Murara

Introduction

The United Nations has recognized that the acts perpetrated in Rwanda between April and July 1994 could justifiably be described as acts of genocide, crimes against humanity and serious breaches of article 3 common to the Geneva Conventions of 1949 and of Protocol II additional thereto.[1] The Statute of the International Criminal Tribunal

---

[1] See the preliminary report of the Independent Commission of Experts established in accordance with Security Council resolution 935 (1994) (S/1994/1125) and the report on the situation of human rights in Rwanda established by the Special Rapporteur of the Commission on Human Rights on the situation of human rights in Rwanda in accordance with Economic and Social Council decision 1994/223 (A/49/508 of 13 October 1994). While these documents are not binding on domestic tribunals, they

for Rwanda, adopted by the United Nations Security Council on 8 November 1994, also confirmed that genocide and crimes against humanity had been committed.

Several thousand minors participated actively in the Rwandan genocide of 1994. A survey of 1,125 women victims of violence conducted in three prefectures of Rwanda shows that 24.7[2] per cent of the violence against women was committed by children, and that 39.3 per cent of women had been sexually assaulted. According to 74.5 per cent of the women victims polled during the survey, women had often been sexually assaulted during the genocide.[3]

On 3 August 1996, the National Transitional Assembly passed an organic law on the organization of criminal proceedings against acts which constitute either the crime of genocide or crimes against humanity.

The main innovations of the law include classification, and juvenile magistrates. Such classification is based on the extent of personal responsibility in the perpetration of a crime of genocide or crimes against humanity. One of the objectives of lawmakers was to strike a balance between the need to ensure that the punishment of the most serious crimes was exemplary and the vital importance of national reconciliation.[4] The intention is to classify the perpetrators, rather than the crimes as such.

---

nonetheless constitute admissible evidence upon which judges may base their sentences.

[2] Avega Agahozo, Etude sur les violences faites aux femmes au Rwanda, Kigali, March 1999, p. 32. More often than not, such acts were perpetrated by men, although it is not uncommon to find that women, children and even foreigners had been actively involved.

[3] Ibid., p. 34.

[4] How many of the crimes committed would not be liable to the death penalty? However, lawmakers also have to consider the future of society. To that end, it is the Government's duty to assist the magistrates, acting as a group, to find a solution to the socio-political problems facing the country. Meting out different punishments for those who gave the orders for those crimes and those who carried them out, respectively, would serve as a lesson for society as a whole (act No. 08/96 of 30 August 1996 — deliberations of Parliament, extracts, 1996 session, Alter Egaux (eds), Kigali, Brussels.II, pp. 9 and 15).

The organic law classifies under category 1, which carries the death penalty, persons who committed acts of sexual torture.

Law applicable to minors

The law applicable to minors is determined by the basic principle established in article 39 of the organic law. "Unless otherwise provided in this organic law, all provisions, including those contained in the Penal Code, the Code of Criminal Procedure and the Code of Judicial Organization and Jurisdiction, shall apply." These provisions comprise the legal texts, general principles of law and international instruments.

Under the Constitution, international human rights instruments are directly applicable and take precedence over any other internal norms. Due to the status enjoyed by international human rights law under domestic law, a court rightly based its ruling on a provision of the Convention on the Rights of the Child[5] (article 40).

As a result of the presence in prisons of many children accused of genocide, the international community has made vigorous efforts to disseminate the Convention on the Rights of the Child, the only international convention for which magistrates are trained. The special nature of proceedings involving genocide and massacres as well as their scope justify the creation of specialized chambers with exclusive jurisdiction over such matters. At least one of the benches of such chambers should be composed of juvenile magistrates, who will have exclusive jurisdiction over offences committed by minors.

Juvenile magistrates have started applying the Convention. In the *Maniraguha* case, the Kigali specialized chamber is basing its decision on article 40, paragraph 3 (a) of the Convention, which requires States Parties to establish a minimum age below which children shall be presumed not to have the capacity to infringe the penal law, and on article 77 of the Penal Code, which establishes a presumption of immunity from criminal responsibility for minors aged 14 and below. In the genocide proceedings, the claimants for criminal indemnification find it difficult to reconcile the concept of minor with acts of genocide.

---

[5] Kigali sp. ch., 4 June 1999, RMP 5250/S12 RP 125/CS, Maniraguha case.

In the majority of cases, magistrates apply only those provisions of the Penal Code concerning special treatment for minors, in accordance with the Convention. A minor who committed an offence when he was at least 14 years and a day old but a day younger than 18 years, shall benefit from the excuse of being a minor. The magistrate shall be bound by the ground for mitigation.[6] Where there is the slightest doubt, it shall be mandatory under law to determine the exact age of the accused. Indeed, several implications of public policy, such as the extent of criminal responsibility, the obligation to refer the matter to a bench composed of juvenile magistrates (art. 19 of the organic law) and the regime of sentences (art. 77 of the Penal Code) flow from this. The State prosecutor's office or the court shall automatically ensure this.[7]

Sometimes, civil register documents establishing age are incomplete, lacking the month and day of birth. In such cases, the principle according to which the accused should be given the benefit of the doubt shall prevail.[8]

The Convention defines a child as a human being below the age of 18 years and paragraph 37 (c) states that "... every child deprived of liberty shall be separated from adults". It only requires that teenagers should be separated from adults as far as detention or imprisonment is concerned. The State prosecutor's office institutes proceedings against young people who are between 14 years + a day and 18 as if they were adults within the meaning of the Penal Code. Where they are impris-

---

[6] Mugenzi, L. M, Droit pénal général-Amategeko rusange ahana, Ministry of Justice, RCN (eds), Kigali, p. 67.

[7] Age is determined on the basis of an extract from the civil register prepared in accordance with the law (art. 106 and ff., 125 and 126 of section one of the Civil Code). Where the State prosecutor and the court are unable to obtain a birth certificate, an affidavit must either be drawn up (art. 138 of the same code) or the court of first instance has to issue a suppletory decision (jugement supplétif) concerning the civil registry document (art. 147 to 149).

[8] Kigali sp. ch., 13 July 1999 RMP 8945/S12/NRV, Niyoyita case. Kigali Appeal Court, 30 November 1998 RPA 25/97/R1/Kig, Mugabo case. The appeal was declared admissible on the grounds that, contrary to the law, the judgement decided that the accused was over 14 when the acts were committed, but failed to conduct the mandatory investigations in Mugabo's commune of origin with a view to establishing his date of birth.

157

oned, they are separated from persons above the age of 18. Article 40 of the Penal Code also establishes the principle of separating minors sentenced as adults.

Article 37 (a) of the Convention provides that neither capital punishment nor life imprisonment without possibility of release shall be imposed for offences committed by persons below 18 years of age. It provides, moreover, that any decisions handed down must take into account the interests of the child. According to article 77 of the Penal Code, where a minor is the perpetrator of or accessory to a criminal act, he shall be sentenced to 10 to 20 years of imprisonment, if he is liable to the death penalty or life imprisonment. Where he is liable to a term of imprisonment or to a fine, the penalties that may be imposed on him may not be more than half of those to which he would have been sentenced, had he been 18 years old.

Thus, accused persons who were minors when the offences were committed, were sentenced to four years of imprisonment.[9] In this particular case, offences that were liable to a sentence of eight years if the accused confessed before criminal proceedings were instituted, were classified as category 2 offences and punished by a sentence of eight years of imprisonment, reduced to four because the offender was a minor.

Administrative measures[10] were also taken by the Government to release detainees classified as vulnerable, namely, minors, the elderly and the sick.

Pursuant to article 37 (d) of the Convention, all minors between 14 and 18 years of age referred to the courts are assisted by defence counsel, while the courts are especially careful in dealing with defendants who are children.[11] In accordance with article 27, the State prosecutor represents the civil interests of minors and other incompetent persons who do not have legal representation.

---

[9] Kibungo sp. ch., 19 November 1997, RMP 89004/S3/ND, case concerning Banzubaze and others.

[10] Decision of the Council of Ministers.

[11] For example, Kibungo, sp. ch., 17 June 1998, RMP 89033/S3/ND/KGO/ST, case concerning Sebarinda and others.

The 1996 organic law, the Rwandan Penal Code and the Convention severely punish acts of violence against women and provide protection for children. Yet attempts to speed up the processing of cases of minors in detention have not been successful notwithstanding the provision of article 37 of the Convention that "No child shall be deprived of his or her liberty unlawfully or arbitrarily. The arrest, detention or imprisonment of a child shall be in conformity with the law and shall be used only as a measure of last resort and for the shortest appropriate period of time."

The complexity of proceedings concerning genocide, the large number of unconvicted prisoners, including minors, constitute a national problem and place a heavy burden on the legal system, which is being reorganized. That is why a draft organic law is now being tabled on the establishment of *"gacaca"*[12] courts, which would be entrusted with some of the functions currently performed by the judicial institutions. The outline of the draft law deals with participatory justice and citizens' assemblies, which would discuss the responsibilities of those who carried out the genocide and massacres; the courts would retain the task of judging those who gave orders for these crimes to be carried out.

While legal experts may find this approach disconcerting, it should be borne in mind that the country's judicial institutions will never be able to judge the 120,000 people currently in detention, including 4,453[13] young people, who were supposed to have been between 14 years and a day old and a day younger than 18 years when the offences constituting genocide and crimes against humanity were committed.

Certain situations and the lack of resources may therefore hamper the implementation of an international convention at the national level.

---

[12] Gacaca is the term used for a traditional conflict resolution mechanism.

[13] Ministry of Justice/UNICEF coordination project, August 1999.

Proposed Amendments to the Philippine Rules of Court, or Proposed Integration with the Rules for Family Courts: Video-Conferencing, and the Convention on the Rights of the Child

Ameurfina A. Melencio Herrera

Introduction

Because of the vulnerability of the child, and because procedural rules have been generally drafted with adults in mind, the child complainant, accused or witness calls for special attention and accommodation.

In the Philippines, our Constitution vests in the Supreme Court rule-making power (art. VIII, sec. 5), which is plenary. Pursuant to this constitutional mandate, the Supreme Court has promulgated our Rules of Court.

Revisions of the Rules have been undertaken. However, they have yet to accommodate the special condition of children. Experience has been that for child victims, the confusing and intimidating atmosphere of a regular courtroom and regular court proceedings can be as traumatizing as their victimization.

It is in this context that the Philippine Judicial Academy (PHILJA) has drafted proposals for the revision of the rules, particularly, on the reception of testimony from and by children. Or, the proposed rules could be integrated into the rules for family courts soon to be organized in the Philippines.

Philippine case

In *People v. Ritter*, a foreigner was charged with having raped a girl-child, purportedly under 12 years old, and with having caused her death by leaving a vibrator within the young girl's vaginal canal. The trial court convicted, but the Supreme Court acquitted, for absence of proof beyond a reasonable doubt. Significantly, the Court observed that one of the witnesses - a minor was "already shaking with fear after he had identified the accused."

Our Rules of Court, however, remain unchanged in that our court-rooms and court proceedings are still intimidating to children. It is this fact that underlies the proposals of PHILJA.

Relevant provisions of the Convention on the Rights of the Child (CRC)

Article 3.1: In all actions concerning children, whether undertaken by ... courts of law, ... the best interests of the child shall be a primary consideration.

PHILJA reads this provision to apply not only to the results of the actions themselves but to the very conduct or process of the actions. Thus, while decisions of courts of law must take into priority consideration the best interests of the child, judicial processes and, in particular, the rules must themselves be cognizant and protective of these interests.

Article 19.2: Such protective measures should, as appropriate, include effective procedures ... and, as appropriate, .. judicial involvement.

The foregoing provision constitutes one of the direct sources for the PHILJA proposals to amend the rules as part of the protective measures the Republic of the Philippines can institute in conformity with its obligation under the CRC.

Subjecting a child to the very same ordeal that adults are subject to in judicial processes does not comply with the directive to take such protective measures.

PHILJA proposals

1. Video conferencing and video-teleconferencing of testimony: The court may direct that the child-witness be subject to direct examination or cross-examination, or both, in a suitable room linked to the session hall or elsewhere by closed circuit television or other necessary electronic and communication facilities. Such equipment must allow the judge, the accused, the lawyers, and the public, unless excluded, to observe and hear the child-witness. During such examination the child-witness may be accompanied by an adult of the child's choice who shall not in any way coach the witness or interfere with the exami-

nation. The adult companion, however, may, with leave of court, do what is necessary to keep the child-witness composed and at ease.

We submit that this proposal does not run afoul of the "confrontation clause". In the Philippines, this basic requirement has been held to have two purposes, the main one being to allow the accused the opportunity to cross-examine a witness against him. The second purpose is to allow the court to observe the demeanour of the witness. Both of these purposes are served by the proposed provision on video-conferencing.

Application of video-conferencing will not be automatic. The party representing the child must file the necessary motion and the court must rule on the basis of evidence it receives as to the necessity of its application.

2. When the witness is a child, answers may be given through, or with the help of drawings, diagrams, representative objects or other devices. For purposes of these rules, ...a child is anyone below the age of 18 years.

We propose this rule because when a girl-child, for example, is sexually abused, it may not be easy for her to describe, for purposes of direct or cross-examination, how she was violated.

3. The court may likewise direct that the child-witness be examined through a suitable child facilitator who may be a psychologist, psychiatrist, social worker, teacher, religious leader or, unless disqualified, a parent or relative. In such a case, counsel, both on direct and on cross-examination, shall raise their questions in the usual manner, but these shall be posed to the child-witness, through said child facilitator. Either counsel may object to the manner or mode in which the question is raised and the court shall direct the court facilitator to pose the question in a manner consistent with the rules.

The reason for the proposed rule is that the child should not be questioned as an adult. The mode of questioning and the kinds of questions asked should be suited to a child.

4. Manner of questioning - that manner of questioning that facilitates narration by the child-witness shall be allowed.

The proposed rule will allow both judge and counsel more flexibility in dealing with questions posed to a child-witness to be able to adapt to the peculiar circumstances of that child witness.

5. Applicability of rules on deposition - in all proceedings, the court shall allow video-taped depositions by a child witness that comply with established rules.

The depositions can substitute for live trial testimony upon showing that taking the witness stand in person would harm the child even more.

Conclusion

Amending the Rules of Court alone will not make the world a better place for children, but it will make the pursuit of justice when they are wronged, or even when they are charged as wrongdoers, less intimidating and daunting than it presently is. It is hoped that the judiciary in our respective lands, inspired by the CRC, and through this Judicial Colloquium will continue to extend a solicitous hand to children who, in their vulnerability, need the guarantees of the law most.

Sexual violence in work-related settings

R. V. Ewanchuk: A Case Study on the Meaning of Consent in Cases of Sexual Violence against Women
Catherine Fraser

Sexual violence against women and CEDAW

In all countries, there is debate around sexual assault and rape laws. Sexual violence, in all its forms, involves a distinct gender dimension because typically the victims are female. In Canada, one study indicated that perpetrators are 99 per cent male; victims 90 per cent female.

How a country's laws protect women from sexual violence is an important issue and a good test of whether the country's laws reflect the requirements of the Convention on the Elimination of All Forms of Discrimination against Women (CEDAW). CEDAW calls for States parties to take all appropriate measures, including legislation, to modify or abolish existing laws, regulations, customs and practices which constitute discrimination against women (article 2(f)) and to repeal all national penal provisions which constitute discrimination against women (article 2(g)).

If there is any doubt that violence against women is a form of discrimination, General Recommendation 19, an interpretive guide to CEDAW on the question of violence against women adopted by the Committee on the Elimination of Discrimination in 1992, states clearly that it is.

General Recommendation 19 states that "[T]he definition of discrimination includes gender-based violence, that is, violence that is directed against a woman because she is a woman or that affects women disproportionately".

B. R. v. Ewanchuk

Recently, there was a prominent case in Canada which showed how CEDAW could have relevance at every step of the analysis of facts and law: assessment of credibility of witnesses, interpretation of rules of evidence, assessment of what is "relevant", what is accepted as evidence, the interpretation of statutory provisions and constitutional guarantees.

The main legal issue was one of consent: did the young girl consent to the sexual conduct initiated by the accused? This involved not only a choice between differing versions of the facts but also differing visions of the law. On the law side, the choice was between a historical approach to consent or an equality-based approach. These differing approaches also influenced how the two levels of appellate courts (the Alberta Court of Appeal and the Supreme Court of Canada) interpreted the clear fact findings made by the trial judge and their relevance to the key issue of consent.

What were the facts? A 17 year old girl, 5'1", met a 6'+ man, about 30, on a hot summer day for a job interview which took place in a trailer. The man closed the door to the trailer. The girl believed he had locked the door after she had entered the trailer and was fearful. The man invited her to massage his back; she complied. He massaged her and attempted to touch her breasts. She said "No" and he stopped. He then lay on top of her, pushing her back and rubbing his pelvic area against hers. She again said "No" and again, he stopped momentarily. While still lying on top of her, the man exposed his penis and the girl said "No" again. He then finally stopped and the girl left the trailer. He gave her $100. He was charged with sexual assault.

The trial judge found that even though the young girl was fearful, she had not communicated that fear to the accused and the accused did not know therefore that she was not consenting. He acquitted the accused.

Historical approach to consent in sexual violence cases vs. equality-based approach

Before explaining what happened on appeal, it is helpful to step back and look at the central issue, consent. How has this been dealt with historically? There have been several variations on the same theme.

- If a woman does not say "No" she means "Yes"

- When a woman says "No", she is really saying "Yes" "Try again" or "Persuade me"

- A man is entitled to presume consent until a woman resists

- A women can give her implied consent to sexual activity through how she dresses or her past sexual conduct

- Non-resistance equals implied consent.

How does an equality-based approach, rooted in CEDAW and a country's human rights and equality guarantees, change the way that consent is viewed?

- Consent to sexual activity must be true consent

- Women have the right to physical and sexual autonomy

- The issue is not whether the woman said ""No" but whether she said "Yes"

- "No" to one level of sexual activity does not mean "Yes" to a higher level of sexual activity

- "No" means "No".

The Supreme Court of Canada unanimously followed an equality-based approach to the issue of consent (convicting the accused), as had Fraser, C.J.A. in dissent at the Alberta Court of Appeal.

a) Supreme Court of Canada (L'Heureux-Dubé, J.): Violence against women takes many forms: sexual assault is one of them. So persuasive is violence against women that the international community adopted ... [CEDAW], which has been described as "the definitive international legal instrument requiring respect for and observance of the human rights of women". The accused cannot rely on the complainant's silence or ambiguous conduct to initiate sexual conduct. Moreover, where a complainant expresses non-consent, the accused has a corresponding escalating obligation to take additional steps to ascertain consent.

b) Supreme Court of Canada (McLachlin, J.): On appeal, the idea also surfaced that if a woman is not modestly dressed, she is deemed to consent. Such stereotypical assumptions find their roots in many cultures, including our own. They no longer, however, find a place in Canadian law.

c) Supreme Court of Canada (Major, J.): It follows from the foregoing, however, that the trier of fact may only come to one of two conclusions: the complainant either consented or not. There is no third option.

d) Alberta Court of Appeal (Fraser, C.J.A. in dissent): Women in Canada are not walking around this country in a state of constant consent to sexual activity unless and until they say "No" or offer resistance to anyone who targets them for sexual activity. The unfairness of this approach and its breach of women's equality rights under the Charter and Canada's international human rights obligations cannot be seriously challenged: CEDAW; see also the Declaration on the Elimination of Violence Against Women (DEDAW).

CEDAW, and the equality norms it reflects, operate on two levels: they call on a country's law-makers to pass laws consistent with

CEDAW; and they also influence judicial decision-making. On this latter point, CEDAW and other international human rights instruments can be used domestically as a foundation of a country's constitution and the rights guaranteed therein; as a declaratory statement of customary international law which is itself part of the law of the land; as an interpretive tool in defining the scope and content of domestic laws; and as evidence of public policy, in the event of an alleged conflict between a statute and the Constitution.

Sometimes, it is easier to see how CEDAW can affect statutory interpretation than other parts of the decision-making process. But CEDAW is also working against all forms of inequality in judicial decision-making including the manner in which appellate judges interpret facts as found by a trial judge. For example, contrast the result of the differing approaches in this case to the facts as found by the trial judge.

Historical approach vs. equality approach to interpretation of facts

Physical disparity is irrelevant.	The fact the accused was twice the size of the complainant is relevant.
What she was wearing (or not wearing) was important and warranted comment.	What she was wearing was irrelevant.
This was a social encounter; a romantic interlude.	This was a job interview.
The accused stopped what he was doing when asked.	The accused did not stop; he simply moved on to a higher level of sexual contact.

Conclusion

While this case study shows how an equality-based approach can influence the way that laws on sexual violence against women are interpreted, there are many other areas where CEDAW and the equality-based approach endorsed by it will also potentially influence judicial decision-making.

167

Application of International Human Rights Law in India
Sujata Manohar

Introduction

The last 50 years have seen the emergence of an internationally accepted enunciation of human rights. These rights are scattered over various international declarations, covenants and the like, starting with the Universal Declaration of Human Rights. CEDAW embodies some of the major human rights that touch the lives of women whether working outside their homes or inside their homes. Many nations have signed, ratified or acceded to this Convention or other such international instruments. Not all have translated the rights they have affirmed into domestic legislation.

As a result, domestic courts have increasingly faced a situation where a person, an institution or an organization complains before the courts of a violation of human rights recognized in international instruments and seeks redress - either in the form of an injunction or compensation for the breach of human rights. If there is domestic legislation affirming these human rights, the task of the court is easier. Problems arise where there is no domestic legislation supporting the claim based on international human rights obligations.

Cases decided by courts in India

In India there has been a spate of litigation covering the last twenty years where increasingly, international human rights norms are invoked in justification of claims based on violation of human rights.

This litigation is often in the form of public interest litigation (PIL). Indian courts have permitted public interest litigation by responsible bodies or individuals on behalf of the downtrodden – whether these be bonded or child laborers, inmates of mental asylums or children's homes, undertrials or prisoners – for the enforcement of their human rights. But for PIL, these groups would have had no access to the legal system for various reasons connected with their present condition. The following discussion refers to several recent cases in the Indian Supreme Court where international human rights norms were invoked by the Supreme Court in support of its decision. The best-known is *Vishakha v. State of Rajasthan [(1997) 6 SCC241]* where I was one of the judges.

Under common-law jurisdiction, the provisions of an international treaty signed by a country do not form part of the law of that country unless its provisions are incorporated in a domestic law. This principle applies in Indian jurisprudence also. However, the courts have interpreted international human rights documents to which India is a signatory, on a somewhat different jurisprudential basis. The Constitution of India contains, in part III, a series of fundamental rights which can be judicially enforced through the law courts. For women, the most important are articles 14, 15, 16 and 21. Article 14 prescribes equality before the law and equal protection of the laws. Article 15 prohibits discrimination on grounds of race, religion, caste, sex or place of birth. Article 16 which covers employment under the State prohibits discrimination on grounds of race, religion, caste, sex, place of birth, descent or place of residence. Article 12 has been judicially interpreted to cover a right to lead one's life with dignity.

All these rights have been interpreted by the courts widely to include within their ambit, whenever possible, international human rights which have been accepted by India by signing the relevant declaration, covenant, etc. As a result, these human rights can now be directly enforced by the courts.

In *D.K. Basu v. State of West Bengal [(1997)1 SCC 416]* the claim for compensation arose out of torture, rape and death in police custody. The Supreme Court held that the expression "life or personal liberty" in article 21 included a right to live with human dignity and would include a guarantee against torture or assault by the State or its functionaries, whether to extract information or otherwise. It is a public wrong committed by the State against a constitutional right and entails remedy in the form of compensation.

The same issue had been taken earlier by the Supreme Court in *Nilabati Behera v. State of Orissa [(1993)2 SCC 746]*. In both cases the Court invoked article 9(5) of the International Covenant on Civil and Political Rights, which provides that "[A]nyone who has been victim of unlawful arrest or detention shall have an enforceable right to compensation". Interestingly India, while ratifying the ICCPR, had

169

made a reservation stating that its legal system did not recognize a right to compensation for victims of unlawful arrest or detention. Yet the Supreme Court expressly held that this reservation was irrelevant because compensation could be awarded for a public wrong involving infringement of a citizen's fundamental right to life.

In *People's Union for Civil Liberties v. Union of India [(1997)3 SCC 433]* the Supreme Court held that the provisions of an international convention to which India was a party, especially one which declares universal fundamental rights, may be used by the courts as a legitimate guide in developing the common law (p.441). The Court cited Australian cases in support. This case also dealt with a death in police custody.

In *Vishakha v. State of Rajasthan [(1997)6 SCC 241]* however, the Supreme Court dealt for the first time with a woman's right to work and her working environment. It was an unusual PIL brought on behalf of a woman social worker employed by the State of Rajasthan to tour villages and educate the rural population against child marriages and dowry. She was raped by some village leaders who were annoyed by her activities. The Supreme Court based the fundamental rights of a working woman on articles 14, 19 and 21 of the Constitution. (Article 14: equality, article 19: the right to carry on any business or profession, article 21: the right to life.)

The Court said that the true concept of gender equality in the work place entails freedom from sexual harassment at the place of work; and since this could be a recurring phenomenon, the writ of mandamus had to be accompanied by directions for prevention, because the fundamental right to carry on any occupation, trade or business depends on the availability of a safe working environment. In the absence of any specific legislation, the Court laid down guidelines to secure the fundamental rights of women under articles 14, 15 and 21. It said that article 32 which casts an obligation on the courts to enforce fundamental rights, entails a duty to ensure and promote observance of human rights and to prevent their violation. Reliance was placed on the Beijing Statement of Principles on the Independence of the Judiciary adopted in Beijing in August 1995 by the Sixth Conference of Chief Justices of Asia and the Pacific.

It is of particular interest that the Court made an extensive use of international conventions and norms in support of its decision. The Court also derived support from articles 11 and 24 of CEDAW. This is the first time that the Indian Supreme Court expressly quoted from CEDAW and the CEDAW Committee's general recommendations. The Court also referred to the official commitments made by India at the Fourth World Conference on Women in Beijing.

Happily, this reasoning has again been reiterated and confirmed in another case relating to sexual harassment which came before the Supreme Court two years later, namely *Apparel Export Promotion Council v. A.K. Chopra [(1999)1 SCC 759]*. The Court relied on the definition of sexual harassment spelt out in *Vishakha* and agreed that the protection against sexual harassment at the workplace was a part of gender equality at the work place.

Protecting women and girls against violence

A Study on Judicial Custody, Popularly Known as Safe Custody
K. M. Hasan

Some recent incidents like rape, killings and torture of females in safe custody have led to the demand by women's rights activists in Bangladesh for the abolition of the system which keeps a minor in so-called "safe custody" in jail. They claim that 'safe custody is not safe anymore'.

The practice of safe custody

There is no law providing for safe custody. It obtained legal status from judicial pronouncements. The concept is directed towards protecting the best interests and the welfare of 'victim girls'. In one of the earlier decisions on safe custody, the case of *Jahanara Begum v The State,* reported in *15 DLR (Dhaka) 148*, it was held that the absence of any specific statutory provision in the Code did not mean prohibition of the detention of the minor where an offence has been alleged to have been committed by someone relating to the said minor. Taking a minor into custody or arranging for his or her detention, with a view to temporarily isolating him or her from certain influences, may be necessitated by the dictates of justice. That custody or detention is different from the custody of an alleged criminal and even of a political detenu. It has the complexion of the custody of a guardian. It has an object different from confinement or placing restriction on the person's movement. In the case of *Ayesha Begum v The State, 13 DLR (Dhaka) 681* it is thought that a person in such a situation is incapable of exercising an independent mind unless kept in a neutral place for a reasonable time. The Appellate Division persisted to hold the view that the detention under safe custody is different from the detention of a criminal or of a political detenu *(Pratulla Chakrabarty v Secretary, Ministry of Home Affairs, 1995 RSCR (Vol. VIII 112).*

Sending a woman to safe custody becomes necessary when she, once recovered by the police from the custody of the accused and produced before a court of law in connection with her kidnapping, has no place to go. After recovery she is detained by the police under section 54 of Criminal Procedure Code, then produced before the Magistrate for necessary action under section 100 of the Criminal Procedure Code. The recovered girl might be a destitute, or carry a social stigma for which she may be unwanted by the family. She might refuse to go with her parents, because hers was a genuine love affair and she voluntarily eloped with the accused. In case of the former, the court sends her to safe custody, to be kept there until the trial is over, as she is a vital witness to the offence alleged against the accused. In the latter case, the court finds itself in a dilemma. It would like to pass an order giving her over to the custody of her parents, but such an order cannot be passed unless it is established that she is a minor. In the absence of a registration of birth, the determination of the victim girl's age becomes most important. It is also important to establish the commission of the offence. If the victim has reached the age of majority and if she denies having been kidnapped by the accused, the case against him will automatically fail. In such a situation the court cannot release her to the custody of her legal guardian nor let her go on her own or throw her out on the street until the determination of her age and completion of investigation of the offence alleged against her. In such circumstances, the court finds it best for all concerned to keep her in safe custody in jail as the country still lacks facilities for sheltering these girls.

The next common feature, in cases where the recovered girl refuses to go to her parents and is sent to safe custody, is an application by the legal guardian or any one interested including the recovered girl before the High Court Division under section 491 of the Criminal Procedure Code for a declaration that the detention of the recovered girl in safe custody is illegal. The criminal proceeding under section 491 is a summary proceeding and remedial in nature but it postulates the existence of a right to personal freedom.

Challenges to safe custody

Recently, the detention of a girl in safe custody in jail has been challenged in the High Court Division of the Supreme Court by way of a pro-bono litigation in the writ petition No. 1563 of 1998, *Rokeya Kabir v Government of Bangladesh* (not yet reported). One of the grounds was that the Convention of the Rights of the Child, which Bangladesh has ratified, did not allow such detention of a victim girl. The petition specifically referred to articles 12(1), 16(1) and 37(1) of the CRC.

The writ of habeas corpus under article 102(2)(b)(I) of the Constitution confers on a person in custody the right to have the High Court Division test and determine the legality of the order or warrant by which he/she is kept in custody and declare it unlawful and of no legal effect. The Court's scope and power under article 102(2)(b)(I) of the Constitution in the matter of granting relief are very wide and beyond the powers conferred under section 491 of the Criminal Procedure Code.

However the rule was finally discharged by the Court observing that "... in a pro bono litigation, the detention of a single person cannot the challenged to espouse a public cause. It can be done but this is not such a case. It does in no way invoke the simple question of detention of a single person, but challenges the legality of a system that has been developed by our Court known as safe custody".

Previously, under article 102 of our Constitution, except in habeas corpus cases, only a directly 'aggrieved person' could invoke the writ jurisdiction of the High Court Division. Since *Dr. Mohiuddin Faroo-que*'s case, reported in *49 DLR (AD)1,* the door that had been long closed to persons other than the constitutionally entitled directly 'aggrieved person' has been opened a little by the Appellate Division to persons representing an indeterminate class of people. Non-governmental organizations and activists may now come before the High Court Division invoking the writ jurisdiction and challenging safe custody by way of a public interest litigation.

However, an observation made by the Appelate Division calls for a note of caution. A NGO or any member of the public, while invoking the writ jurisdiction, should not act in a manner that might be construed that they are acting more for the sake of publicity rather than the cause.

Conclusion

A lot can be said against safe custody, for example that it is not safe anymore, or that it holds an innocent girl in custody for an indefinite period of time without even furnishing her the grounds. But the Court has to take into consideration many facts, including the socio-economic condition of the country and economic constraints that so far have prevented the construction of sufficient shelter homes. In a society like ours, which is basically conservative and has followers of different religions, the Court must consider communal harmony and custodial rights of the legal guardian of a minor, especially when the parties involved belong to different communities. Where two communities are concerned, the question of maintaining communal harmony becomes one of the dominant factors in the mind of the Court. The judges are to debate not only the constitutional and textual position of a case but also the socio-economic realities of the country.

The courts are fully aware that a system that was developed for the welfare of the minor girl has now become a source of misery. They are trying to find a better solution which might take time. In the meantime, two recommendations for immediate relief are offered. First, there is a need for strict application of the existing law of compulsory registration of birth, and second, shelter homes for young women need to be opened at local level to provide an alternative for cases where safe custody is presently used.

"Honour" Killing
Nasir-ul-Mulk

Introduction

This paper concerns not the application, but rather the need to apply, international human rights law in Pakistan in matters relating to honour killing. Killings for "honour" are an extreme form of violence against women. Though the concept of honour killing is old and tacitly, if not openly, approved by a large section of the population, a national debate was triggered in early 1999 by the tragic murder of a young married woman, Samia Sarwar, from a well placed family. She was murdered, reportedly by members of her family, in the office of her lawyer where she had gone for consultation for dissolution of her marriage with her cousin against the wishes of family. Samia lost her life but her tragic death drew the attention of the nation to this inhuman practice of killing for "honour". It generated discussions in the news media, debates in Parliament, and some soul searching by the people. However it came as no surprise that a section of the people openly approved of the practice, calling it a part of their culture and tradition.

Killings of women in the name of honour take place for a variety of reasons. The most common is the indulgence of the victim in extramarital sex and the execution is invariably carried out by a male family member of the victim. Mere suspicion of sexual impropriety of a woman has at times proved sufficient for a male member of the family to take her life, because the primary motive for honour killing is to restore the honour of the assailant or his family which is perceived to have been lost on account of the deceased woman's misdemeanor. And that is why women are not even provided with an opportunity to explain before they are put to death. A woman's choice to marry against the wishes of the male members of the family, or to obtain a divorce may put her life at risk. A woman may also be killed in the name of honour for a very trivial cause. The list of reasons is long, and new reasons are constantly being added.

The treatment of "honour" killing under the law and in practice

It is unfortunate that many of the perpetrators of honour killings are never brought to justice, thus encouraging such killings. In our criminal justice system, the police is obliged to register a case if it receives information, even though not formally, of the commission of a serious crime, like murder. The police personnel are then bound to carry out an investigation, collect evidence, arrest the accused and prosecute them in a court of law. However, where an honour killing is carried out with the approval, tacit or explicit, of the elders of the community or the victim's family, the crime is invariably not formally reported to the police and it is very likely that the police may never come to know of the commission of the crime. But even if informal information is received by the police, the officials are generally reluctant to initiate criminal proceedings because they believe that it would be an exercise in futility as no one would volunteer, or dare to, furnish information or testify in court. Added to this may be the personal belief of the male police officials that honour killing is after all not as serious a crime as plain murder. The cases that do get investigated and tried are those where a relative of the murdered woman does not approve of her killing and reports the matter to the police or when the accused, in the excitement of having redeemed his honour, goes to the police station and admits the commission of the crime.

There is a dire need to educate the police force on gender-based crimes and provide them with special training to investigate cases of honour killing. Pakistan is a State party to the Convention on the Elimination of All Forms of Discrimination against Women. It participated in the adoption, by consensus, of the United Nations Declaration on the Elimination of Violence against Women. Under article 4(c) of the Declaration, States have a duty to exercise due diligence to prevent, investigate, and in accordance with the national legislation, punish acts of violence against women. In order to bring to justice those responsible for honour killing, no new legislation is required in Pakistan as the existing Criminal Procedure Code casts a duty on law enforcement agencies to investigate all crimes and prosecute the criminals.

There is no special provision in our penal statutory laws for killing in the name of honour. In murder cases, the courts have all along accepted the plea of killing for personal or family honour. Prior to the amendments brought about by the 1989 Qisas and Diyat Ordinance to the Pakistan Penal Code, murder which was punishable with death or imprisonment for life, would be reduced to culpable homicide not amounting to murder (manslaughter) if the killing was the result of grave and sudden provocation, for which the punishment was imprisonment for life or imprisonment for up to 10 years. The courts allowed the lesser plea to an accused charged with the murder of a female relative if it was found that he was provoked by the sexual impropriety of the deceased. Sentences meted out in such cases ranged from three to ten years.

Though the statutory partial defence of grave and sudden provocation has been repealed by the Qisas and Diyat Ordinance, the plea has been held by the Supreme Court of Pakistan to be still available under the new dispensation of criminal justice (*Ali Muhammad Vs Ali Muhammad*, PLD 1996 Supreme Court 274). Thus the old criteria for awarding sentences in murder cases will continue to be applied when grave and sudden provocation is established.

Even in the absence of provocation, the plea of killing for honour has always been considered as a mitigating circumstance for reducing the normal penalty of sentence of death for murder to that of imprisonment for life. The courts have accepted various instances as mitigating circumstances, including the break up of an engagement by the deceased fiancée of the accused (*Muhammad Ali vs The State*, NLR 1987 criminal 405); marriage by the deceased sister of the accused against the wishes of the family (*Mulazim Hussain vs The State*, NLR 1988 criminal 594); and refusal of a marriage proposal of the accused by the murdered woman (*Muhammad Younas vs The State*, PLD 1978 Lahore 82).

Conclusion

Bringing the accused to justice and imposing stiff sentences may serve as a deterrence, but to effectively eradicate or arrest the menace of honour killing, the state must plan and take steps to bring about change in the attitudes of the people by educating them.

Victims' rights in legislation and court practice

The Responsibility of Judges in Handling Cases of Violence Against Women, with Particular Attention to Rape Cases
A.K. Badrul Huq

Introduction

Gender equality is enshrined in the Constitution of Bangladesh, and enunciated in the Directive Principles of State Policy. Article 28 mandates that no person shall suffer discrimination on the ground of sex. Article 27 provides that all citizens are equal before the law and are entitled to the equal protection of the law. According to article 31, no action detrimental to life, liberty, body, reputation or property of any person can be taken except in accordance with the law. Under article 32, no person shall be deprived of life or personal liberty save in accordance with the law. Accordingly, the right to life is a fundamental right, and articles 44 and 102 of the Constitution provide for the realization and enforcement of all those rights.

Women as a group are subjected to discrimination in various fields and remain in a disadvantaged position in society because of social barriers and impediments, and as such have been the victims of discrimination and violence at the hands of a male-dominated community and society. Under the Constitution and the law, women enjoy the fundamental right to life, as well as the right to be properly respected and treated as equal citizens of the land. Women's honour and dignity may not be violated, and they are entitled to lead an honourable and dignified life.

Bangladesh is a State party to the Convention on the Elimination of All Forms of the Discrimination against Women (CEDAW). Based on the Convention, together with the Committee's General Recommendation 19 on violence against women, States are mandated to ensure that laws against family violence and abuse, rape, sexual assault and other gender-based violence give adequate protection to all women, and respect their integrity and dignity.

The rights of women victims of violence and the role of judges

Stringent legislation has been enacted in Bangladesh to protect women against such crimes. The 1995 Nari-O-Shishu Nirjatan (Bishesh Bidhan) Ain (Women and Children Repression Special Provision Act) was enacted to punish offences committed against women and children. This notwithstanding, women are subject to atrocities, torture and violence in the form of Fatwa by alleged Moulavis and Mathbars in the locality, acid burning, domestic violence like dowry repression, rape and other heinous crimes. Crimes against women in general and rape in particular are on the increase. Offenders escape justice not because of any shortcomings in the law, but under the protective principle of criminal jurisprudence of the 'benefit of doubt'.

In *Al-Amin and others Vs. State* (1999) 51 DLR HCD 154 - (1999) 19 BLD 307, in the observation of a Division Bench of the Supreme Court of Bangladesh consisting of Muhammad Abdul Mannan and A.K. Badrul Huq J, the issue of corroborative evidence in rape cases, which is relevant to resolve the question of benefit of doubt for the accused, is couched in the following language :

"Corroborative evidence is not an imperative component of judicial credence in every case of rape. Corroboration as a condition for judicial reliance on the testimony of a victim of sex crime is not a requirement of law but merely a guidance of prudence under a given circumstances. The rule is not that corroboration is essential before there can be a conviction. The testimony of the victim of sexual assault is vital and unless there are compelling reasons which necessite looking for corroboration of her statement, the court should find no difficulty in acting on the testimony of a victim of sex crime alone to convict an accused where her testimony inspires confidence and is found to be reliable."

In case of rape, offenders have been acquitted under the protective principle of criminal jurisprudence of 'reasonable benefit of doubt'. The dedication to the doctrine of 'benefit of doubt' should not be allowed to reign supreme in rape cases. Justice is as much due to the accuser as to the accused. The balance must be maintained. Too frequent acquittals of the guilty persons may tend to bring criminal law itself into contempt.

In *Al-Amin and others Vs. State* (supra) it is posited : "The principle of benefit of doubt accepted in England as a matter of public policy is available to an accused on the same ground or to the same extent in our country. Proof beyond reasonable doubt does not mean proof beyond the shadow of a doubt. This doubt is not an imaginary doubt. Benefit of doubt to the accused would be available provided there is supportive evidence on record. For creating doubt or granting benefit of doubt, the evidence is to be such which may lead to such doubt. The law would fail to protect the community, the society, if fanciful possibilities is admitted, thus, deflecting the course of justice".

A woman who is raped undergoes two crises, that of the rape and of the subsequent investigation and trial. Consequently, the investigation of the offence of sexual assault on a girl or women should be conducted by a female police officer, and more women police officers need to appointed for that purpose, as was stated in *Al-Amin and others Vs. State*. Furthermore, rape victims should be medically examined by women doctors.

In Bangladesh, trials of rape cases are held in open court since courts are, and always have been public places. Rape trials, however, should be held *in camera* as a rule. Consideration should also be given to having women judges try cases of sexual assault, wherever available and possible, to facilitate the testimony of the victim of sexual assault.

Judges trying rape cases have the inherent jurisdiction to award compensation against the offenders of sex crimes, along with appropriate punishment. The High Court Division of the Supreme Court of Bangladesh in *Al-Amin and others Vs. State* commented:

"Every citizen of the land has the fundamental right to life as enshrined in article 31 of the Constitution. Rape is a breach of the raped woman's fundamental right to life. It is the violation of human dignity. Rape being an indictable crime, mere punishment of the offenders of sexual assault cannot give solace to the victim of a sex crime and her family members. In the assessment of compensation, the emphasis has to be on the compensatory rather than the punitive element. The quantum of compensation will depend upon the peculiar facts of each and every case. No rigid formula may be evolved. This compensation has to be awarded independently, having no nexus with the provision of imposition of fine embodied in the Penal Code and the same has to be inserted in the Ain (Act) itself. A permanent mode of compensation has to be worked out".

The treatment of victims of sexual assault in the courts by defence lawyers during cross-examination must not be overlooked. In total disregard of the provisions of the Evidence Act regarding the relevancy of facts, some defence lawyers attempt to cast a stigma on the character of the victim of a sex crime and twist the interpretation of events given by her so as to make her appear inconsistent with her allegations. Judges must effectively control the recording of evidence in the court.

Conclusion

The role of the judges is primarily the administration and dispensation of justice. Justice is that which ensures fair treatment for all citizens of the land, which does not compromise to any pressure, which is effective and accessible to all. Legislation enacted for the benefit of women will be ineffective unless judges see it in a gender-sensitive attitude when dispensing justice. The judiciary cannot be a conservative institution, it must not fail to recognize, uphold and enforce women's human rights. Judges should not only be aware of international human rights law and jurisprudence, but should feel obliged to follow it. They should also invite the executive branch to comply with international treaty obligations in carrying out administrative functions, unless there is an express and insuperable bar under domestic law to doing so.

Society expects a great deal from judges. It expects them to be objective, independent, practical, sensitive, neutral: but neutrality can not mean that judges have no prior conception, opinion or sensibilities about values of societies. Prior conceptions and sensibilities must not influence the minds of the judges who will be free in their minds to the evidences and materials brought on record in coming to a just decision. In cases of violence against women, especially rape, acid burning and dowry repression, the court must take account not only of the rights of the accused, but also of the rights of the victims of crime. The interest of the victim in getting the offender punished cannot be ignored or completely subordinated to the interest of the accused who is interested to have an order of acquittal on the principle of criminal jurisprudence of the benefit of doubt.

Botswana Legislation on Rape
Stella Dabutha

Introduction

Section 141 of the Penal Code of Botswana defined rape as "[A]ny male person who has unlawful carnal knowledge of a woman or girl, without her consent, or with her consent if the consent is obtained by force or means of threat or intimidation of any kind, by fear of bodily harm, or by means of false representation as to the nature of the act, or in the case of a married woman, by personating her husband, is guilty of the offence of rape".

Rape was punishable by a sentence to imprisonment for life, with or without corporal punishment. The application and interpretation of the rape laws contained in the Penal Code prior to 1998 proved that the law was defective or inadequate in actually protecting women as victims of rape. In particular, the law required corroboration of the woman's allegations, proceedings were public, relatively light sentences were imposed by the courts on men convicted of rape and rape was narrowly defined.

The present legislative situation

The Penal Code (Amendment) Act of 1998 was a response to some of these concerns. The amendment defines rape as "[A]ny person who has unlawful carnal knowledge of another person, or who causes the penetration of a sexual organ or instrument, of whatever nature, into the person of another for the purposes of sexual gratification, or who causes the penetration of another person's sexual organ into his or her person, without the consent of such other person, or with such person's consent if the consent is obtained by force or means of threats or intimidation of any kind, by fear of bodily harm, or by means of false pretences as to the nature of the act, or, in the case of a married person, by personating that person's spouse, is guilty of the offence of rape".

The Amendment brought about the following five major developments:

1. denial of bail to anyone accused of rape;

2. introduction of a minimum sentence of 10 years imprisonment for those convicted;

3. where an act of rape is attended by violence resulting in injury to the victim, the person convicted of rape shall be sentenced to a minimum term of 15 years imprisonment or to a maximum term of life imprisonment with or without corporal punishment;

4. a person convicted of the offence of rape who tests positive for the human immunodeficiency virus (HIV) shall be sentenced to a minimum term of 15 years imprisonment or a maximum term of life imprisonment with corporal punishment, where it is proved that such person was aware of being HIV positive; or to a minimum term of 20 years imprisonment or to a maximum term of life imprisonment with corporal punishment where it is proved that on a balance of probabilities, such person was aware of being HIV positive; and

5. the introduction of gender neutrality in the definition of rape.

The issue therefore is whether the Penal Code Amendment of 1998 went far enough in protecting women against rape. The amendment has already been challenged in *Ishmael Dintwa v. The State* where the applicant, Dintwa, alleged that the mandatory denial of access to bail was unconstitutional. He argued that the Act contravened section 5(3)(b) of the Constitution of Botswana which section protects one's right to personal liberty. He further argued that the amendment contravened the presumption of innocence as enshrined under section 10(2)(a) of the Constitution, and that the amendment curtailed the discretionary powers of the courts as provided for under the Criminal Procedure and Evidence Act to grant bail to an accused person. The Judge held that "a person charged with a criminal offence is presumed innocent and that a person awaiting trial should not be subjected to total confinement or deprivation of his liberty. As such, I have no hesitation in holding that section 142(1)(a) of the Penal Code, as amended by Act No. 5 of 1998 goes against the Constitution of Botswana because, by providing for the denial of bail to any person charged with rape, it not only imposes a limitation on the liberty of a person awaiting trial beyond the limitations found to be permissible and provided for under section 5(3)(b) of the Constitution. The Act also takes away even the already existing mandatory Constitutional right for an accused person to be released on bail in the event such accused person is not tried within a reasonable time, as provided for under section 5(3)(b) of the Constitution".

In July 1997, the Women's Affairs Department of the Ministry of Labour and Home Affairs of Botswana commissioned a comprehensive study of laws affecting the status of women, with a view to expanding the rights and hereby enhancing the position of women in terms of the law. The specific terms of reference of the study were *inter alia* to review all statutes and subsidiary legislation affecting women and to review all relevant United Nations Conventions and other documents concerning women, especially the Convention on the Elimination of All Forms of Discrimination against Women, with the view to assessing the extent to which the law of Botswana complies with United Nations standards, and their possible ratification.

With regard to rape, the study found that, although the definition of rape and the minimum sentences for sexual offences laid down in the Penal Code Amendment Act of 1998 had been revised, the following issues and concerns with direct bearing on women's status remained:

1. the problems of corroboration of the woman's story;

2. the procedure in rape trials; and

3. the inadequacies in the definition of rape.

The following recommendations were made:

1. the onus of proof on the prosecution should be limited to establishing the occurrence of the sexual act only, while the accused should be required to prove consent;

2. the requirement for corroboration in rape cases should be abolished and evidence of a woman's chastity and her previous acquaintance with the alleged rapist should be inadmissible;

3. medical evidence from nurses should be admissible in rape trials;

4. only qualified lawyers should be assigned to prosecute rape cases;

5. the police, magistrates, judges and other law enforcement officers should receive gender training, and be sensitized to the fact that rape and sexual abuse are violations of women's human rights which should attract their sympathy and serious consideration;

6. the holding of rape trials *in camera* should be monitored to ensure that the measure introduced by the Criminal Procedure and Evidence Amendment Act of 1997 (viz, that rape cases should be held *in camera*) is indeed useful; and

7. the legal definition of rape should be further revised to include marital rape, and should move away from the view of rape as a crime against morality to a crime against the person.

It suffices to point out that the law with regard to rape, in particular the Penal Code (Amendment) Act of 1998 decided to be harsher on sexual offenders in the light of the increasing rate of sexual offences and the associated risk of contracting sexually transmitted diseases in particular the human immunodeficiency virus which causes AIDS. This may seem like an overreaction on the part of the law to what is a problem which cannot be addressed by harsh sentencing alone. The concern should therefore be education to raise awareness in the community on the issue of violence against women. The Government, with the help of community-based organizations, should commit itself to dismantling the social structures that tolerate violence against women.

Next steps

The Deputy Director of the Criminal Investigation Department recently told a crime prevention seminar in Botswana that the police force was worried at the increase of incidences of rape in spite of the stiff penalties introduced by the Penal Code (Amendment) Act of 1998. This has prompted a study on causes of rape in Botswana. The purpose of the study is to provide a clear picture of incidence and prevalence of the crime of rape in Botswana to enable the police to control and combat the crime more effectively and reassess its operational strategies. The data will

1. assist the Botswana Police to refocus crime prevention strategies and to strengthen partnerships with all stakeholders in the fight against rape;

2. assist in refocusing and strengthening public education programmes to fight rape;

3. provide data to assist and inform decision makers in Government
   and non-governmental agencies; and

4. provide data through which to evaluate the impact of public education programmes upon male attitudes.

New Ways and Forms of Cooperation in Austrian Courts in the Fight Against Trafficking in Women
Petra Smutny

Article 6 of the Convention on the Elimination of All Forms of
Discrimination against Women (CEDAW) deals with the sexual abuse
of women and requires States parties to "take all appropriate measures,
including legislation, to suppress all forms of traffic in women and exploitation of prostitution of women". Other United Nations achievements to combat traffic in women followed, and activities have
increased in recent years.

While the introduction of a new government policy may not be as
dramatic as a constitutional change or a victory in high court, a good
policy can lead to widespread and concrete changes and effective results. This will be illustrated with a case decided by the Regional Penal
Court in Vienna in July 1999.

The framework

Section 217 of the Austrian Criminal Code prohibits trafficking in
human beings. It provides for imprisonment from six months to five
years of any person who introduces another person to prostitution in a
country of which this person is neither a citizen nor a resident, or re-
cruits a person for prostitution under the same circumstances, regardless
of whether the recruited person has been a prostitute prior to the recruitment or not. If trafficking is carried out as a business, i.e. if the
perpetrator aims at securing a continuous income from this activity, the
penalty is one to ten years of imprisonment. The law also defines as
trafficking in human beings if a person wants to introduce another person to prostitution in another country, and for that purpose deceives or

186

coerces him/her through violence or violent threats to travel to this other country, or uses deception or violence to transport him/her to this other country. This would include the case of a woman who is promised work as a dancer while in reality she is brought to a brothel. Under Austrian law, promotion of prostitution and pimping are also criminal offences. The sentence can be up to two years imprisonment, whereas the prostitute is not subject to punishment under the Criminal Code.

If a female victim of trafficking decides to report anyone to the police as a trafficker, she must expect problems with her residence status in Austria. If she is in the country illegally, deportation may follow. Turning to the authorities means leaving the cover of anonymity and making her illegal status public. From a legal point of view, residence issues do not directly relate to the Austrian Criminal Code. Such issues are dealt with under the Aliens Law, the Residence Law, and the Foreign Nationals Employment Law. However, the resolution of residence issues is crucial for women's willingness to report traffickers to the authorities.

According to the Alien Law of 1997, limited residence may be granted due to humanitarian reasons, in particular to women victims of trafficking in accordance with section 217 of the Criminal Code so that they can testify, and pursue civil remedies.

Arrests of trafficked women occur mostly during raids of brothels, and women put in custody are in a very poor psychological state. Their working situation is traumatizing and humiliating, and involves violence and coercion. These women do not know what to expect after being arrested. Until recently, they had no possibility to communicate or to seek help with necessary matters. In the worst cases, they had no contact at all with the outside world. They suffered from poor conditions in police prisons and did not know when they would be deported.

These women urgently needed assistance to support them psychologically, take care of their private affairs, and help them to prepare for repatriation. Therefore, the authorities sought the cooperation of support organizations and counseling facilities such as LEFÖ (a women's non-governmental organization serving as intervention centre and victim protection institution, and focussing on migrant women victims of trafficking). At best, these counseling facilities also have contact with similar organizations in the countries of origin of these women and work with those groups to support returned women.

If a woman decides to report a criminal offence to the authorities (this may also be done by a third person or an institution, such as LEFÖ), the case is referred to the public prosecutor's office which has the legal obligation to prosecute all criminal offences that are brought to the office's attention.

The trafficked woman has to testify before court. According to an administrative ordinance of the Minister of Justice from 1998, judges and prosecutors are advised to inform LEFÖ about a planned interrogation of a victim of trafficking so that LEFÖ can provide support and protection measures to the witness.

Court proceedings are conducted in German. If the woman's knowledge of the language is inadequate, she is entitled to an interpreter. The court and other persons involved in the proceedings do not have an unrestricted right to ask questions. For example, questions relating to the woman's intimate life may be asked only if the answers to such questions appear to be indispensable to arrive at a judgement. The witness may also refuse to provide information about her name or other personal data if that would create a serious danger to life, health, bodily integrity or liberty of the witness or another person. The witness may also request that a person of her confidence be present during the questioning. Since that person's presence is intended as psychological support, he/she has no standing at the questioning.

According to the Austrian Code of Criminal Procedure, a witness may be questioned by the investigating judge in the presence of the defendant, the defence counsel, the prosecutor and any private plaintiff suing for damages, if legal or factual reasons would prevent the witness from appearing in the subsequent trial. This questioning may also be videotaped without the defendant's and the other participants' presence in the same room, and in special cases it may be conducted by an expert witness (usually a psychiatrist). Audiovisual recording of this interrogation may be used at the trial where the victim is allowed to refuse any further questioning. Victims of sexual offences have the right to insist on this kind of interrogation. The Austrian Code of Criminal Procedure requires that the jury-court has a minimum number of members of the same sex as the victim.

Any person whose rights have been violated by a criminal offence and who has suffered (economic) damage as a result of the crime may participate as a private plaintiff in the criminal proceedings up to the end of the trial. In 1996 the Austrian Civil Code was amended so that all victims of sexual offences may also obtain redress for immaterial harm suffered.

The facts of the case and the trial

In June 1998, the Romanian citizen Nico persuaded his country-woman Iona to move with him to Vienna to work there as a dancer in a bar that belonged to one of his friends. Iona had never before been to Austria. On her explicit inquiry he confirmed that she would have to dance only and that nobody expected her to have sexual intercourse with customers, although he already planned to make her work as a prostitute. Because she owed him quite a big sum of money she accepted his offer. As Iona did not have a legal entry permit, Nico provided her with a forged passport.

A few days after her arrival in Vienna , Nico brought Iona to a bar. He knew that the barmaids who worked there were forced to have sexual intercourse with paying customers in a separate room. When Iona tried to resist, he beat her several times and forced her to follow his "advice" by threatening to continue the violence. He underlined his threats by raping her several times during the following weeks. Furthermore he threatened to report her to the police repeating – as he had already done in Romania - that she would have to prostitute herself to the policemen, too, should she dare to tell the whole story of her arrival in Austria. Iona lived in complete isolation in Vienna and did not speak German. She did not receive any money but had to give her earnings to Nico who watched her nearly constantly.

When Iona became pregnant, Nico battered her with the calculated aim to cause an abortion, and causing a life-threatening hemorrage. Iona had to be brought to a hospital, where she was again in such great fear that she followed Nico's instructions and showed another forged passport to disguise her true identity.

At the beginning of September, Iona met a man who offered her his flat for a few days and who covered her daily expenses. When Nico was reported to the police by an anonymous person, Iona was also arrested and was at first put into police custody and interrogated. Subsequently she was deported and a residence-prohibition was issued against her. Between her arrest and deportation, the staff of LEFÖ who had been informed by the police about her case immediately after her interrogation, took care of Iona.

When the judicial authorities were seized of the matter and criminal proceedings were opened against Nico for trafficking in human beings, rape, intentional serious bodily harm, causing an abortion, forging of documents, violation of the law on arms and other offences, Iona was already back in Romania. The defendant and his Romanian associates put heavy pressure on the witness.

The trial judge and LEFÖ established contact. An "adversarial interrogation" was arranged, whereby

- a Romanian advisory board cooperating with the Austrian institutions looked after Iona in Romania;

- the trial judge determined a convenient date for the interrogation of the witness, arranged for it to take place in a courtroom equipped for video-transmitted interrogations and had the summons served to the witness, who lived in hiding, with the assistance of LEFÖ and and her relatives;

- LEFÖ provided the witness with lodging during her necessary stay in Austria, the costs of which were borne by the court,

- the trial judge, with reference to the date of the interrogation, obtained a short-term exception to the residence-prohibition by the Ministry of the Interior.

In the spring of 1999, Iona finally could testify "softly", that is by means of video-transmission, before the Viennese criminal court of first instance. Her personal testimony decisively contributed to Nico's conviction by the court on 25 June 1999.

Legislation to protect women against violence

Violence Against Women and the Family in Ecuador: Addressing and Eradicating Gender Bias in the Application of the Penal Law
María Leonor Jiménez de Viteri

In the section on vulnerable groups (articles 47 to 54), the Constitution of Ecuador undertakes to give priority, preferential and specialized attention to girls, teenagers and pregnant women. It guarantees that the best interests of children shall prevail and that they shall be consulted in matters that affect them. It provides protection against all forms of exploitation of minors, including sexual exploitation, which is covered by article 19 of the Convention on the Rights of the Child. Article 23 of the Constitution reaffirms civil rights with respect to equality before the law, freedom, development and personal integrity. Paragraph 2 provides for the adoption of necessary measures to prevent, eliminate and punish, in particular, violence against children, teenagers, women and senior citizens. The article guarantees freedom and considers the rape of minors and women as well as indecent assault offences against sexual freedom.

The act on domestic violence has filled a gap in the previous legislation that afforded no protection to the victims of domestic violence. It tackles the traditional cultural and legal system by characterizing acts or omissions that constitute physical, mental or sexual abuse committed by a member of a family against a woman or other members of the family group by introducing a timely and innovative system of protective measures, marking a departure from the previous approach that considered domestic violence a private matter and making it a subject of public and legal debate of interest to society as a whole.

New article 58 of the Penal Code prohibiting the imprisonment of a pregnant woman or notification to her of the imposition of a term of imprisonment or confinement until 90 days after she has given birth seems inadequate, since there may be instances where flagrant offences are committed. Legislation should have been enacted on house arrest, which is not covered by our legislation, and which prevents the application of the guarantee. As a result of the definition of sexual harassment committed by a superior in the workplace, in a teaching establishment or similar situation as an offence punishable by six months to two years of imprisonment, we now have an explicit provision that did not exist before, despite the abolition of articles 268 and 269 of the Penal Code which defined sexual solicitation. Moreover, the definition of rape has been broadened to include, in addition to penetration by the male organ, the insertion of any other object. Where rape also constitutes incest, the punishment has been increased by four years. The age for statutory rape was raised from 12 to 14 years. Chapter VIII of the Penal Code, on procuring and corruption of minors, was changed.

The promotion of greater awareness within the judiciary by involving both the National Association of Female Judges and the National Bar Association remains critical so that, in keeping with the commitment to gender equality, women judges may participate in the implementation of criminal justice, in which only very few are currently engaged. There are many opportunities for change, but they are largely dependent on raising the awareness of the judiciary.

Legislative Framework and the Administration of Justice in Venezuela
Maria Cristina Parra de Rojas

Background and introduction

On signing the Convention on the Elimination of All Forms of Discrimination against Women in 1982, Venezuela made a commitment to eliminate discrimination against women. This was confirmed on 2 May 1983 with its ratification of the Convention. Accordingly, Venezuela has progressively recognized the principle of equality of women before the law in its domestic legislation and it prohibits discrimination on grounds of sex. The partial reform of the Civil Code, also conducted in 1982, established equality within the family by providing that parental rights over children, as well as the administration of common property, are shared by women and men. In 1993, the Equal Opportunities for Women Act, based on the Convention on the Elimination of All Forms of Discrimination against Women, was adopted, guaranteeing equality before the law, equality of opportunity and non-discrimination. Similarly, on 3 September 1998 Venezuela promulgated the Violence against Women and the Family Act, which entered into force on 1 January 1999. Venezuelan courts have begun to apply these laws effectively.

On 29 June 1999, the Supreme Court of Justice, meeting in plenary, ruled partially null and void the second part of article 395 of the Penal Code, which provided that "persons guilty of seduction, rape or abduction shall, unless marriage takes place, be sentenced to pay civil compensation to the victim, if she is single or a widow and, in either case, chaste ...". The appeal, filed on 25 September 1996 by lawyers Alfonzo Albornoz Niño and Gloria de Vicentini, was based on the conflict of that provision with the preamble and articles 46 and 61 of the National Constitution, with articles 3, 5 and 6 of the Equal Opportunities for Women Act and with the Convention on the Elimination of All Forms of Discrimination against Women.

The Court indicated in its ruling that this provision was a breach of article 61 of the Constitution and article 6 of the Equal Opportunities for Women Act, in that the last part of the second section of article 395 of the Penal Code, and specifically the expression "if she is single or a widow and, in either case, chaste", established a form of discrimination. On these grounds, the Court declared the provision in question partially null and void, so as to preserve the right to a compensatory judgement through civil compensation but without the discrimination, amending it to read as follows "... persons guilty of seduction, rape or abduction shall, unless marriage takes place, be sentenced to pay civil compensation to the victim ..." (ruling of the Supreme Court of Justice of Venezuela dated 29 June 1999).

Legislative framework and administration of justice in Venezuela

The system for the administration of justice in Venezuela comprises the Supreme Court of Justice, the Council of the Judiciary, the courts and the Public Prosecutor's Office. In 1997, the judiciary had 1,150 judges, or approximately one judge for every 20,000 inhabitants. Of this total, 96 were family and children's judges. There are 36 family attorneys, as well as 80 attorneys for minors — attached to the Office of the Attorney-General — whose task is to protect the rights of children and adolescents. According to the source of these statistics, "the capacity to deliver judicial services has collapsed. Citizens do not effectively enjoy the right to defence and to justice because the justice system is expensive, complex and slow. The judiciary responds to 14 per cent of the cases brought before the courts, and 30 per cent of the prison population has not yet been sentenced."

With regard to the functioning and efficiency of the justice system in cases of violence against women and children, prior to the entry into force of the Act on this subject, existing laws did not deal specifically with the problem and were inadequate to the situation. The intervention of the authorities focused primarily on getting the couple involved in the act of domestic violence to sign a non-aggression commitment. In cases of recurrence or of refusal to sign such a commitment, the civil authorities had the power to order arrest for up to 72 hours. If the injuries were very serious, the case was referred to the precinct of the district concerned. The provisions of the Penal Code were not designed to deal with offences taking place in the privacy of the home, and this created obstacles to intervening and verifying the facts. Family members could not act as witnesses, although it was they who were really familiar with the problem within the home. In the civil as compared with the penal sphere, there were more legal remedies for the protection of women as members of the family, specifically in the case of married women physically abused by their husbands, for whom serious injury constituted grounds for divorce. In such cases, the judge was able to order measures such as authorizing the woman to be given protection and to remain in the conjugal home. A judge could not expressly order the husband to move out, because the home is a common asset forming part of the conjugal property which is apportioned at the time of divorce. In addition, the State saw preserving the institution of the family as a fundamental role, and hence there were no free legal services for pursuing divorce cases on grounds of physical separation and many women could not afford to retain a lawyer. Separation from the husband was therefore difficult in cases where divorce was the woman's preferred alternative. Women were also indirectly protected under the law in cases where the interests of the children were affected, through the intervention of the offices of the attorneys for minors.

Thus, the interests of women as victims of violence were legally protected to some extent, whether as members of the family group, by virtue of their marital status or as mothers. This was confirmed by the Fundamental Labour Act, which recognized the social function of maternity and protected women from this standpoint. The auxiliary bodies of the justice system (for example, the Office of the Attorney-General) and other government agencies providing services for women (the National Women's Council) lacked the human resources to deal with the problem. They generally took in battered women and offered them valuable support and general guidance on their rights, but did not give them legal assistance, including with court proceedings. This affected the speed and effectiveness of the proceedings and meant that the women ended up alone and gave up legal action. For non-governmental organizations, demand for legal assistance on the part of women referred by government agencies created a major additional workload.

The recent adoption of the Violence against Women and the Family Act and the classification of the various forms of violence against women as crimes have expanded the range of institutions that can receive complaints, as well as their obligation to respond to the complaint regardless of the type of offence (the unacceptability of psychological violence, for example, has come to be properly appreciated). The institutions are courts of the peace and family courts, criminal courts of first instance, prefectures and civil authorities, police bodies and the Public Prosecutor's Office.

The main causes of women's limited access to the justice system are their "lack of information about their rights and the various ways of exercising them, the cost of judicial proceedings, the lack of facilities for providing legal assistance to women, the lack of credibility extended to women in the administration of justice, women's lack of representation in the legislative area and women's low level of participation in the political running of the State".

Materials consulted: Asociación Venezolana para una Educación Sexual Alternativa (AVESA), "Violencia de Genero contra las Mujeres", Caracas, 1999.

Some Problems of Domestic Violence against Woman in Latvia: Legal Aspects
Anita Usacka

The situation with regard to violence against women

The independence of the Republic of Latvia was proclaimed for the first time in 1918 but in 1940, the Soviet Union occupied Latvia. Independence was *de facto* re-established in 1991, restoring Latvia's pre-war status as a sovereign independent country. Since then, Latvia has experienced transitional difficulties both in the economic and social spheres, as well as the legal field. The effects of economic and social change are felt most of all by women, who make up 53.7 per cent of the population of Latvia.

The negative attitude and distrust of the general public towards law enforcement institutions in Latvia constitutes a serious obstacle in determining the scope of domestic violence. According to survey data of the Criminological Research Centre on public attitudes towards the police, 58.2 per cent of all respondents evaluate police work negatively, with only 10.8 percent positively. This attitude also influences the willingness of the public to report crimes. When asked why they were unwilling to report to the police, the majority of respondents stated that the police would not be able to do anything. Although the survey does not mention domestic violence, the answers of female respondents about their willingness to report sexual incidents might be an indicator of similar attitudes towards reporting cases of domestic violence.

According to 1997 data from the Criminological Research Centre, 45 out of 769 women respondents, or 5.8 per cent, were victims of sexual harassment. The fact that in 20 cases they were acquainted with the assailant is also an indicator of domestic violence. Many women suffer violence in the family, and seek neither legal nor social assistance. They prefer not to speak about it.

The situation is further complicated by a lack of knowledge about the nature of domestic violence and limited possibilities which exist to change the existing situation. Although a women's shelter has been in operation in Riga since 1996, it is not specifically meant for victims of domestic abuse and has limited capacity (20 places). Due to the lack of shelters or alternative housing arrangements for victims of domestic violence, women are often forced to live with their abuser under the same roof. Although some efforts are under way, a network of shelters has yet to be developed.

Latvia has no official statistics, research or data on gender-based violence. While some attempts have been made to collect such data, none have been comprehensive and none have yielded entirely reliable results. For example, according to data compiled by the United Nations Population Fund (UNFPA) and the Ministry of Welfare, only 6.6 per cent of women respondents acknowledged that they were victims of sexual violence, 9.4 per cent that they were victims of physical violence and 18.7 per cent that they were victims of psychological violence. Reliable data from countries all around the world have highlighted that anywhere from one in four to one in two women are victims of some form of gender-based violence. Consequently, we can expect similar figures in Latvia. From the experience of other countries we can also assume that Latvian women face greater risks of violence at home than outside the home. Women are much more likely to suffer violence, including rape and murder, from their husbands, partners, family members and acquaintances than from strangers.

The Latvian Human Rights Bureau, the State's human rights machinery established in 1995, very seldom receives complaints concerning domestic violence. In 1997 the Bureau received 611 written complaints and 2,595 oral complaints and only one complaint was about violence, a son against his mother. In 1998, of 3,558 complaints, only two were connected with domestic violence against women.

Despite the lack of official statistics, some information has become available through the research of new non-governmental organizations (NGOs). Research undertaken by NGOs, although on a smaller scale, has furnished results more in line with global statistics. For example, the Latvian Center for Human Rights and Ethnic Studies, a non-governmental human rights research organization, conducted a study on domestic violence cases that reached the chief medical insurance company from the Riga City ambulance service. The doctor at the site of the crime, or, in case the victim goes directly to the hospital, completes a report on the injury. From these reports, the research identified 120 cases of domestic violence throughout the period of 1996 and the beginning of 1997. 71.6 per cent of victims were women, and 85.8 per cent of offenders were men. Although the information provided in these reports is too limited to provide a comprehensive picture, women undoubtedly constitute the vast majority of domestic violence victims.

A second study by the same organization focused on women in prison who had suffered long term domestic violence and then inflicted grievous bodily injury or even murdered their husbands or partners. In 1992, 70 per cent of all women in prison were there as a result of crimes of property (burglary, theft, fraud), but only 6.1 per cent for violent crimes. In 1994 and 1995, the share of women in prison for violent crimes rose to 22.7 and 26.8 per cent respectively, and to 36.1 per cent by May 1997. Thus, in five years there has been a six-fold increase in the percentage of women in prison for violent offences. Women interviewed in the Ilguciema prison suggest that as many as 90 per cent were subjected to regular physical intimidation, and 81 per cent had been raped. More than one half had been subjected to long term violence. Their explanations for not resisting violence reflected all the prevailing myths about domestic violence, as well as the limited opportunities for escaping violence.

The lack of official statistics and underreporting suggest that there is insufficient understanding in society of what exactly domestic violence is, and thus a failure to recognize it and name it. The silence impedes a more meaningful dialogue in society that could raise awareness of the causes and effects of such violence, while also curtailing concrete action against perpetrators and in support of victims. All gender-based violence poses a serious threat to sustainable human development and the development of a stable and democratic society. From a health perspective, violence has debilitating effects on survivors, ranging from stress and fear, to serious injury, to death. This violence can have very practical consequences in terms of economic productivity and growth. Similarly, the distress, psychological impact and physical injury endured by survivors of violence can impede them from participating in political, civil and social life. Violence, and particularly violence within the home, is also cyclical, passed from generation to generation, which means that children learn from behavior they observe in their parents. For all of these reasons, gender-based violence needs to be urgently addressed to ensure the safety of survivors and potential victims, but also for the benefit of society as a whole.

Legislation on the rights of women in Latvia

According to the Latvian Constitution "[A]ll people in Latvia shall be equal before the law and the courts. Human rights shall be realized without discrimination of any kind". Therefore the equality of men and women in Latvia is guaranteed by the Constitution as well as by international agreements.

Latvia ratified the Convention on the Elimination of All Forms of Discrimination against Women in April 1992, and the Convention on the Political Rights of Women and the Convention on the Nationality of Married Women on July 1992. In Latvia, the norms of international agreements ratified by Parliament have supremacy over national law, with an exception concerning the norms of the Constitution. Latvia has also ratified other treaties in the field of human rights both in the United Nations system and the European human rights system.

These human rights treaties have become an integral part of the national legal system. To date, there are only two cases of direct application in Latvian courts of legal norms of international human rights conventions. The main reason of the non-application is that although Latvia has ratified international human rights instruments and is developing a modern western legal system, there are problems in Latvia with application of the law. Not only judges but also civil servants and other administrative authorities charged with applying the norms of human rights were mainly educated before 1990 in the Soviet legal tradition. We need to educate our judges and administrative authorities. The training in legal methodology to use international instruments as sources of law is very important and necessary.

Conclusion

In solving the problem of domestic violence it is necessary not only to amend the legislation but also to improve the application of the law as well as to inform and educate society. Additional comprehensive and in-depth research on the situation in Latvia is urgently needed as well as the provision of more accessible and quality services for survivors.

Women's rights in the work place

The Convention on the Elimination of All Forms of Discrimination against Women in Case Law on Equal Treatment in the Netherlands, with Special Attention to the Equal Treatment Commission
Jenny E. Goldschmidt

Introduction

This paper provides a bird's eye view of how a semi-judicial authority such as the Equal Treatment Commission relates to the Convention on Elimination of All Forms of Discrimination against Women (CEDAW), and how it is applied by the judiciary. In the Netherlands, the impact of other international human rights instruments on national law has sometimes been greater. Thus, after the *Broeks* case (referred to in Marc Bossuyt's paper) national courts have found certain social security legislation to be in contravention to article 26 of the International Covenant on Civil and Political Rights, and application of article 8 of the European Convention for the Protection of Human Rights and Fundamental Freedoms by the courts led to a fundamental restructuring of the Family Code.

The Equal Treatment Commission (ETC)

The Equal Treatment Commission was established in 1994 by the Equal Treatment Act, which also created its competence to hear cases related to this, and several other legislative acts. While the Commission's 'opinions' are not legally binding, they are in practice adhered to by the parties concerned and by the legal profession. The Commission is an independent, semi-judicial body consisting of nine members (the President and two vice-presidents serve full-time, and the nine members part-time), with a staff of approximately thirty officers, including legal officers, a communication expert, and specialists in job evaluation. The members are appointed for a period of up to six years by the Minister of

Justice after consultation with the ministers of the Interior, Education, Health, Labour and Social Affairs. Members can be reappointed.

Individuals as well as organizations (through class actions) can bring cases before the Commission. The Commission can also be requested to issue an opinion on an entity's internal rules or practices. While in theory courts can request the Commission to investigate the equal treatment aspects of cases, this has not yet happened in practice. Finally, the Commission can initiate an investigation if it suspects unequal treatment in a specific area. Admittance to the Commission is free, and parties do not need legal representation. The Commission has powers to investigate cases and to ask the parties concerned, as well as third parties, to provide relevant information and documents. The Commission also has *locus standi* before the courts and thus the power to take a case to court. While the Commission has no official powers of mediation, it tries to bring parties together if this seems possible.

Once the Commission has issued an opinion in a case, it monitors implementation through a follow-up policy with the parties concerned to assess whether the opinion leads to a more equal treatment in practice. If relevant, the Commission also contacts other relevant organizations to broaden the impact of the equal treatment law. Finally, the Commission advises the Government on bills and proposals that affect the work of the Commission.

The Commission's competence

The Commission's competence is limited by the legislative acts upon which it is based. These acts cover only specific forms of discrimination, i.e. discrimination based on race, religion, sexual preference, nationality, marital status, gender, conviction, political preference and part-time work. Secondly, the acts cover only specific areas. Generally speaking, they cover the whole area of labour law, including sexual harassment, and considerable parts of contract law. Administrative law is covered only to the extent that a public authority acts as a private person, for example by renting a house or offering a job. The Commission is not competent to assess possible infringements of other national or international non-discrimination law. Thus, the Commission cannot give an opinion on questions related to the CEDAW Convention or the Convention on the Rights of the Child.

Relevance of CEDAW for the work of the Commission

Although the Commission is not competent to review the compatibility of specific acts or practices with the CEDAW, this does not mean that the CEDAW is entirely irrelevant to its work. The relevance is established in different ways. First, the Commission uses the CEDAW and other relevant international human rights law, especially ILO Conventions, in interpreting national equal treatment laws in a way comparable to the examples given by Krisztina Morvai in her paper (see page 79). In the Commission's experience, article 5 of the Convention can be especially effective in preventing a 'gender-blind' and formal approach of equality.

For example, the Commission has held an employer's affirmative action policy that gives priority to female workers in the provision of limited child care facilities to be acceptable in the short term, but not indefinitely. In the long term such a practice can amount to a reaffirmation of stereotyped roles of men and women, which is no longer allowed under article 5 of CEDAW. Likewise, age limits have been characterized as suspect under article 5, because they usually reflect a male pattern of life.

A second way of invoking the CEDAW occurs when a case is outside the scope of the Commission's competence. In such cases the Commission can pay attention to the relevance of the CEDAW in an *obiter dictum*. This was done in a case on the legality of the refusal of a political party to admit female members, where the Commission referred to article 7 of CEDAW. Also, the Commission can raise the compatibility of a specific rule or practice with CEDAW by sending a letter to the Government and/or Parliament. This was done in a Commission letter on the treatment of pregnant workers. In the Dutch Disability Insurance Act, pregnancy and maternity leave are included in the period of sickness, which means that women are at greater risk of becoming 'disabled' within the meaning of this law, and thus to qualify for a lower allowance than the sickness benefit, which is given during the first year of sickness. The Commission considers that this is not in accordance with the article 11 (2) (b) of CEDAW. The case is still under consideration.

The Convention can also be invoked in the Commission's advice to the Government on specific bills and policies, as has been done recently in a comment on legislative proposals to facilitate combining paid work and care. The Commission raised the question as to whether the fact that the proposed 'care-leave' was unpaid leave would reaffirm stereotyped roles of men and women and therefore not be in accordance with article 5 of the Convention. The provision has since been amended to make paid leave possible.

Domestic reporting under CEDAW

Application of the Convention in the national legal system is stimulated also by a domestic reporting procedure in the Netherlands which exists in addition to the Convention's requirement under article 18 of reporting periodically to the Committee on the Elimination of Discrimination against Women. The first national report was prepared by independent experts, who also consulted organs such as the ETC. One of the report's recommendations proposed the extension of the Commission's competence to other national and international equal treatment provisions. This recommendation will probably be reconsidered in the coming period when the Equal Treatment Act is scheduled for evaluation.

As a result of the national report, more attention is paid to the expertise of the judiciary in the fields covered by the Convention. Workshops and training are offered, and the establishment of a centre of expertise to provide information and support on the obligations under the Convention and other international human rights law is being considered.

Dutch case law

Dutch case law shows that the judiciary is not very eager to apply the relevant provisions of the Convention. The Dutch Constitution does not permit constitutional review of legislation, but international law can be applied without any further legislation if the relevant provision is sufficiently clear. Directly applicable provisions of international law have to be applied by the courts in the Dutch legal system. The courts have to test the conformity of statutes with self-executing provisions of international treaties. It seems that the reluctance to apply the provisions of the CEDAW Convention is often caused by doubts as to whether these provisions contain legal duties or only 'obligations to make efforts'. This matter is closely related to the discussion on the applicability of social and economic rights. Apart from this aspect, it has been suggested that, since most cases on equal treatment and discrimination in the field of work are taken to the Equal Treatment Commission, there is insufficient pressure on the courts to develop expertise in the field of legal instruments against discrimination. In other words, the Commission's success is seen as the cause of inaction by the courts. In future, the Commission will therefore provide legal education to change this attitude. Finally, the existence of supra-national European law (the law of the European Union), which has an elaborate system of sex-discrimination law makes the CEDAW somewhat less relevant in the day-to-day practice of work-related cases in the Netherlands. CEDAW can be an influence in areas where the Court of Justice of the European Community interprets equal treatment provisions rather formally. An example is the way the Court dealt with preferential treatment. In one case, the Attorney-General also referred to the CEDAW but gave a rather restricted interpretation.

I hope that the new Optional Protocol on individual complaints will offer a new opportunity to give more concrete meaning to the provisions of the Convention and to provide examples to the judiciary on the interpretation of discrimination against women. I expect that this will broaden the possibilities for national application and interaction between national and international interpretations. And I hope that these joint efforts will bring about a levelling of the standard of legal protection of women's rights.

Conclusion

In the field of work, a semi-judicial body such as the Equal Treatment Commission can contribute to the application of the law of the Convention at the domestic level, provided that such a Commission has power to apply it. But even if not, the Convention has indirect effects. The new Optional Protocol can be an important instrument to enforce the application of the Convention in the national context.

Work and Work-Related Rights in the Philippine Setting
Consuelo Ynares-Santiago

Discrimination in the work place

Discrimination in hiring is covered by legislation including the Republic Act No. 6725, which is the Philippine's anti-discrimination law. Article 135 of the Labour Code also applies. Both concentrate on discrimination during employment.

The following jurisprudence on discrimination in hiring, with reference to the Convention on the Elimination of All Forms of Discrimination against Women (CEDAW) can be cited:

Philippine Telegraph and Telephone Company v. National Labor Relations Commission[1]. This decision declared illegal the dismissal of a woman worker, grounded as it was on the company policy of not accepting married women for employment. CEDAW was seen as the cause for the emergence of more frequent corrective labour and social laws on gender inequality.

Discrimination against women workers extends to wages, with women workers earning less than half of what their male counterparts earn for similar work. Consider this: For every peso earned by a male, a female gets .358 pesos in agriculture, fishery and forestry; .341 pesos in mining and quarrying; .371 pesos in wholesale and retail trade; .394 in manufacturing; .461 in financing, insurance and business services; and .433 in community, social and personal services.

Sexual harassment

In 1995, the Philippines enacted the Republic Act No. 7877, the "anti-sexual harassment act". In doing so, the Philippines became the first Asian country to enact a law against sexual harassment.

The following limitations of the law may be pointed out:

---

[1] G.R. No. 118978, 272 SCRA 596 (1997).

1. Coverage is limited to the workplace, education or training environment; other venues of commission of sexual harassment are not covered;

2. It requires as an essential element "authority, influence, or moral ascendancy" on the part of the person committing the act for there to be a crime of sexual harassment; sexual harassment between peers is, therefore, not covered;

3. No liability is provided for workplaces which fail to comply with the mandate to promulgate rules and regulations on sexual harassment and to create a committee on decorum and investigation.

Reference to international law and international standards and practices may successfully be made, in conjunction with the spirit of the anti-sexual harassment law. In *Vedaña v. Valencia*[2], a judge was suspended for one year on account of charges of gross misconduct and immoral acts filed by his branch court interpreter. Although the anti-sexual harassment act does not cover the judiciary and its members, our Supreme Court went on to give its stand on its implications on the judiciary and used it as a model in reaching its verdict.

Utilization of human rights treaty law, specifically CEDAW

To date, reference to CEDAW has been made in only two decisions of the Philippine Supreme Court: *Romualdez-Marcos v. Commission of Elections*[3] and *Philippine Telegraph and Telephone Company v. National Labor Relations Commission.*[4] There is no data on the utilization of human rights treaty law in the municipal, regional and appellate court levels.

Migrant workers

Filipinos have been employed as overseas contract workers (OCW) for nearly 100 years. Such workers have experienced all forms of abuses including those which result in death. Yet this has not stopped

[2] Adm. Mat. No. RTJ-96-1351, 295 SCRA 1 (1998).

[3] G.R. No. 119976, 248 SCRA 300 (1995).

[4] See Note 1.

Filipino women from becoming migrant workers, and they now comprise the greater number of overseas workers. By 1992, there were more women OCWs than men in land-based occupations. In 1994, some 60 percent of Filipinos who left the country for overseas jobs were women. Most of these women are employed as domestic helpers or entertainers. A considerable number experience abuses in their place of employment, and return to broken homes and mismanaged funds.

The cases of Flor Contemplacion and of Sarah Balabagan received broad international attention. Ms. Contemplacion went to work as a domestic helper in Singapore in 1989. In 1991, she was arrested for the killing of another domestic helper and her four-year old ward. On trial, she pleaded guilty on account of temporary insanity, believing that such a plea would earn her a lesser sentence. Instead, her plea of insanity was rejected and she was convicted of the crime and sentenced to death. Appeals from various sectors of the international community and from Filippine President Fidel V. Ramos to the authorities for a stay of the execution and reopening of the case were did not prevent her hanging in 1995. Fourteen-year old Sarah Balabagan was found guilty, after a second trial in 1995, of murdering her male employer and sentenced to be beheaded. Approximately two months after arriving in the United Arab Emirates, she killed her employer after he had raped her at knifepoint. Prior to that, he had offered her gold and money in exchange for her virginity and had subjected her to sexual advances. The circumstances surrounding the killing and the fact that Sarah was a minor were initially ignored, but subsequently she was pardoned, and the Court's verdict was reversed.

Philippine legislation, namely the Republic Act No. 8042 on "Migrant Workers and Overseas Filipinos Act of 1995", was passed in response to the problems facing our migrant workers; posed stricter requirements for recruitment agencies and limited the deployment of workers to countries where the rights of migrant workers are protected.

Problems, however, persist. While the Philippines is a State party to the International Convention for the Protection of All Migrant Workers and their Families, this Convention has not attracted widespread ratification from other states. It has also offered to host an international conference on migrant workers.

The Philippine courts and government should continue to work for better terms for migrant workers. As was proven in the case of Sarah Balabagan, bringing the issues to the international arena can be instrumental in achieving gains where domestic or local laws are inadequate.

Suggestions for utilization of international human rights law in judicial decisions

1. Judicial Conferences can draw attention to human rights treaty law and disseminate materials during such conferences. In this manner, judges busy unclogging their dockets become acquainted with the latest relevant international treaties and are encouraged to use these in their own decision-making;

2. Advocates play an important role in increasing public, specifically judicial awareness, of international human rights treaty law;

3. Government agencies, particularly quasi-judicial agencies, should be provided with continuing education and information regarding international human rights treaty laws pertinent and relevant to their work. This would ensure that such treaty law is incorporated into the resolutions and decisions of these agencies. CEDAW, for instance, should be commonly drawn from and used as a source by the Department of Social Welfare and Development, the Department of Labor, including the Philippine Overseas Employment Agency, and by the Civil Service Commission;

International gatherings such as this judicial colloquium, play an important role in the dissemination of international human rights treaty law.

Work and Law: The Tunisian Example
Hamida Laarif

In accordance with article 6 of the Tunisian Constitution ("*Destour*"), dating from 1959, "all citizens have the same rights and the same duties; they are equal before the law". On the basis of this principle and in full respect for the cultural specificities of the Arab-Muslim countries, the Labour Code explicitly incorporates a provision barring discrimination between men and women to put an end to all forms of discrimination against women with regard to their occupational status.

The legal framework for the protection of women's rights

As employees on an equal footing with men under article 5 of the Tunisian Labour Code, women have equal access to employment, remuneration and promotion. Article 234 of the Labour Code expressly states that violation of this principle is punishable. Hence, the collective labour agreements adopted a number of rules on women's equal rights with regard to employment status, remuneration, paid leave, promotion, the social-security regime, the regime of compensation for industrial accidents and occupational disease, and the retirement regime.

Furthermore, in order to ensure the preservation of women's health in the workplace and on the basis of the relevant provisions of international treaty law, the Labour Code contains provisions protecting women from arduous and hazardous work. Thus, women may not be recruited for work underground in mines and quarries (art. 77 of the Labour Code) or in companies or divisions thereof and sites for the recovery, processing or storage of scrap metal (art. 78 of the Labour Code). A law also governs the maximum load women can carry at work (Ministerial decree of 5 May 1988).

Since 1996, following the approval of the 1990 protocol, the Labour Code provides that the prohibition of night work by women may be waived, subject to certain conditions to ensure the health and safety of female employees, particularly pregnant women. Article 68 of the Labour Code also specifies that the waiver of the prohibition on night work by women may not constitute grounds for terminating an employment contract.

With respect to pregancy and maternity, article 20 of the Labour Code provides that an employer may not terminate an employment contract on the grounds that a woman stops work during the period before and after delivery, and will be liable in such case for the payment of damages. Also, pregnant women may leave work without giving prior notice and therefore without having to pay a fine for terminating an employment contract (art. 18).

Following delivery, female civil servants are granted fully paid maternity leave, which may be combined with annual leave (Act of 12 December 1983). Nursing mothers, on their return to work after maternity leave, are given one hour free at the beginning or end of each working day for six months (circular of 11 September 1992). Similarly, a special nursing room must be set up in every establishment which employs at least 50 women (art. 64 of the Labour Code). In order to enable working mothers to raise their children, various attempts have been made in Tunisia to allow women to work flexible hours, for example, by arriving at work one hour later (1982), or to work part-time at half pay in the private sector (1985). In the public sector, at the end of maternity leave, a mother, at her request, may be granted either a four-month post-natal leave at half pay or a two-year temporary leave of absence, renewable twice, in order to raise one or more children under six years of age or tend to a sick child requiring constant care. She can even exercise her right to early retirement (Act of 5 March 1985).

In order to allow working women to reconcile employment responsibilities and family obligations, the Social Security Fund assumes the cost of placing children of working mothers in child-care facilities (Act of 26 July 1994). The Government offers incentives for the creation of and increase in the number of centres for preschool children.

These measures also apply to rural women. Since 1993, article 135 of the Labour Code has explicitly rescinded any discriminatory provisions against rural women, particularly with regard to pay. An agricultural investment code giving major advantages to women working in agriculture has been promulgated. Accordingly, projects for the promotion of rural women's activities in the agricultural, fishing and crafts sectors, similar to those for men, have been developed.

The role of courts in the protection of the rights of working women

With respect to the courts, the *Conseils de Prud'homme*, which are labour courts, are competent to resolve conflicts which arise at work and contravene the rules of labour law. Moreover, Tunisian case law attaches great importance to conflict settlement related to the violation of women's labour rights.

For example, decisions have been handed down concerning the termination of a female employee's employment contract for absence on certified medical leave related to a pregnancy or childbirth which prevented her from resuming work (art. 20 of the Labour Code). Under case law, this was considered an improper termination of an employment contract, entailing liability for the payment of damages. The same is true of decisions requiring an employer to ensure respect for the rules of morality and decent moral conduct towards women and children in the workplace (arts. 76 and 373 of the Labour Code) (appellate decision no. 41509 of 25 November 1996, which established that the mere sending of morally offensive love letters by a school employee to a girl student constituted gross misconduct on the employee's part).

In cases of physical violence against or sexual harassment of women in the workplace, the court has applied the relevant provisions of the Tunisian Penal Code (arts. 233, 218, 219 and 220).

With regard to married women, case law has not upheld divorce proceedings instituted by the husband on the grounds that his wife refused to terminate her employment contract.

It should be noted, however, that there is no specific case law with regard to discrimination between the sexes in the application of workplace rules, for the simple reason that this question does not arise in practice, taking into account political and social considerations related to the promotion of women's work and, consequently, their integration into public and working life, including access to managerial and political posts.

Several mechanisms are in place to protect women's labour rights, including:

i)   The Labour Inspection Corps (Act of 21 February 1994), composed of Government employees responsible for ensuring the application of the legal, regulatory and treaty provisions governing labour relations in all fields of activity. These officials report violations to the Government Procurator's Office for the purposes of prosecution, such as the employment of girls under the legal working age. They may also assist the magistrates on the *Conseils de Prud'homme* in any inquiry deemed necessary during a trial, given that most employee-employer conflicts are first submitted for mediation by the Labour Inspectorate.

ii) Payment by the Social Security Fund, without discrimination as to sex, of compensation owed to employees laid off for economic or technological reasons and protection of their legal rights, should it be determined that they are unable to recover the monies owed to them in the event of a company's suspension of payments (Act of 18 November 1996).

iii) The establishment of the Health and Safety at Work Institute (Act of 7 August 1990) to promote the health and safety of men and women in the workplace.

iv) Medical workplace inspections (Act of 15 July 1996, art. 289 of the Labour Code), in which doctors, acting as labour inspectors are responsible for ensuring the application of health and safety legislation at work, in conjunction with the regular labour inspectors.

Conclusion

The reforms undertaken in Tunisia with regard to women, particularly after the change of Government of 7 November 1987, have enabled Tunisian women to strengthen their position in all areas relating to education, training, health and employment. These measures also extended to children, with the promulgation in November 1995 of the Code on Child Protection containing all rights, actions and measures designed to protect children. Particular attention is devoted to children in difficult circumstances. New mechanisms for their benefit are planned in order to ensure more effective exercise of their rights and, at the same time, complementarity between the objectives of social prevention and legal protection.

Judicial training

Moving Towards a Jurisprudence of Equality: A Judicial Training Programme Addressing Women's Human Rights
Arline Pacht

In the beginning

In 1989, 50 women judges from every continent assembled in Washington, DC to celebrate the tenth anniversary of the United States National Association of Women Judges. Realizing that similar problems confronted them in their quest for equal justice, they agreed to act in concert in order to more effectively advance the legal status of all women. That historic meeting led to the formation of the International Association of Women Judges (IAWJ), an organization that today includes over 4,000 jurists at every level of the judiciary in 78 nations. Several years later, the International Women Judges Foundation (IWJF) was established to support the IAWJ in attaining its goals.

The IAWJ members recognized that notwithstanding differences in culture, language and legal-judicial systems, they shared a common legal language – that of the international human rights conventions. However, they also were aware that although these instruments uniformly guarantee non-discrimination on the basis of sex, they were not being applied to redress violations of women's rights.

At the Fourth World Conference in Beijing, 189 nations affirmed their commitment to promote and protect human rights for all people, but the principles enshrined in widely-ratified international human rights instruments rarely are cited as authority in cases involving egregious violations of women's human rights. Thus, the most flagrant of human rights abuses of women and girls -- domestic violence, rape, sexual slavery, trafficking -- continue unremedied and unabated.

One of the significant causes for this deficiency lies in the judiciary's lack of knowledge of the protective provisions in these international covenants and their overriding authority in cases which come before them in their own judicial systems. Moreover, judges often are unaware that they have the power to declare that both private individuals and public officials must comply with the provisions set forth in human rights treaties. Jurists are reluctant, even fearful, to invoke human rights law and declare it controlling in their courts.

Thus, a jurisprudence of inequality prevails.

Determined to convert abstract promises of international human rights law into the concrete reality of daily life, the IWJF designed and in 1995, began implementing a pilot project in Costa Rica, the Philippines and Romania titled "Towards a Jurisprudence of Equality: Women, Judges and Human Rights Law" (JEP). Based on experiences in these countries, and with financial support from the Inter-American Development Bank, the JEP was restructured and introduced next to the judiciary in Argentina, Brazil, Chile, Ecuador and Uruguay. Now in its third year of delivery in South America, the JEP is equipping judges with the knowledge and skills needed to resolve cases arising in national courts that involve discrimination and/or violence against women, in accordance with the principles enshrined in international and regional human rights treaties.

The project's structure in a nutshell

The JEP is implemented in the following interrelated steps:

Task forces and '3 Ts' training workshops

Initially, IAWJ members in each participating country form a task force, that is, a committee charged with administering all operational aspects of the project in their respective countries. Among their earliest and most important duties, the task forces are responsible for selecting two-member teams composed of a judge and a legal academic or NGO advocate who attend a 10-day 'train the trainers (3 Ts) workshop, led by the IWJF human rights education facilitators.

IWJF human rights educational experts, relying on their own instructional materials and employing interactive teaching methods, lead the workshops which are designed to prepare the training teams to conduct human rights seminars for jurists in their respective countries. Specifically, at each workshop offered during the three year period, the training teams became familiar with the terms of the relevant human rights conventions, learned to apply these terms to real and hypothetical cases typical of those that would be filed in their nation's courts, practiced the use of progressive techniques and prepared model agendas for the seminars they subsequently would lead. Through these means, teams of trainers are prepared to train others.

The seminars

In the six-month period following their 3 Ts workshop, the training teams prepare and present between two and four JEP seminars for groups of approximately 30 jurists in various locations throughout their countries. While trainers are encouraged to model their seminars on the 3 Ts workshop, both in substance and in teaching methodology, they are free to tailor the curriculum so that it addresses legal issues and practices of particular concern to women in their respective nations. Thus, in one country, a training team may concentrate on human rights norms that redress domestic violence while in another, they may focus on gender discrimination in the workplace.

Follow-up

At the end of each project year, the task forces and training teams conduct follow-up meetings with JEP participants in their countries. These sessions have a threefold purpose: to review the curriculum in light of any legal changes that may have occurred; to discuss the ways in which they have applied their training; and to elicit suggestions on ways to improve the curriculum for future sessions.

The cycle described above, that is, a ten-day training workshop followed by two, three or four day in-country seminars and an annual review session, are repeated in each of the project's three year term.

Although the JEP curriculum originally was designed with civil law judicial systems in mind, it provides a template that can be readily adapted to common law systems as well. Thus, the IWJF and project partners in Kenya, South Africa, Tanzania, Uganda and Zimbabwe now are planning to introduce the JEP to the judiciary in their countries.

Measuring success

Currently, the IAWJ-IWJF and their South American partners are examining ways to measure the impact of the project. Although it is difficult to quantify results in concrete terms, some numerical gauges are available. For example, as the project nears its conclusion, over 1,000 South American jurists have benefited directly from the JEP training. Each participant can be expected to share his or her experience with colleagues, particularly those on appellate courts. While 1,000 JEP-trained judges spread throughout four countries may not constitute a critical mass, they are numerous enough to provide substantial collegial support to one another in their efforts to apply the human rights conventions in local cases. Moreover, the multiplier effect will continue even beyond the term of the IADB-funded project. A number of judicial districts in Argentina and Uruguay have requested that the JEP be offered to judges and prosecutors in their regions. In addition, a few trainers have integrated the JEP materials into their law school courses. Another trainer is planning a human rights training programme for police officers in her community.

Since the ultimate objective of the Jurisprudence of Equality project is to supplant laws and practices that disadvantage and oppress women and girls with judgements that invoke human rights norms, the number of human rights rulings issued by JEP-trained judges in South America should be a significant indicator of the project's value. Given this criteria, the JEP is well on the road to success. Judges in the participating nations have issued dozens of decisions that rely on human rights principles to rationalize equitable results. After these judgements are translated, they will be analyzed and entered into a Website under IADB's auspices.

However, many JEP participants have cautioned that the success of the programme should not be measured solely on the basis of the number of human rights decisions issued. Instead, they point to other outcomes that while favorable, are difficult to quantify. For example, South American participants assessed their training sessions very positively. Many said that the project transformed their lives; others that it changed their attitudes. By way of illustration, several prosecutors stated that the JEP experience caused them to pay far more attention to victims' rights than they had prior to the training, leading them to introduce evidence that they would not previously have considered relevant.

In the final analysis, although the project partners are intent on transforming the law, success in changing the discriminatory social, cultural and legal-judicial environment that women throughout the world experience, will happen only gradually. The true worth of JEP training is long range. However, organized and united under the IAWJ-IWJF's mantle, women judges are uniquely positioned to lead the way toward a jurisprudence of equality.

Annexes

Biographical notes on keynote presenters

Emna AOUIJ is the President of the Court of Cassation (*Cour des Comptes*) of Tunisia. Having been the first woman judge in her country, Ms. Aouij served as Juvenile Magistrate Judge, and Judge at the Court of Appeals, before being appointed to the Court of Cassation in 1989. She was a member of Parliament for two terms, and was active in international Parliamentarians' issues. She also represented her country in international conferences, including on women, and on human rights. Ms. Aouij has been a member of the United Nations Committee on the Elimination of Discrimination against Women since 1990, and was its Vice-Chairperson from 1994-1996. Ms. Aouij is a national of Tunisia.

Marc BOSSUYT is Professor of international law at the University of Antwerp, Belgium. He is also a Judge at the Court of Arbitration, the Belgian Constitutional Court. Mr. Bossuyt has been a member of the United Nations Sub-Commission on the Promotion and the Protection of Human Rights (from 1981-1985, and from 1992-1999), for which he served as Special Rapporteur for a study on the concept of affirmative action. He was the representative of Belgium to the United Nations Commission on Human Rights, and chaired the Commission in 1989. He has published and lectured extensively on international law and human rights issues. Mr. Bossuyt is a national of Belgium.

Christine CHINKIN is a Professor of international law at the London School of Economics and Political Science. Prior to that, she was Dean and Head of Department at the Faculty of Law, Southampton University. She was an Assistant Professor at the University of Sydney, and taught at the University of Singapore, the University of London, and Lincoln College, Oxford. Her research and teaching interests include public international law, human rights with particular emphasis on the human rights of women, and international dispute resolution. She has published widely on these and other subjects. Ms. Chinkin holds British and Australian citizenship.

Claudio GROSSMAN is Dean of Washington College of Law (WCL), American University, Washington DC, a position he has held since 1995. Prior to this appointment, he served as Dean of Graduate Studies, Acting Dean of WCL, and Director of International Legal Studies Programme. Mr. Grossman has litigated cases before the Inter-American Court of Human Rights. In 1993, he was elected to the Inter-American Commission on Human Rights of the Organization of American States, and appointed its Special Rapporteur on Women's Human Rights in 1995. He has written extensively in the area of international law. Mr. Grossman is from Chile.

Krisztina MORVAI is Associate Professor of Law at Eötvös Loránd University School of Law and Political Science in Budapest, Hungary. She was a Fulbright Visiting Professor at the University of Wisconsin at Madison Law School. She has served as staff attorney at the European Commission of Human Rights in Strasbourg. Her fields of teaching and research include criminal law, human rights law, constitutional dimensions of the democratic transitions in Eastern and Central Europe, and has a particular interest in gender and the law. She has lectured and published on these and other topics. Ms. Morvai is a national of Hungary.

Navanethem PILLAY is the President of the International Criminal Tribunal for Rwanda. She was first elected a Judge by the United Nations General Assembly in May 1995, and re-elected for a second term to expire in 2003. Ms. Pillay was the first black woman to start a law practice in Natal, South Africa. and was also the first black woman attorney to be appointed acting judge of the Supreme Court in South Africa. She was a lecturer at Natal University, Department of Public Law, and served as Vice-President of the Council of the University of Durban Westville. She remains involved in national and international activities to promote women's human rights. Ms. Pillay is a national of South Africa.

Participants

ANTIGUA & BARBUDA

Mr. Ephraim GEORGES
Resident Judge
Judges Chambers, High Court of Justice
High Street, St. John's
Antigua
Tel: (1 268) 562 1969
Fax: (1 268) 462 3929
Email: igeorges@hotmail.com

AUSTRIA

Ms. Lilian HOFMEISTER
Judge at the Vienna Superior Commercial Court
Substitute Justice at the Austrian Constitutional Court
Riemergasse 7
A-1010 Vienna
Austria
Tel: (43 1) 515 282 99
Fax: (43 1) 515 285 76

Ms. Petra SMUTNY
Judge
Adviser in the Federal Ministry of Justice
Museumstrasse 7
A-1070 Vienna
Austria
Tel: (43 1) 52 152 2152
Fax: (43 1) 52 152 2753

BANGLADESH

Mr. A.K. Badrul HUQ
Judge, Supreme Court of Bangladesh
Chamber No. 21 (ka)
Supreme Court Building, Rama

Dhaka
Bangladesh
Tel: (880 2) 956 29 45, Ext. 146
Fax: (880 2) 956 24 74
Email: amit@bol-online.com

Mr. Khandker HASAN
Judge, Supreme Court of Bangladesh
House No. 18, Road No. 5
Dhanmondi
Dhaka 1205
Bangladesh
Tel: (880 2) 861 816 (home)
Fax: (880 2) 831 966
Email: amber@citechco.net

BENIN

Mme. Conceptia D. OUINSOU
Président de la Cour Constitutionelle du Benin
Cotonou
Benin
Tel: (229) 31 16 10
Fax: (229) 31 37 12
Email: courconstitu@planben.intnet.bj

Mme. Clotilde MEDEGAN-NOUGBODE
Membre de la Cour Constitutionelle du Benin
Cotonou
Benin
Tel: (229) 31 16 10
Fax: (229) 31 37 12
Email: courconstitu@planben.intnet.bj

BOTSWANA

Ms. Naledi Stella DABUTHA
Senior State Counsel
P.O. Box 40414
Gaborone
Botswana
Tel: (267) 354 781

Fax: (267) 357 089
Email: sdabutha@gov.bw

Ms. Unity DOW
Justice, High Court of Botswana
Private Bag 1
Lobatse
Botswana
Tel: (267) 330 396
Fax: (267) 332 317
Email: udow@info.bw

BURKINA FASO

Ms. Amina OUEDRAOGO
Vice Président de la Cour Suprême
Ouagadougou
Burkina Faso
Tel: (226) 306 415 / 16 / 18
Fax: (226) 310 271
Email: alioune@fast.univ-ouaga.bf

CAMBODIA

Ms. Sathavy KIM
Judge detache
Legal Advisor to the Vice Prime Minister
23 E2, Stree 178
Khan Daun Penh
Phnom Penh
Cambodia
Tel: (855) 238 806 35
Fax: (855) 238 806 34
Email: hangsa@forum.org.kh
　　　Guest@fcc.forum.org.kh

CAMEROON

Ms. Florence ARREY
Chief Justice
Court of Appeal, Buea
South West Province

Cameroon
Tel: (237) 32 26 65
Fax: (237) 43 25 08 / 43 24 98
Email: pelican@camnet.cm
    pelican@douala1.com

Mme. Madeleine SAO
Ministre Plénipotentiare
Responsable des questions Femme et
  Genre au Cabinet du Ministre
Ministère des Relations Extérieures
Yaounde
Cameroun
Tel. (237) 20 50 38
Fax: (237) 21 02 04
Email: madeleine_sao@hotmail.com

CANADA

Mr. Michel BASTARACHE
Justice, Supreme Court of Canada
Ottawa, Ontario
Canada KIA 0J1
Tel: (613) 996 91 97
Fax: (613) 952 18 82

Mr. Douglas R. CAMPBELL
Justice, Federal Court of Canada
Supreme Court of Canada Building
Kent and Wellington Streets
Ottawa, Ontario
Canada KIA 0H9
Tel: (613) 947 78 71
Fax: (613) 947 41 61
Email: dr_campbell@bc.sympatico.ca

Ms. Catherine Anne FRASER
The Honourable Chief Justice of Alberta
Law Courts Building, 5th Floor
1A Sir Winston Churchill Square
Edmonton, Alberta

Canada T5J OR1
Tel: (780) 422 24 33; 422 22 82
Fax: (780) 427 5507
Email: cfraser@just.gov.ab.ca

CONGO

Ms. Delphine Edith EMMANUEL née ADOUKI
Directrice de cabinet au Ministère de la fonction publique,
  des réformes administratives et de la promotion de la femme
Brazzaville
Congo
Tel: (242) 81 41 53
Fax: (242) 81 41 55

CUBA

Ms. Eulogia PRIETO
Vice President, People's Supreme Court of Havana
Boyeros e/ Tulipán y Lombillo
Plaza de la Revolución
Cuidad de La Habana
Cuba
Tel: (53 7) 81 03 89
Fax: (53 7) 24 24 91 (UNFPA office)
Email: alfonso.farnos@undp.org /graciela.puebla@undp.org

DEMOCRATIC PEOPLE'S REPUBLIC OF KOREA

Mr. Ri JAE RIM
Magistrate
Department of Legislation, Presidium, SPA, DPRK
Nam mun-dong, Chungsong Distr.
Pyongyang City
DPRK
Tel: (85 02) 382 9743
Fax: (85 02) 381 4560

Mr. Rim YONG CHOL
Legal Adviser of International
  Human Rights Law
Department of Laws and Treaties

Chung song-dong, Chungu Distr.
Pyongyang City
DPRK
Tel: (85 02) 382 7222
Fax: (85 02) 381 4660

DENMARK

Mr. John LUNDUM
High Court/Appeals Court Judge
Vestre Landsret
Graabroedre Kirkestraede 3
8800 Viborg
Denmark
Tel: (45 86) 626 200
Fax: (45 86) 626 365

ECUADOR

Ms. Maria Leonor JIMENEZ DE VITERI
Ministra Juez de la Cuarta Sala de la H. Corte Superior
 De Justicia de Guayaquil
Av. 9 de Octubre y Av. Quito, cuarto piso, Cuarta Sala
Guayaquil
Ecuador
Tel/Fax: (593 4) 531 533

EGYPT

Mr. Sanaa KHALIL
Counsellor
Ministry of Justice
Nasr City, 10th District
Swiss Area, Building 29 A, Apt. 4
Cairo
Egypt
Tel: (20 2) 271 30 27

ETHIOPIA

Ms. Mekedes TESFAYE
Judge, Federal Supreme Court
Box 6166

Addis Ababa
Ethiopia
Tel: (251 1) 11 64 42

FIJI

Mr. D.V. FATIAKI
Judge of the High Court of Fiji
PO Box 2215
Government Buildings
Suva, Fiji
Tel: (679) 211 308
Fax: (679) 300 674

Ms. Gwen PHILLIPS
Resident Magistrate
C/-Judicial Department
P.O. Box 2217, Government Buildings
Suva, Fiji
Tel: (679) 306 025 / 315 623
Fax: (679) 300 327

Ms. Madhuri SHARMA
Resident Magistrate
Magistrates Court
PO Box 22 17
Government Buildings
Suva
Fiji
Tel: (679) 211 485 / 211 203
Fax: (679) 300 674

FINLAND

Ms. Elina DEGENER
Justice
Supreme Administrative Court
P.O. Box 180
00131 Helsinki
Finland
Tel: (358 9) 1853 346
Fax: (358 9) 1853 382

GUINEE

Mme. Mariama CAMARA
Juge de Paix de Coyah
Guinee
Fax: (224) 42 39 97 (attn: Mme Bangoura Sylla)
Email: ceci@mirinet.net.gn

Mme. Paulette KOUROUMA
Presidente du Tribunal de Premiere Instance de Conakry
PO Box 564
Conakry
Guinee
Tel: (224) 11 212 392
Fax: (224) 41 24 85, or 45 10 58 (UNFPA)

GUINEE BISSAU

Mr. Emiliano NOSOLINI DOS REIS
President de la Cour Supreme
BP 341
Bissau
Tel: (245) 20 13 65, or 20 40 15, or 21 10 03
Fax: (245) 20 13 65

Mr. Augusto MENDES
Juge
BP 341
Bissau
Tel: (245) 21 10 03
Fax: (245) 20 13 65

INDIA

Ms. Sujata MANOHAR
Former Judge, Supreme Court of India
National Human Rights Commission
Sardar Patel Bhawan, Sansad Narg
New Delhi 110001
India
Tel.: (91-11) 334-8476
Fax: (91-11) 334-0016/336-6537

INDONESIA

Mr. Maruarar SIAHAAN
Judge, Court of Appeal
Jalan Kayu Mas Tengah II/31
Jakarta Timur
Indonesia
Tel: (62 21) 425 20 69
Fax: (62 21) 426 55 03

IRAQ

Mr. Ibrahim AL-AZZI
Magistrate
Court of Appeal
C/UNICEF Baghdad
Tel: (873) 555 1636 (home)
Fax: (873) 761 473 376 (UNICEF)
Email: tsutton@unicef.org

IRELAND

Ms. Mella CARROLL
Justice, The High Court
Four Courts
Dublin 7
Ireland
Tel./Fax: (353 1) 872 03 24

ITALY

Ms. Antonietta CARESTIA
Magistrata di Cassazione
Adviser, Ministry of Justice, Legislative Office
Via Aremula, 70
Rome
Italy
Tel (39 06) 688 52 706
Fax: (39 06) 688 97 531

JAMAICA

Ms. Rosemary NEALE-IRVING
Senior Judge (Acting)
Family Court Kingston & St. Andrew
74B King Street
Kingston
Jamaica
Tel: (876) 922 10 00
Fax: (876) 922 03 26
Email: rosemary@jamweb.net

JORDAN

Ms. Malak GHAZAL
Reconciliation Judge
Justice Palace
P.O. Box 450
Amman, 11953
Jordan
Tel: (96 26) 562 1315 ext. 2333
Fax: (96 26) 562 2362
Email: attiehm@go.com.jo

Mr. Turky HADDAD
Adviser to the Legislative Board at the Prime Ministry
Prime Ministry
PO Box 80
Amman
Jordan
Tel: (96 26) 464 12 11
Fax: (96 26) 463 32 68

KENYA

Ms. Mary Atieno ANG'AWA
The Honourable Lady Justice of the High Court of Kenya
Puisne Judge, Judge of Appeal
P.O. Box 30041
Nairobi
Kenya
Tel: (254 2) 338 293 (direct)

(254 2) 221 221
Fax: (254 2) 333 449 / 214 632
Email: Mang'awa@rapid.africaonline.com

Ms. Winny KAMANDE
Senior Practising Lawyer and Arbitrator in Nairobi
Council Member of the Federation of Women Lawyers
Nairobi
Kenya
Tel: (254 2) 22 66 98, or 21 56 99
Fax: (254 2) 21 56 99
Email: wkamande@insightkenya.com

LATVIA

Ms. Anita UŠACKA
Associate Professor, Ph.D.
Justice of the Constitutional Court of the Republic of Latvia
Alunana 1, Riga, LV-1010
Latvia
Tel: (371) 7221 512
Fax: (371) 7220 572
Email: anita.u@satv.tiesa.gov.lv

LIBERIA

Ms. Gloria M. SCOTT
Chief Justice
Supreme Court of Liberia
Capitol Hill
Monrovia
Liberia
Tel: (231) 226 071, or 227 778, or 227 604
Fax: (231) 226 071

MALAWI

Ms. Anastasia S.E. MSOSA
Judge, High Court of Malawi
P.O. Box 30244
Blantyre 3
Malawi

Tel: (265) 670 255
Fax: (265) 670 213
Email: hightones@sdnp.org.mw

MALDIVES

Mr. Ahmed MUIZZU
Legal Counsel
Ministry of Women's Affairs and Social Affairs
Male
Maldives
Tel: (960) 31 71 64

MALI

Ms. Awa Kouyate KANTE
Magistrate, Cour d'Appel
Bamako
Mali
Tel: (223) 22 84 20 (home)
Fax: (223) 23 04 53 / 21 65 23
Email: ceci-dcf@cefib.com

MOROCCO

Ms. Saadia BELMIR
Président de Chambre á la Cour Suprême
Membre du Conseil Constitutionnel
Av. Al Nakil-Hay-Ryad
BP 2007
Rabat
Maroc
Tel: (212 7) 714 936 / 714 937
Email: coursup@iam.net.ma

MOZAMBIQUE

Mr. Afonso FORTES
Juiz Conselheiro
Tribunal Supremo
Maputo
Mozambique

Tel: (258 1) 310 672
Fax: (258 1) 340 01

Mr. Ozias PONDJA
Juiz Conselheiro
Tribunal Supremo
Maputo
Mozambique
Tel: (258 1) 310 672
Fax: (258 1) 420 699
Email: BibliotecaTS@Teledata.mz

Ms. Claudina Ernesto MACUACUA
Magistrada Judicial
Tribunal Judicial da Provincia de Maputo
Maputo
Mozambique
Tel: (258 1) 720 389
Fax: (258 1) 720 389

NAMIBIA

Mr. Uutoni D. NUJOMA
Chairperson, Law Reform & Development Commission
Ministry of Justice
Private Bag 13248
Windhoek
Namibia
Tel: (264 61) 280 53 34
Fax: (264 61) 250 868 / 221 615

NEPAL

Mr. Krishana Jung RAYAMAJHI
Judge, Supreme Court of Nepal
Supreme Court of Nepal, Ramashahapath
Kathmandu
Nepal
Tel: (977 1) 250 937
Fax: (977 1) 262 878

NETHERLANDS ANTILLES

Mr. Luis Alberto Jose de LANNOY
Chief Justice of the High Court of Justice
of the Netherlands Antilles & Aruba
Wilhelminaplein 4, Willemstad
Curacao
Netherlands Antilles
Tel: (5999) 463 41 40/463 41 65
Fax: (5999) 461 83 41
Email: hofcur@cura.net

NETHERLANDS

Ms. Jenny E. GOLDSCHMIDT
President of the Equal Treatment Commission of the Netherlands
Professor of Law, University of Leiden
P.O. Box 16001
3500 DA Utrecht
The Netherlands
Tel: (31 30) 233 51 11
Fax: (31 30) 230 06 06
Email: Cgb@support.nl
janpeter@worldonline.nl

Ms. Marjet OUDE SOGTOEN
Assistant to Ms. Goldschmidt

NIGER

Mme. Fassouma MAHAMANE
Magistrat auprés de la Cour d'Appel
BP 662
Niamey
Niger
Tel: (227) 75 21 79
Fax: (227) 74 08 88

NIGERIA

Ms. A. O. IGE
Judge
Court of Appeal

Lagos
Nigeria
Tel: (234 1) 263 59 20
Fax: (234 1) 263 50 67

Ms. Zainab A. BULKACHUWA
Judge
Court of Appeal
P.M.B. 722
Garki Abuja
Nigeria
Tel: (234 9) 234 27 03

Ms. Hansine DONLI
Judge
High Court of Justice
Kaduna
Nigeria
Tel: (234 62) 240 990
Fax: (234 62) 240 622

Ms. Agnes USIFO AMAESHI
Judge, High Court of Justice
Owerri, Imo State
Nigeria
Tel: (234 83) 234 212, or 232 618
Fax: (234 83) 234 212

Ms. Amina Adamu AUGIE
Judge, High Court of Justice
Sokoto, Sokoto State
Nigeria
Tel: (234 60) 232 954
Fax: (234 9) 234 0367, or (234 62) 240 622

Ms. Aloma MOUKHTAR
Judge, Court of Appeal
Ibadan, Oyo State
Nigeria
Tel: (234 2) 31 20 89
Fax: (234 2) 31 03 86

OMAN

Ms. Thuwayba Bint Ahmed AL-BARWANI
Under-Secretary for Social Affairs
Ministry of Social Affairs, Labour & Vocational Training
P.O. Box 560, Postal Code 113
Muscat
Sultanate of Oman
Tel: (968) 602 753 / 602 773
Fax: (968) 694 609

Mr. Khalifa Mohammed Abdullah AL-HADRAMI
Judge, Director of the Office of the Magistrate Court
P.O. Box 549, Postal Code 111 Al Seeb
Shatti-al-Qurum
Muscat
Sultanate of Oman
Tel: (968) 693 304, or 933 40 16
Fax: (968) 693 309

PAKISTAN

Mr. Nasir-ul-MULK
Judge, Peshawar High Court
1/9 Raza Shah Shaheed Road
Peshawar Cantonment, NWFP
Pakistan
Tel: (92 91) 921 01 41
Fax: (92 91) 285 122
Email: Chin@pes.comsats.net.pk

Mr. Tassaduq Hussain JILANI
Judge, Lahore High Court
8-Tollinton Road, GOR-1
Lahore
Pakistan
Tel: (92 42) 920 02 36 / 731 12 19
Fax: (92 42) 735 58 88 / 735 77 33
Email: justicejillani@hotmail.com

PALESTINE

Mr. Ibrahim AL DAGHMA
Head of Diwan Al Fatwa Wa Al Tashri
Ministry of Justice Diwan Al Fatwa Wa Al Tashri
Palestine
Tel: (972 7) 282 91 97
Fax: (972 7) 282 91 97
Email: diwan@mail.hally.net

Ms. Salwa K. SAYEGH
Judge
PO Box 51 37
El Remal, Gaza
Tel: (972 7) 286 13 80
Fax: (972 7) 286 563
Email: salwa.jadd@marna.com

PANAMA

Ms. Esmeralda Arosemena de TROITINO
Magistrada del Tribunal Superior de Ninez y Adolescencia del
   Organo Judicial de la Republica de Panama
Edificio Dolchester, Via Espana, Oficina 306
Panama
Republic of Panama
Tel: (507) 264 00 79
Fax: (507) 264 72 03
Email: lilah@pty.com

PHILIPPINES

Mr. Reynato S. PUNO
Associate Justice, Supreme Court of the Philippines
Supreme Court
Manila
Philippines
Tel: (632) 536 95 36
Fax: (632) 525 32 08

Ms. Consuelo YNARES-SANTIAGO
Associate Justice, Supreme Court of the Philippines

Supreme Court
Manila, Philippines
Tel: (632) 536 95 36
Fax: (632) 525 32 08

Ms. Erlinda NICOLAS-ALVARO
Prosecutor, Department of Justice
Lot 10 Blk. 3 Jade St. San Pedro 6, Tandang Sora
Quezon City, Philippines
Tel: (632) 527 09 86
Fax: (632) 527 50 01/ 536 04 52

PORTUGAL

Ms. Regina TAVARES DA SILVA
Adviser, Commission for Equality and Women's Rights
Av. Da República, 32/1
P 1050/193 Lisboa Códex
Portugal
Tel: (351) 21 798 30 00/ 3014
Fax: (351) 21 798 30 98
Email: regina.tavares@mail.sitepac.pt

PUERTO RICO

Ms. María M. NAVEIRA
Associate Justice of the Supreme Court
 of the Commonwealth of Puerto Rico
Supreme Court of the Commonwealth of Puerto Rico
P.O. Box 902 2392
San Juan
Puerto Rico 00902-2392
Tel: (787) 721 66 25
Fax: (787) 725 23 01
Email: naveira@caribe.net

ROMANIA

Ms. Viorica COSTINIU
Judge at the Appeal Court of Bucharest
The General Secretary, Romanian Magistrate Association
Bucarest

Romania
Tel/Fax: (401) 250 31 21
Email: costiniu@hades.ro

RWANDA

Ms. Odette MURARA
Présidente de la Cour d'Appel de Kigali
B.P. 101
Kigali
Rwanda
Tel: (250) 78 189 / 781 94
Fax: (250) 78 193

SLOVAK REPUBLIC

Ms. Beata VRTOVA
Judge
976 61 Lucatin 190
Slovak Republic
Tel: (421 88) 41 91 138
Fax: (421 88) 41 91 253
Email: sk-puto@isternet.sk

SOLOMON ISLANDS

Ms. Ester FERAH
Ministry of Justice
Box G 17
Honiara
Solomon Islands
Tel: (667) 213 54, or 213 55

SOUTH AFRICA

Ms. Catherine O'REGAN
Judge of the Constitutional Court of South Africa
Private Bag X32
Braamfontein
Gauteng 2017
South Africa
Tel: (27 11) 359 74 14

Fax: (27 11) 403 88 98
Email: O'Regan@concourt.org.za

Ms. Belinda MOLAMU
Magistrate
Justice College
Private Bag x659
Pretoria 0001
South Africa
Tel: (12) 334 77 00
Fax: (12) 326 42 88
Email: belindaM@justcol.org.za

SUDAN

Ms. Aisha Abu El Gasim HAG HAMED
Former Judge
Deputy of Human Rights and Humanitarian Law Department
Chairman of Women's Desk
Ministry of Justice
Khartoum
Sudan
Tel: (249 11) 772 696
Fax: (249 11) 778 446

TUNISIA

Ms. Hamida LAARIF
General Attorney
Ministère de la Justice
Boulevard Bab-Bnat
La Kasba-Tunis
Tunisia
Tel: (216 1) 568 613
Fax: (216 1) 568 106

TURKEY

Ms. Gonul Basaran ERONEN
Supreme Court Justice
Supreme Court
Lefkosa

Kibris Mersin 10
Turkey
Tel/Fax: (90 392) 22 86 001 (direct)
Tel: (90 392) 22 73 690 (chambers)
Fax: (90 392) 22 85 265 (court)
Email: yego@north-cyprus.net

UGANDA

Ms. Stella ARACH
Judge
The High Court of Uganda
P.O. Box 7085
Kampala
Uganda
Tel: (256 41) 254 866
Fax: (256 41) 259 680
Email: eacodev@infocom.co.ug

Mr. Albert Frank RUGADYA-ATWOKI
Justice
The High Court of Uganda
P.O. Box 7085
Kampala
Uganda
Tel: (256 41) 345 384

UNITED KINGDOM OF GREAT BRITAIN AND NORTHERN IRELAND

Ms. Teresa DOHERTY
Judge
263 Ballywalter Road
Millisle, Co. Down
BT22 2LZ
Northern Ireland
Tel./Fax: (1247) 86 14 40

UNITED STATES OF AMERICA

Ms. Arline PACHT
Director

International Association of Women Judges (IAWJ)
International Women Judges Foundation (IWJF)
3212 Pickwick Lane
Chevy Chase, MD, 20815
USA
Tel: (301) 986 01 84
Fax: (301) 652 78 18
Email: APachtIWJF@igc.apc.org

URUGUAY

Ms. Marta Elena BATTISTELLA DE SALABERRY
Doctor in Law and Social Sciences
Martin C. Martinez 2568
Montevideo, 11.800
Uruguay
Tel: (598 2) 209 58 90
Fax: (598 2) 208 64 03
Email: salabat@adinet.com.uy

VANUATU

Mr. Vincent LUNABEK
Acting Chief Justice of Vanuatu
Supreme Court Building
Private Mail Bag 041
Port Lila
Vanuatu
Tel: (678) 22 420
Fax: (678) 22 692

VENEZUELA

Ms. Maria Cristina PARRA
Jueza Superior de Familia y Ninos
Calle Juan Griego, Qta Agua Miel.
Santa Ana, Cafetal
Caracas
Venezuela
Tel: (58 2) 986 83 96 / 482 92 12
Fax: (58 2) 985 92 65
Email: mcp54@yahoo.com

VIETNAM

Ms. Hoa Thi TRUONG
Vice-President, HoChiMinh City Bar Association
91 Nguyen Du St., District 1
HoChiMinh City
Vietnam
Tel: (84 8) 829 05 67
Fax: (84 8) 829 85 40

ZAMBIA

Ms. Elizabeth MUYOVWE
Judge
High Court of Zambia
Box 50067
Lusaka
Zambia
Tel: (260 1) 25 48 58, or 25 17 43
Fax: (260 1) 22 44 75
Email: wlsazam@zamnet.zm

ZIMBABWE

Mr. Anthony GUBBAY
Chief Justice of Zimbabwe
Supreme Court of Zimbabwe
P.O. Box CY 870
CAUSEWAY
Harare
Zimbabwe
Tel: (263 4) 721 528
Fax: (263 4) 731 867

Ms. Elizabeth C. GWAUNZA
Justice, High Court of Zimbabwe
45 Lavenham Drive East
Bluff Hill, P.O. Westgate
Harare
Zimbabwe
Tel: (263 4) 736 430
Fax: (263 4) 736 431

KEYNOTE SPEAKERS / RESOURCE PERSONS

Ms. Emna AOUIJ
Présidente de la Cour des Comptes
25, Avenue de la Liberté
Tunis
Tunisia
Fax: (216 1) 797 285

Mr. Marc BOSSUYT
Judge at the Court of Arbitration
Professor at the University of Antwerp (UIA)
B-2650 Edegem
Belgium
Tel/Fax: (32 3) 440 61 36

Ms. Christine CHINKIN
Professor of Law
London School of Economics
Houghton Street
London, WC2A-SAE
United Kingdom of Great Britain and
  Northern Ireland
Tel: (44-171) 405-7686
Fax: (44-171) 995-7366
Email: C.Chinkin@lse.ac.uk

Mr. Claudio GROSSMAN
Special Rapporteur of the Inter-American Commission on Human
Rights
  On the Status of Women
Dean, Washington College of Law
American University
4801 Massachusetts Avenue, NW, Suite 366
Washington, DC 20016-8192, USA
Tel: (202) 274 4004
Fax: (202) 274-4005

Ms. Krisztina MORVAI
Professor of Law
Eötvös Loránd University

School of Law
Egyetem tér 1-3
Budapest, Hungary
Tel: (36 1) 2670 820/2405
Fax: (36-1) 2670 820/3263
Email: womensrightscenter@matavnet.hu

Ms. Navanethem PILLAY
President, International Criminal Tribunal for Rwanda
PO Box 6016
Arusha
Tanzania
Tel: (255 57) 4207-11 / 4367-72
Fax: (255 57) 4000 / 4373
Email: pillayn@un.org

UNITED NATIONS

Ms. Angela E.V. KING
Assistant Secretary-General
Special Adviser to the Secretary-General on Gender Issues and
  the Advancement of Women
United Nations
DC 2 -1220
New York, NY 10017
Tel: (212) 963 5086
Fax: (212) 963 0534
Email: king@un.org

Ms. Yakin ERTÜRK
Director
Division for the Advancement of Women
United Nations
DC 2 -1250
New York, NY 10017
Tel: (212) 963 9750
Fax: (212) 963 3463
Email: erturk@un.org

Ms. Jane CONNORS
Chief, Women's Rights Unit

Division for the Advancement of Women
United Nations
DC 2 - 1226
New York, NY 10017
Tel: (212) 963 3162
Fax: (212) 963 3463
Email: connorsj@un.org

Ms. Christine A. BRAUTIGAM
Social Affairs Officer, Women's Rights Unit
Division for the Advancement of Women
United Nations
DC 2 - 1206
New York, NY 10017
Tel: (212) 963 0535
Fax: (212) 963 3463
Email: brautigamc@un.org

Ms. Abigail LOREGNARD-KASMALLY
Information Officer, Coordination and Outreach Unit
Division for the Advancement of Women
United Nations
DC 2 - 1212
New York, NY 10017
Tel: (212) 963 3137
Fax: (212) 963 3463
Email: loregnard-kasmally@un.org

UNICEF

Ms. Sree GURURAJA
Senior Adviser, Gender and Development
Gender and Programme Partnership Section
UNICEF
Three UN Plaza, (TA-24-84)
New York, NY 10017, USA
Tel: (212) 824 6671
Fax: (212) 824 6486
Email: sgururaja@unicef.org

UNITED NATIONS VOLUNTEERS

Mr. Youssef EL BARODI
Child and Women's Rights Coordinator
UNV
PO Box 25 141
Jerusalem
Tel: (02) 583 00 13/4
Fax: (02) 583 08 06

OBSERVERS FROM ACADEMIC AND RESEARCH INSTITUTIONS

Ms. Ameurfina MELENCIO HERRERA
Chancellor, Philippine Judicial Academy
Philippine Judicial Academy
Supreme Court, 3rd Floor, Taft Avenue Building
Manila
Philippines
Tel: (632) 523 62 77
Fax: (632) 523 90 75; 525 89 39
Email: PHILJA@EVOSERVE.COM

Ms. Margaret REYNOLDS
Chair, International Advisory Commission
Commonwealth Human Rights Initiative
Professor, Department of Government
University of Queensland
St. Lucia
Q 4067 Australia
Tel: (617) 3365 1756
Fax: (617) 3365 1388
Email: margaret.reynolds@bigpond.av

Ms. Susanne ZWINGEL
Hamburg School of Economy and Politics
Binderstrasse 34
20146 Hamburg
Germany
Tel: (49-40) 42838 6766
Fax: (49 40) 42838 6762
Email: ZwingelS@hwp.uni-hamburg.de

Ms. Ulrike GRIESHOFER
University of Vienna Law School
A-1010 Vienna
Austria
Fax: (43 1) 815 29 14
Email: Ulrike.Grieshofer@oeh.ac.at

Convention on the Elimination of All Forms of Discrimination against Women

Adopted and opened for signature, ratification and accession by
General Assembly resolution 34/180 of 18 December 1979

The States Parties to the present Convention,

Noting that the Charter of the United Nations reaffirms faith in
fundamental human rights, in the dignity and worth of the human person
and in the equal rights of men and women,

Noting that the Universal Declaration of Human Rights affirms the
principle of the inadmissibility of discrimination and proclaims that all
human beings are born free and equal in dignity and rights and that everyone is entitled to all the rights and freedoms set forth therein, without
distinction of any kind, including distinction based on sex,

Noting that the States Parties to the International Covenants on
Human Rights have the obligation to ensure the equal right of men and
women to enjoy all economic, social, cultural, civil and political rights,

Considering the international conventions concluded under the
auspices of the United Nations and the specialized agencies promoting
equality of rights of men and women,

Noting also the resolutions, declarations and recommendations
adopted by the United Nations and the specialized agencies promoting
equality of rights of men and women,

Concerned, however, that despite these various instruments extensive discrimination against women continues to exist,

Recalling that discrimination against women violates the principles
of equality of rights and respect for human dignity, is an obstacle to the
participation of women, on equal terms with men, in the political, social, economic and cultural life of their countries, hampers the growth
of the prosperity of society and the family and makes more difficult the
full development of the potentialities of women in the service of their
countries and of humanity,

Concerned that in situations of poverty women have the least access to food, health, education, training and opportunities for employment and other needs,

Convinced that the establishment of the new international economic order based on equity and justice will contribute significantly towards the promotion of equality between men and women,

Emphasizing that the eradication of apartheid, of all forms of racism, racial discrimination, colonialism, neo-colonialism, aggression, foreign occupation and domination and interference in the internal affairs of States is essential to the full enjoyment of the rights of men and women,

Affirming that the strengthening of international peace and security, relaxation of international tension, mutual co-operation among all States irrespective of their social and economic systems, general and complete disarmament, and in particular nuclear disarmament under strict and effective international control, the affirmation of the principles of justice, equality and mutual benefit in relations among countries and the realization of the right of peoples under alien and colonial domination and foreign occupation to self-determination and independence, as well as respect for national sovereignty and territorial integrity, will promote social progress and development and as a consequence will contribute to the attainment of full equality between men and women,

Convinced that the full and complete development of a country, the welfare of the world and the cause of peace require the maximum participation of women on equal terms with men in all fields,

Bearing in mind the great contribution of women to the welfare of the family and to the development of society, so far not fully recognized, the social significance of maternity and the role of both parents in the family and in the upbringing of children, and aware that the role of women in procreation should not be a basis for discrimination but that the upbringing of children requires a sharing of responsibility between men and women and society as a whole,

Aware that a change in the traditional role of men as well as the role of women in society and in the family is needed to achieve full equality between men and women,

Determined to implement the principles set forth in the Declaration on the Elimination of Discrimination against Women and, for that purpose, to adopt the measures required for the elimination of such discrimination in all its forms and manifestations,

Have agreed on the following:

PART I

Article 1

For the purposes of the present Convention, the term "discrimination against women" shall mean any distinction, exclusion or restriction made on the basis of sex which has the effect or purpose of impairing or nullifying the recognition, enjoyment or exercise by women irrespective of their marital status, on a basis of equality of men and women, of human rights and fundamental freedoms in the political, economic, social, cultural, civil or any other field.

Article 2

States Parties condemn discrimination against women in all its forms, agree to pursue by all appropriate means and without delay a policy of eliminating discrimination against women and, to this end, undertake:

a) To embody the principle of the equality of men and women in their national constitutions or other appropriate legislation if not yet incorporated therein and to ensure, through law and other appropriate means, the practical realization of this principle;

b) To adopt appropriate legislative and other measures, including sanctions where appropriate, prohibiting all discrimination against women;

c) To establish legal protection of the rights of women on an equal basis with men and to ensure through competent national tribunals and other public institutions the effective protection of women against any act of discrimination;

d) To refrain from engaging in any act or practice of discrimination against women and to ensure that public authorities and institutions shall act in conformity with this obligation;

e) To take all appropriate measures to eliminate discrimination against women by any person, organization or enterprise;

f) To take all appropriate measures, including legislation, to modify or abolish existing laws, regulations, customs and practices which constitute discrimination against women;

g) To repeal all national penal provisions which constitute discrimination against women.

Article 3

States Parties shall take in all fields, in particular in the political, social, economic and cultural fields, all appropriate measures, including legislation, to ensure the full development and advancement of women, for the purpose of guaranteeing them the exercise and enjoyment of human rights and fundamental freedoms on a basis of equality with men.

Article 4

1. Adoption by States Parties of temporary special measures aimed at accelerating de facto equality between men and women shall not be considered discrimination as defined in the present Convention, but shall in no way entail as a consequence the maintenance of unequal or separate standards; these measures shall be discontinued when the objectives of equality of opportunity and treatment have been achieved.

2. Adoption by States Parties of special measures, including those measures contained in the present Convention, aimed at protecting maternity shall not be considered discriminatory.

Article 5

States Parties shall take all appropriate measures:

a) To modify the social and cultural patterns of conduct of men and women, with a view to achieving the elimination of prejudices and customary and all other practices which are based on the idea of the inferiority or the superiority of either of the sexes or on stereotyped roles for men and women;

b) To ensure that family education includes a proper understanding of maternity as a social function and the recognition of the common responsibility of men and women in the upbringing and development of their children, it being understood that the interest of the children is the primordial consideration in all cases.

Article 6

States Parties shall take all appropriate measures, including legislation, to suppress all forms of traffic in women and exploitation of prostitution of women.

PART II

Article 7

States Parties shall take all appropriate measures to eliminate discrimination against women in the political and public life of the country and, in particular, shall ensure to women, on equal terms with men, the right:

a) To vote in all elections and public referenda and to be eligible for election to all publicly elected bodies;

b) To participate in the formulation of government policy and the implementation thereof and to hold public office and perform all public functions at all levels of government;

c) To participate in non-governmental organizations and associations concerned with the public and political life of the country.

Article 8

States Parties shall take all appropriate measures to ensure to women, on equal terms with men and without any discrimination, the opportunity to represent their Governments at the international level and to participate in the work of international organizations.

Article 9

1. States Parties shall grant women equal rights with men to acquire, change or retain their nationality. They shall ensure in particular that neither marriage to an alien nor change of nationality by the husband during marriage shall automatically change the nationality of the wife, render her stateless or force upon her the nationality of the husband.

2. States Parties shall grant women equal rights with men with respect to the nationality of their children.

PART III

Article 10

States Parties shall take all appropriate measures to eliminate discrimination against women in order to ensure to them equal rights with men in the field of education and in particular to ensure, on a basis of equality of men and women:

a) The same conditions for career and vocational guidance, for access to studies and for the achievement of diplomas in educational establishments of all categories in rural as well as in urban areas; this equality shall be ensured in preschool, general, technical, professional and higher technical education, as well as in all types of vocational training;

b) Access to the same curricula, the same examinations, teaching staff with qualifications of the same standard and school premises and equipment of the same quality;

c) The elimination of any stereotyped concept of the roles of men and women at all levels and in all forms of education by encouraging coeducation and other types of education which will help to achieve this aim and, in particular, by the revision of textbooks and school programmes and the adaptation of teaching methods;

d) The same opportunities to benefit from scholarships and other study grants;

e) The same opportunities for access to programmes of continuing education including adult and functional literacy programmes, particularly those aimed at reducing, at the earliest possible time, any gap in education existing between men and women;

f) The reduction of female student drop-out rates and the organization of programmes for girls and women who have left school prematurely;

g) The same opportunities to participate actively in sports and physical education;

h) Access to specific educational information to help to ensure the health and well-being of families, including information and advice on family planning.

Article 11

1. States Parties shall take all appropriate measures to eliminate discrimination against women in the field of employment in order to ensure, on a basis of equality of men and women, the same rights, in particular:

a) The right to work as an inalienable right of all human beings;

b) The right to the same employment opportunities, including the application of the same criteria for selection in matters of employment;

c) The right to free choice of profession and employment, the right to promotion, job security and all benefits and conditions of service and the right to receive vocational training and retraining, including apprenticeships, advanced vocational training and recurrent training;

d) The right to equal remuneration, including benefits, and to equal treatment in respect of work of equal value, as well as equality of treatment in the evaluation of the quality of work;

e) The right to social security, particularly in cases of retirement, unemployment, sickness, invalidity and old age and other incapacity to work, as well as the right to paid leave;

f) The right to protection of health and to safety in working conditions, including the safeguarding of the function of reproduction.

2. In order to prevent discrimination against women on the grounds of marriage or maternity and to ensure their effective right to work, States Parties shall take appropriate measures:

a) To prohibit, subject to the imposition of sanctions, dismissal on the grounds of pregnancy or of maternity leave and discrimination in dismissals on the basis of marital status;

b) To introduce maternity leave with pay or with comparable social benefits without loss of former employment, seniority or social allowances;

c) To encourage the provision of the necessary supporting social services to enable parents to combine family obligations with work responsibilities and participation in public life, in particular through promoting the establishment and development of a network of child-care facilities;

d) To provide special protection to women during pregnancy in types of work proved to be harmful to them.

3. Protective legislation relating to matters covered in this article shall be reviewed periodically in the light of scientific and technological knowledge and shall be revised, repealed or extended as necessary.

Article 12

1. States Parties shall take all appropriate measures to eliminate discrimination against women in the field of health care in order to ensure, on a basis of equality of men and women, access to health care services, including those related to family planning.

2. Notwithstanding the provisions of paragraph 1 of this article, States Parties shall ensure to women appropriate services in connection with pregnancy, confinement and the post-natal period, granting free services where necessary, as well as adequate nutrition during pregnancy and lactation.

Article 13

States Parties shall take all appropriate measures to eliminate discrimination against women in other areas of economic and social life in order to ensure, on a basis of equality of men and women, the same rights, in particular:

a) The right to family benefits;

b) The right to bank loans, mortgages and other forms of financial credit;

c) The right to participate in recreational activities, sports and all aspects of cultural life.

Article 14

1. States Parties shall take into account the particular problems faced by rural women and the significant roles which rural women play in the economic survival of their families, including their work in the non-monetized sectors of the economy, and shall take all appropriate measures to ensure the application of the provisions of this Convention to women in rural areas.

2. States Parties shall take all appropriate measures to eliminate discrimination against women in rural areas in order to ensure, on a basis of equality of men and women, that they participate in and benefit from rural development and, in particular, shall ensure to such women the right:

a) To participate in the elaboration and implementation of development planning at all levels;

b) To have access to adequate health care facilities, including information, counselling and services in family planning;

c) To benefit directly from social security programmes;

d) To obtain all types of training and education, formal and non-formal, including that relating to functional literacy, as well as, inter alia, the benefit of all community and extension services, in order to increase their technical proficiency;

e) To organize self-help groups and co-operatives in order to obtain equal access to economic opportunities through employment or self-employment;

f) To participate in all community activities;

g) To have access to agricultural credit and loans, marketing facilities, appropriate technology and equal treatment in land and agrarian reform as well as in land resettlement schemes;

h) To enjoy adequate living conditions, particularly in relation to housing, sanitation, electricity and water supply, transport and communications.

PART IV

Article 15

1. States Parties shall accord to women equality with men before the law.

2. States Parties shall accord to women, in civil matters, a legal capacity identical to that of men and the same opportunities to exercise that capacity. In particular, they shall give women equal rights to conclude contracts and to administer property and shall treat them equally in all stages of procedure in courts and tribunals.

3. States Parties agree that all contracts and all other private instruments of any kind with a legal effect which is directed at restricting the legal capacity of women shall be deemed null and void.

4. States Parties shall accord to men and women the same rights with regard to the law relating to the movement of persons and the freedom to choose their residence and domicile.

Article 16

1. States Parties shall take all appropriate measures to eliminate discrimination against women in all matters relating to marriage and family relations and in particular shall ensure, on a basis of equality of men and women:

a) The same right to enter into marriage;

b) The same right freely to choose a spouse and to enter into marriage only with their free and full consent;

c) The same rights and responsibilities during marriage and at its dissolution;

d) The same rights and responsibilities as parents, irrespective of their marital status, in matters relating to their children; in all cases the interests of the children shall be paramount;

e) The same rights to decide freely and responsibly on the number and spacing of their children and to have access to the information, education and means to enable them to exercise these rights;

f) The same rights and responsibilities with regard to guardianship, wardship, trusteeship and adoption of children, or similar institutions where these concepts exist in national legislation; in all cases the interests of the children shall be paramount;

g) The same personal rights as husband and wife, including the right to choose a family name, a profession and an occupation;

h) The same rights for both spouses in respect of the ownership, acquisition, management, administration, enjoyment and disposition of property, whether free of charge or for a valuable consideration.

2. The betrothal and the marriage of a child shall have no legal effect, and all necessary action, including legislation, shall be taken to specify a minimum age for marriage and to make the registration of marriages in an official registry compulsory.

PART V

Article 17

1. For the purpose of considering the progress made in the implementation of the present Convention, there shall be established a Committee on the Elimination of Discrimination against Women (hereinafter referred to as the Committee) consisting, at the time of entry into force of the Convention, of eighteen and, after ratification of or accession to the Convention by the thirty-fifth State Party, of twenty-three experts of high moral standing and competence in the field covered by the Convention. The experts shall be elected by States Parties from among their nationals and shall serve in their personal capacity, consideration being given to equitable geographical distribution and to the representation of the different forms of civilization as well as the principal legal systems.

2. The members of the Committee shall be elected by secret ballot from a list of persons nominated by States Parties. Each State Party may nominate one person from among its own nationals.

3. The initial election shall be held six months after the date of the entry into force of the present Convention. At least three months before the date of each election the Secretary-General of the United Nations shall address a letter to the States Parties inviting them to submit their nominations within two months. The Secretary-General shall prepare a list in

alphabetical order of all persons thus nominated, indicating the States Parties which have nominated them, and shall submit it to the States Parties.

4. Elections of the members of the Committee shall be held at a meeting of States Parties convened by the Secretary-General at United Nations Headquarters. At that meeting, for which two thirds of the States Parties shall constitute a quorum, the persons elected to the Committee shall be those nominees who obtain the largest number of votes and an absolute majority of the votes of the representatives of States Parties present and voting.

5. The members of the Committee shall be elected for a term of four years. However, the terms of nine of the members elected at the first election shall expire at the end of two years; immediately after the first election the names of these nine members shall be chosen by lot by the Chairman of the Committee.

6. The election of the five additional members of the Committee shall be held in accordance with the provisions of paragraphs 2, 3 and 4 of this article, following the thirty-fifth ratification or accession. The terms of two of the additional members elected on this occasion shall expire at the end of two years, the names of these two members having been chosen by lot by the Chairman of the Committee.

7. For the filling of casual vacancies, the State Party whose expert has ceased to function as a member of the Committee shall appoint another expert from among its nationals, subject to the approval of the Committee.

8. The members of the Committee shall, with the approval of the General Assembly, receive emoluments from United Nations resources on such terms and conditions as the Assembly may decide, having regard to the importance of the Committee's responsibilities.

9. The Secretary-General of the United Nations shall provide the necessary staff and facilities for the effective performance of the functions of the Committee under the present Convention.

Article 18

1. States Parties undertake to submit to the Secretary-General of the United Nations, for consideration by the Committee, a report on the

legislative, judicial, administrative or other measures which they have adopted to give effect to he provisions of the present Convention and on the progress made in this respect:

a) Within one year after the entry into force for the State concerned; and

b) Thereafter at least every four years and further whenever the Committee so requests.

2. Reports may indicate factors and difficulties affecting the degree of fulfilment of obligations under the present Convention.

Article 19

1. The Committee shall adopt its own rules of procedure.

2. The Committee shall elect its officers for a term of two years.

Article 20

1. The Committee shall normally meet for a period of not more than two weeks annually in order to consider the reports submitted in accordance with article 18 of the present Convention.

2. The meetings of the Committee shall normally be held at United Nations Headquarters or at any other convenient place as determined by the Committee.

Article 21

1. The Committee shall, through the Economic and Social Council, report annually to the General Assembly of the United Nations on its activities and may make suggestions and general recommendations based on the examination of reports and information received from the States Parties. Such suggestions and general recommendations shall be included in the report of the Committee together with comments, if any, from States Parties.

2. The Secretary-General shall transmit the reports of the Committee to the Commission on the Status of Women for its information.

Article 22

The specialized agencies shall be entitled to be represented at the consideration of the implementation of such provisions of the present

Convention as fall within the scope of their activities. The Committee may invite the specialized agencies to submit reports on the implementation of the Convention in areas falling within the scope of their activities.

PART VI

Article 23

Nothing in this Convention shall affect any provisions that are more conducive to the achievement of equality between men and women which may be contained:

a)   In the legislation of a State Party; or

b)   In any other international convention, treaty or agreement in force for that State.

Article 24

States Parties undertake to adopt all necessary measures at the national level aimed at achieving the full realization of the rights recognized in the present Convention.

Article 25

1. The present Convention shall be open for signature by all States.

2. The Secretary-General of the United Nations is designated as the depositary of the present Convention.

3. The present Convention is subject to ratification. Instruments of ratification shall be deposited with the Secretary-General of the United Nations.

4. The present Convention shall be open to accession by all States. Accession shall be effected by the deposit of an instrument of accession with the Secretary-General of the United Nations.

Article 26

1. A request for the revision of the present Convention may be made at any time by any State Party by means of a notification in writing addressed to the Secretary-General of the United Nations.

2. The General Assembly of the United Nations shall decide upon the steps, if any, to be taken in respect of such a request.

Article 27

1. The present Convention shall enter into force on the thirtieth day after the date of deposit with the Secretary-General of the United Nations of the twentieth instrument of ratification or accession.

2. For each State ratifying the present Convention or acceding to it after the deposit of the twentieth instrument of ratification or accession, the Convention shall enter into force on the thirtieth day after the date of the deposit of its own instrument of ratification or accession.

Article 28

1. The Secretary-General of the United Nations shall receive and circulate to all States the text of reservations made by States at the time of ratification or accession.

2. A reservation incompatible with the object and purpose of the present Convention shall not be permitted.

3. Reservations may be withdrawn at any time by notification to this effect addressed to the Secretary-General of the United Nations, who shall then inform all States thereof. Such notification shall take effect on the date on which it is received.

Article 29

1. Any dispute between two or more States Parties concerning the interpretation or application of the present Convention which is not settled by negotiation shall, at the request of one of them, be submitted to arbitration. If within six months from the date of the request for arbitration the parties are unable to agree on the organization of the arbitration, any one of those parties may refer the dispute to the International Court of Justice by request in conformity with the Statute of the Court.

2. Each State Party may at the time of signature or ratification of this Convention or accession thereto declare that it does not consider itself bound by paragraph 1 of this article. The other States Parties shall not be bound by that paragraph with respect to any State Party which has made such a reservation.

3. Any State Party which has made a reservation in accordance with paragraph 2 of this article may at any time withdraw that reservation by notification to the Secretary-General of the United Nations.

Article 30

The present Convention, the Arabic, Chinese, English, French, Russian and Spanish texts of which are equally authentic, shall be deposited with the Secretary-General of the United Nations.

IN WITNESS WHEREOF the undersigned, duly authorized, have signed the present Convention

Optional Protocol to the Convention on the Elimination of All Forms of Discrimination against Women

Adopted and opened for signature, ratification and accession by General Assembly resolution 54/4 of 6 October 1999

The States Parties to the present Protocol,

Noting that the Charter of the United Nations reaffirms faith in fundamental human rights, in the dignity and worth of the human person and in the equal rights of men and women,

Also noting that the Universal Declaration of Human Rights proclaims that all human beings are born free and equal in dignity and rights and that everyone is entitled to all the rights and freedoms set forth therein, without distinction of any kind, including distinction based on sex,

Recalling that the International Covenants on Human Rights and other international human rights instruments prohibit discrimination on the basis of sex,

Also recalling the Convention on the Elimination of All Forms of Discrimination against Women ("the Convention"), in which the States Parties thereto condemn discrimination against women in all its forms and agree to pursue by all appropriate means and without delay a policy of eliminating discrimination against women,

Reaffirming their determination to ensure the full and equal enjoyment by women of all human rights and fundamental freedoms and to take effective action to prevent violations of these rights and freedoms,

Have agreed as follows:

Article 1

A State Party to the present Protocol ("State Party") recognizes the competence of the Committee on the Elimination of Discrimination against Women ("the Committee") to receive and consider communications submitted in accordance with article 2.

Article 2

Communications may be submitted by or on behalf of individuals or groups of individuals, under the jurisdiction of a State Party, claiming to be victims of a violation of any of the rights set forth in the Convention by that State Party. Where a communication is submitted on behalf of individuals or groups of individuals, this shall be with their consent unless the author can justify acting on their behalf without such consent.

Article 3

Communications shall be in writing and shall not be anonymous. No communication shall be received by the Committee if it concerns a State Party to the Convention that is not a party to the present Protocol.

Article 4

1. The Committee shall not consider a communication unless it has ascertained that all available domestic remedies have been exhausted unless the application of such remedies is unreasonably prolonged or unlikely to bring effective relief.

2. The Committee shall declare a communication inadmissible where:

a) The same matter has already been examined by the Committee or has been or is being examined under another procedure of international investigation or settlement;

b) It is incompatible with the provisions of the Convention;

c) It is manifestly ill-founded or not sufficiently substantiated;

d) It is an abuse of the right to submit a communication;

e) The facts that are the subject of the communication occurred prior to the entry into force of the present Protocol for the State Party concerned unless those facts continued after that date.

Article 5

1. At any time after the receipt of a communication and before a determination on the merits has been reached, the Committee may transmit to the State Party concerned for its urgent con-

268

sideration a request that the State Party take such interim measures as may be necessary to avoid possible irreparable damage to the victim or victims of the alleged violation.

2. Where the Committee exercises its discretion under paragraph 1 of the present article, this does not imply a determination on admissibility or on the merits of the communication.

Article 6

1. Unless the Committee considers a communication inadmissible without reference to the State Party concerned, and provided that the individual or individuals consent to the disclosure of their identity to that State Party, the Committee shall bring any communication submitted to it under the present Protocol confidentially to the attention of the State Party concerned.

2. Within six months, the receiving State Party shall submit to the Committee written explanations or statements clarifying the matter and the remedy, if any, that may have been provided by that State Party.

Article 7

1. The Committee shall consider communications received under the present Protocol in the light of all information made available to it by or on behalf of individuals or groups of individuals and by the State Party concerned, provided that this information is transmitted to the parties concerned.

2. The Committee shall hold closed meetings when examining communications under the present Protocol.

3. After examining a communication, the Committee shall transmit its views on the communication, together with its recommendations, if any, to the parties concerned.

4. The State Party shall give due consideration to the views of the Committee, together with its recommendations, if any, and shall submit to the Committee, within six months, a written response, including information on any action taken in the light of the views and recommendations of the Committee.

5. The Committee may invite the State Party to submit further information about any measures the State Party has taken in response to its views or recommendations, if any, including as

deemed appropriate by the Committee, in the State Party's subsequent reports under article 18 of the Convention.

Article 8

1. If the Committee receives reliable information indicating grave or systematic violations by a State Party of rights set forth in the Convention, the Committee shall invite that State Party to cooperate in the examination of the information and to this end to submit observations with regard to the information concerned.

2. Taking into account any observations that may have been submitted by the State Party concerned as well as any other reliable information available to it, the Committee may designate one or more of its members to conduct an inquiry and to report urgently to the Committee. Where warranted and with the consent of the State Party, the inquiry may include a visit to its territory.

3. After examining the findings of such an inquiry, the Committee shall transmit these findings to the State Party concerned together with any comments and recommendations.

4. The State Party concerned shall, within six months of receiving the findings, comments and recommendations transmitted by the Committee, submit its observations to the Committee.

5. Such an inquiry shall be conducted confidentially and the cooperation of the State Party shall be sought at all stages of the proceedings.

Article 9

1. The Committee may invite the State Party concerned to include in its report under article 18 of the Convention details of any measures taken in response to an inquiry conducted under article 8 of the present Protocol.

2. The Committee may, if necessary, after the end of the period of six months referred to in article 8.4, invite the State Party concerned to inform it of the measures taken in response to such an inquiry.

Article 10

1. Each State Party may, at the time of signature or ratification of the present Protocol or accession thereto, declare that it does not recognize the competence of the Committee provided for in articles 8 and 9.

2. Any State Party having made a declaration in accordance with paragraph 1 of the present article may, at any time, withdraw this declaration by notification to the Secretary-General.

Article 11

A State Party shall take all appropriate steps to ensure that individuals under its jurisdiction are not subjected to ill treatment or intimidation as a consequence of communicating with the Committee pursuant to the present Protocol.

Article 12

The Committee shall include in its annual report under article 21 of the Convention a summary of its activities under the present Protocol.

Article 13

Each State Party undertakes to make widely known and to give publicity to the Convention and the present Protocol and to facilitate access to information about the views and recommendations of the Committee, in particular, on matters involving that State Party.

Article 14

The Committee shall develop its own rules of procedure to be followed when exercising the functions conferred on it by the present Protocol.

Article 15

1. The present Protocol shall be open for signature by any State that has signed, ratified or acceded to the Convention.

2. The present Protocol shall be subject to ratification by any State that has ratified or acceded to the Convention. Instruments of ratification shall be deposited with the Secretary-General of the United Nations.

3. The present Protocol shall be open to accession by any State that has ratified or acceded to the Convention.

4. Accession shall be effected by the deposit of an instrument of accession with the Secretary-General of the United Nations.

Article 16

1. The present Protocol shall enter into force three months after the date of the deposit with the Secretary-General of the United Nations of the tenth instrument of ratification or accession.

2. For each State ratifying the present Protocol or acceding to it after its entry into force, the present Protocol shall enter into force three months after the date of the deposit of its own instrument of ratification or accession.

Article 17

No reservations to the present Protocol shall be permitted.

Article 18

1. Any State Party may propose an amendment to the present Protocol and file it with the Secretary-General of the United Nations. The Secretary-General shall thereupon communicate any proposed amendments to the States Parties with a request that they notify her or him whether they favour a conference of States Parties for the purpose of considering and voting on the proposal. In the event that at least one third of the States Parties favour such a conference, the Secretary-General shall convene the conference under the auspices of the United Nations. Any amendment adopted by a majority of the States Parties present and voting at the conference shall be submitted to the General Assembly of the United Nations for approval.

2. Amendments shall come into force when they have been approved by the General Assembly of the United Nations and accepted by a two-thirds majority of the States Parties to the present Protocol in accordance with their respective constitutional processes.

3. When amendments come into force, they shall be binding on those States Parties that have accepted them, other States Parties still being bound by the provisions of the present Protocol and any earlier amendments that they have accepted.

Article 19

1. Any State Party may denounce the present Protocol at any time by written notification addressed to the Secretary-General of the United Nations. Denunciation shall take effect six months after the date of receipt of the notification by the Secretary-General.

2. Denunciation shall be without prejudice to the continued application of the provisions of the present Protocol to any communication submitted under article 2 or any inquiry initiated under article 8 before the effective date of denunciation.

Article 20

The Secretary-General of the United Nations shall inform all States of:

a) Signatures, ratifications and accessions under the present Protocol;

b) The date of entry into force of the present Protocol and of any amendment under article 18;

c) Any denunciation under article 19.

Article 21

1. The present Protocol, of which the Arabic, Chinese, English, French, Russian and Spanish texts are equally authentic, shall be deposited in the archives of the United Nations.

2. The Secretary-General of the United Nations shall transmit certified copies of the present Protocol to all States referred to in article 25 of the Convention.

Convention on the Rights of the Child
Adopted by General Assembly resolution 44/25 of 20 November 1989.

The States Parties to the present Convention,

Considering that, in accordance with the principles proclaimed in the Charter of the United Nations, recognition of the inherent dignity and of the equal and inalienable rights of all members of the human family is the foundation of freedom, justice and peace in the world,

Bearing in mind that the peoples of the United Nations have, in the Charter, reaffirmed their faith in fundamental human rights and in the dignity and worth of the human person, and have determined to promote social progress and better standards of life in larger freedom,

Recognizing that the United Nations has, in the Universal Declaration of Human Rights and in the International Covenants on Human Rights, proclaimed and agreed that everyone is entitled to all the rights and freedoms set forth therein, without distinction of any kind, such as race, colour, sex, language, religion, political or other opinion, national or social origin, property, birth or other status,

Recalling that, in the Universal Declaration of Human Rights, the United Nations has proclaimed that childhood is entitled to special care and assistance,

Convinced that the family, as the fundamental group of society and the natural environment for the growth and well-being of all its members and particularly children, should be afforded the necessary protection and assistance so that it can fully assume its responsibilities within the community,

Recognizing that the child, for the full and harmonious development of his or her personality, should grow up in a family environment, in an atmosphere of happiness, love and understanding,

Considering that the child should be fully prepared to live an individual life in society, and brought up in the spirit of the ideals proclaimed in the Charter of the United Nations, and in particular in the spirit of peace, dignity, tolerance, freedom, equality and solidarity,

Bearing in mind that the need to extend particular care to the child has been stated in the Geneva Declaration of the Rights of the Child of 1924 and in the Declaration of the Rights of the Child adopted by the General Assembly on 20 November 1959 and recognized in the Universal Declaration of Human Rights, in the International Covenant on Civil and Political Rights (in particular in articles 23 and 24), in the International Covenant on Economic, Social and Cultural Rights (in particular in article 10) and in the statutes and relevant instruments of specialized agencies and international organizations concerned with the welfare of children,

Bearing in mind that, as indicated in the Declaration of the Rights of the Child, "the child, by reason of his physical and mental immaturity, needs special safeguards and care, including appropriate legal protection, before as well as after birth,

Recalling the provisions of the Declaration on Social and Legal Principles relating to the Protection and Welfare of Children, with Special Reference to Foster Placement and Adoption Nationally and Internationally; the United Nations Standard Minimum Rules for the Administration of Juvenile Justice (The Beijing Rules); and the Declaration on the Protection of Women and Children in Emergency and Armed Conflict,

Recognizing that, in all countries in the world, there are children living in exceptionally difficult conditions, and that such children need special consideration,

Taking due account of the importance of the traditions and cultural values of each people for the protection and harmonious development of the child,

Recognizing the importance of international co-operation for improving the living conditions of children in every country, in particular in the developing countries,

Have agreed as follows:

PART I

Article 1

For the purposes of the present Convention, a child means every human being below the age of eighteen years unless under the law applicable to the child, majority is attained earlier.

Article 2

1. States Parties shall respect and ensure the rights set forth in the present Convention to each child within their jurisdiction without discrimination of any kind, irrespective of the child's or his or her parent's or legal guardian's race, colour, sex, language, religion, political or other opinion, national, ethnic or social origin, property, disability, birth or other status.

2. States Parties shall take all appropriate measures to ensure that the child is protected against all forms of discrimination or punishment on the basis of the status, activities, expressed opinions, or beliefs of the child's parents, legal guardians, or family members.

Article 3

1. In all actions concerning children, whether undertaken by public or private social welfare institutions, courts of law, administrative authorities or legislative bodies, the best interests of the child shall be a primary consideration.

2. States Parties undertake to ensure the child such protection and care as is necessary for his or her well-being, taking into account the rights and duties of his or her parents, legal guardians, or other individuals legally responsible for him or her, and, to this end, shall take all appropriate legislative and administrative measures.

3. States Parties shall ensure that the institutions, services and facilities responsible for the care or protection of children shall conform with the standards established by competent authorities, particularly in the areas of safety, health, in the number and suitability of their staff, as well as competent supervision.

Article 4

States Parties shall undertake all appropriate legislative, administrative, and other measures for the implementation of the rights recognized in the present Convention. With regard to economic, social and cultural rights, States Parties shall undertake such measures to the maximum extent of their available resources and, where needed, within the framework of international co-operation.

Article 5

States Parties shall respect the responsibilities, rights and duties of parents or, where applicable, the members of the extended family or community as provided for by local custom, legal guardians or other persons legally responsible for the child, to provide, in a manner consistent with the evolving capacities of the child, appropriate direction and guidance in the exercise by the child of the rights recognized in the present Convention.

Article 6

1. States Parties recognize that every child has the inherent right to life.

2. States Parties shall ensure to the maximum extent possible the survival and development of the child.

Article 7

1. The child shall be registered immediately after birth and shall have the right from birth to a name, the right to acquire a nationality and. as far as possible, the right to know and be cared for by his or her parents.

2. States Parties shall ensure the implementation of these rights in accordance with their national law and their obligations under the relevant international instruments in this field, in particular where the child would otherwise be stateless.

Article 8

1. States Parties undertake to respect the right of the child to preserve his or her identity, including nationality, name and family relations as recognized by law without unlawful interference.

2. Where a child is illegally deprived of some or all of the elements of his or her identity, States Parties shall provide

appropriate assistance and protection, with a view to re-establishing speedily his or her identity.

Article 9

1. States Parties shall ensure that a child shall not be separated from his or her parents against their will, except when competent authorities subject to judicial review determine, in accordance with applicable law and procedures, that such separation is necessary for the best interests of the child. Such determination may be necessary in a particular case such as one involving abuse or neglect of the child by the parents, or one where the parents are living separately and a decision must be made as to the child's place of residence.

2. In any proceedings pursuant to paragraph 1 of the present article, all interested parties shall be given an opportunity to participate in the proceedings and make their views known.

3. States Parties shall respect the right of the child who is separated from one or both parents to maintain personal relations and direct contact with both parents on a regular basis, except if it is contrary to the child's best interests.

4. Where such separation results from any action initiated by a State Party, such as the detention, imprisonment, exile, deportation or death (including death arising from any cause while the person is in the custody of the State) of one or both parents or of the child, that State Party shall, upon request, provide the parents, the child or, if appropriate, another member of the family with the essential information concerning the whereabouts of the absent member(s) of the family unless the provision of the information would be detrimental to the well-being of the child. States Parties shall further ensure that the submission of such a request shall of itself entail no adverse consequences for the person(s) concerned.

Article 10

1. In accordance with the obligation of States Parties under article 9, paragraph 1, applications by a child or his or her parents to enter or leave a State Party for the purpose of family reunification shall be dealt with by States Parties in a positive, humane and expeditious manner. States Parties shall further ensure that the submission of such a request shall entail no

adverse consequences for the applicants and for the members of their family.

2. A child whose parents reside in different States shall have the right to maintain on a regular basis, save in exceptional circumstances personal relations and direct contacts with both parents. Towards that end and in accordance with the obligation of States Parties under article 9, paragraph 1, States Parties shall respect the right of the child and his or her parents to leave any country, including their own, and to enter their own country. The right to leave any country shall be subject only to such restrictions as are prescribed by law and which are necessary to protect the national security, public order (ordre public), public health or morals or the rights and freedoms of others and are consistent with the other rights recognized in the present Convention.

Article 11

1. States Parties shall take measures to combat the illicit transfer and non-return of children abroad.

2. To this end, States Parties shall promote the conclusion of bilateral or multilateral agreements or accession to existing agreements.

Article 12

1. States Parties shall assure to the child who is capable of forming his or her own views the right to express those views freely in all matters affecting the child, the views of the child being given due weight in accordance with the age and maturity of the child.

2. For this purpose, the child shall in particular be provided the opportunity to be heard in any judicial and administrative proceedings affecting the child, either directly, or through a representative or an appropriate body, in a manner consistent with the procedural rules of national law.

Article 13

1. The child shall have the right to freedom of expression; this right shall include freedom to seek, receive and impart information and ideas of all kinds, regardless of frontiers, either

orally, in writing or in print, in the form of art, or through any other media of the child's choice.

2. The exercise of this right may be subject to certain restrictions, but these shall only be such as are provided by law and are necessary:

d) For respect of the rights or reputations of others; or

e) For the protection of national security or of public order (ordre public), or of public health or morals.

Article 14

1. States Parties shall respect the right of the child to freedom of thought, conscience and religion.

2. States Parties shall respect the rights and duties of the parents and, when applicable, legal guardians, to provide direction to the child in the exercise of his or her right in a manner consistent with the evolving capacities of the child.

3. Freedom to manifest one's religion or beliefs may be subject only to such limitations as are prescribed by law and are necessary to protect public safety, order, health or morals, or the fundamental rights and freedoms of others.

Article 15

1. States Parties recognize the rights of the child to freedom of association and to freedom of peaceful assembly.

2. No restrictions may be placed on the exercise of these rights other than those imposed in conformity with the law and which are necessary in a democratic society in the interests of national security or public safety, public order (ordre public), the protection of public health or morals or the protection of the rights and freedoms of others.

Article 16

1. No child shall be subjected to arbitrary or unlawful interference with his or her privacy, family, home or correspondence, nor to unlawful attacks on his or her honour and reputation.

2. The child has the right to the protection of the law against such interference or attacks.

Article 17

States Parties recognize the important function performed by the mass media and shall ensure that the child has access to information and material from a diversity of national and international sources, especially those aimed at the promotion of his or her social, spiritual and moral well-being and physical and mental health. To this end, States Parties shall:

f)   Encourage the mass media to disseminate information and material of social and cultural benefit to the child and in accordance with the spirit of article 29;

g)   Encourage international co-operation in the production, exchange and dissemination of such information and material from a diversity of cultural, national and international sources;

h)   Encourage the production and dissemination of children's books;

i)   Encourage the mass media to have particular regard to the linguistic needs of the child who belongs to a minority group or who is indigenous;

j)   Encourage the development of appropriate guidelines for the protection of the child from information and material injurious to his or her well-being, bearing in mind the provisions of articles 13 and 18.

Article 18

1. States Parties shall use their best efforts to ensure recognition of the principle that both parents have common responsibilities for the upbringing and development of the child. Parents or, as the case may be, legal guardians, have the primary responsibility for the upbringing and development of the child. The best interests of the child will be their basic concern.

2. For the purpose of guaranteeing and promoting the rights set forth in the present Convention, States Parties shall render appropriate assistance to parents and legal guardians in the performance of their child-rearing responsibilities and shall ensure the development of institutions, facilities and services for the care of children.

3. States Parties shall take all appropriate measures to ensure that children of working parents have the right to benefit from child-care services and facilities for which they are eligible.

Article 19

1. States Parties shall take all appropriate legislative, administrative, social and educational measures to protect the child from all forms of physical or mental violence, injury or abuse, neglect or negligent treatment, maltreatment or exploitation, including sexual abuse, while in the care of parent(s), legal guardian(s) or any other person who has the care of the child.

2. Such protective measures should, as appropriate, include effective procedures for the establishment of social programmes to provide necessary support for the child and for those who have the care of the child, as well as for other forms of prevention and for identification, reporting, referral, investigation, treatment and follow-up of instances of child maltreatment described heretofore, and, as appropriate, for judicial involvement.

Article 20

1. A child temporarily or permanently deprived of his or her family environment, or in whose own best interests cannot be allowed to remain in that environment, shall be entitled to special protection and assistance provided by the State.

2. States Parties shall in accordance with their national laws ensure alternative care for such a child.

3. Such care could include, inter alia, foster placement, kafalah of Islamic law, adoption or if necessary placement in suitable institutions for the care of children. When considering solutions, due regard shall be paid to the desirability of continuity in a child's upbringing and to the child's ethnic, religious, cultural and linguistic background.

Article 21

States Parties that recognize and/or permit the system of adoption shall ensure that the best interests of the child shall be the paramount consideration and they shall:

k) Ensure that the adoption of a child is authorized only by competent authorities who determine, in accordance with

applicable law and procedures and on the basis of all pertinent and reliable information, that the adoption is permissible in view of the child's status concerning parents,
relatives and legal guardians and that, if required, the persons concerned have given their informed consent to the
adoption on the basis of such counselling as may be necessary;

l) Recognize that inter-country adoption may be considered
as an alternative means of child's care, if the child cannot
be placed in a foster or an adoptive family or cannot in
any suitable manner be cared for in the child's country of
origin;

m) Ensure that the child concerned by inter-country adoption
enjoys safeguards and standards equivalent to those existing in the case of national adoption;

n) Take all appropriate measures to ensure that, in inter-
country adoption, the placement does not result in improper financial gain for those involved in it;

o) Promote, where appropriate, the objectives of the present
article by concluding bilateral or multilateral arrangements or agreements, and endeavour, within this framework, to ensure that the placement of the child in another
country is carried out by competent authorities or organs.

Article 22

1. States Parties shall take appropriate measures to ensure that
a child who is seeking refugee status or who is considered a
refugee in accordance with applicable international or domestic law and procedures shall, whether unaccompanied or accompanied by his or her parents or by any other person,
receive appropriate protection and humanitarian assistance in
the enjoyment of applicable rights set forth in the present Convention and in other international human rights or humanitarian instruments to which the said States are Parties.

2. For this purpose, States Parties shall provide, as they consider appropriate, co-operation in any efforts by the United
Nations and other competent intergovernmental organizations
or non-governmental organizations co-operating with the
United Nations to protect and assist such a child and to trace

the parents or other members of the family of any refugee child in order to obtain information necessary for reunification with his or her family. In cases where no parents or other members of the family can be found, the child shall be accorded the same protection as any other child permanently or temporarily deprived of his or her family environment for any reason , as set forth in the present Convention.

Article 23

1. States Parties recognize that a mentally or physically disabled child should enjoy a full and decent life, in conditions which ensure dignity, promote self-reliance and facilitate the child's active participation in the community.

2. States Parties recognize the right of the disabled child to special care and shall encourage and ensure the extension, subject to available resources, to the eligible child and those responsible for his or her care, of assistance for which application is made and which is appropriate to the child's condition and to the circumstances of the parents or others caring for the child. 3. Recognizing the special needs of a disabled child, assistance extended in accordance with paragraph 2 of the present article shall be provided free of charge, whenever possible, taking into account the financial resources of the parents or others caring for the child, and shall be designed to ensure that the disabled child has effective access to and receives education, training, health care services, rehabilitation services, preparation for employment and recreation opportunities in a manner conducive to the child's achieving the fullest possible social integration and individual development, including his or her cultural and spiritual development

4. States Parties shall promote, in the spirit of international cooperation, the exchange of appropriate information in the field of preventive health care and of medical, psychological and functional treatment of disabled children, including dissemination of and access to information concerning methods of rehabilitation, education and vocational services, with the aim of enabling States Parties to improve their capabilities and skills and to widen their experience in these areas. In this regard, particular account shall be taken of the needs of developing countries.

Article 24

1. States Parties recognize the right of the child to the enjoyment of the highest attainable standard of health and to facilities for the treatment of illness and rehabilitation of health. States Parties shall strive to ensure that no child is deprived of his or her right of access to such health care services.

2. States Parties shall pursue full implementation of this right and, in particular, shall take appropriate measures:

a) To diminish infant and child mortality;

b) To ensure the provision of necessary medical assistance and health care to all children with emphasis on the development of primary health care;

c) To combat disease and malnutrition, including within the framework of primary health care, through, inter alia, the application of readily available technology and through the provision of adequate nutritious foods and clean drinking-water, taking into consideration the dangers and risks of environmental pollution;

d) To ensure appropriate pre-natal and post-natal health care for mothers;

e) To ensure that all segments of society, in particular parents and children, are informed, have access to education and are supported in the use of basic knowledge of child health and nutrition, the advantages of breastfeeding, hygiene and environmental sanitation and the prevention of accidents;

f) To develop preventive health care, guidance for parents and family planning education and services.

3. States Parties shall take all effective and appropriate measures with a view to abolishing traditional practices prejudicial to the health of children.

4. States Parties undertake to promote and encourage international co-operation with a view to achieving progressively the full realization of the right recognized in the present article. In this regard, particular account shall be taken of the needs of developing countries.

Article 25

States Parties recognize the right of a child who has been placed by the competent authorities for the purposes of care, protection or treatment of his or her physical or mental health, to a periodic review of the treatment provided to the child and all other circumstances relevant to his or her placement.

Article 26

1. States Parties shall recognize for every child the right to benefit from social security, including social insurance, and shall take the necessary measures to achieve the full realization of this right in accordance with their national law.

2. The benefits should, where appropriate, be granted, taking into account the resources and the circumstances of the child and persons having responsibility for the maintenance of the child, as well as any other consideration relevant to an application for benefits made by or on behalf of the child.

Article 27

1. States Parties recognize the right of every child to a standard of living adequate for the child's physical, mental, spiritual, moral and social development.

2. The parent(s) or others responsible for the child have the primary responsibility to secure, within their abilities and financial capacities, the conditions of living necessary for the child's development.

3. States Parties, in accordance with national conditions and within their means, shall take appropriate measures to assist parents and others responsible for the child to implement this right and shall in case of need provide material assistance and support programmes, particularly with regard to nutrition, clothing and housing.

4. States Parties shall take all appropriate measures to secure the recovery of maintenance for the child from the parents or other persons having financial responsibility for the child, both within the State Party and from abroad. In particular, where the person having financial responsibility for the child lives in a State different from that of the child, States Parties shall promote the accession to international agreements or the con-

clusion of such agreements, as well as the making of other appropriate arrangements.

Article 28

1. States Parties recognize the right of the child to education, and with a view to achieving this right progressively and on the basis of equal opportunity, they shall, in particular:

a) Make primary education compulsory and available free to all;

b) Encourage the development of different forms of secondary education, including general and vocational education, make them available and accessible to every child, and take appropriate measures such as the introduction of free education and offering financial assistance in case of need;

c) Make higher education accessible to all on the basis of capacity by every appropriate means;

d) Make educational and vocational information and guidance available and accessible to all children;

e) Take measures to encourage regular attendance at schools and the reduction of drop-out rates.

2. States Parties shall take all appropriate measures to ensure that school discipline is administered in a manner consistent with the child's human dignity and in conformity with the present Convention.

3. States Parties shall promote and encourage international cooperation in matters relating to education, in particular with a view to contributing to the elimination of ignorance and illiteracy throughout the world and facilitating access to scientific and technical knowledge and modern teaching methods. In this regard, particular account shall be taken of the needs of developing countries.

Article 29

1. States Parties agree that the education of the child shall be directed to:

a) The development of the child's personality, talents and mental and physical abilities to their fullest potential;

b)   The development of respect for human rights and fundamental freedoms, and for the principles enshrined in the Charter of the United Nations;

c)   The development of respect for the child's parents, his or her own cultural identity, language and values, for the national values of the country in which the child is living, the country from which he or she may originate, and for civilizations different from his or her own;

d)   The preparation of the child for responsible life in a free society, in the spirit of understanding, peace, tolerance, equality of sexes, and friendship among all peoples, ethnic, national and religious groups and persons of indigenous origin;

e)   The development of respect for the natural environment.

2. No part of the present article or article 28 shall be construed so as to interfere with the liberty of individuals and bodies to establish and direct educational institutions, subject always to the observance of the principle set forth in paragraph 1 of the present article and to the requirements that the education given in such institutions shall conform to such minimum standards as may be laid down by the State.

Article 30

In those States in which ethnic, religious or linguistic minorities or persons of indigenous origin exist, a child belonging to such a minority or who is indigenous shall not be denied the right, in community with other members of his or her group, to enjoy his or her own culture, to profess and practise his or her own religion, or to use his or her own language.

Article 31

1. States Parties recognize the right of the child to rest and leisure, to engage in play and recreational activities appropriate to the age of the child and to participate freely in cultural life and the arts.

2. States Parties shall respect and promote the right of the child to participate fully in cultural and artistic life and shall encourage the provision of appropriate and equal opportunities for cultural, artistic, recreational and leisure activity.

Article 32

1. States Parties recognize the right of the child to be protected from economic exploitation and from performing any work that is likely to be hazardous or to interfere with the child's education, or to be harmful to the child's health or physical, mental, spiritual, moral or social development.

2. States Parties shall take legislative, administrative, social and educational measures to ensure the implementation of the present article. To this end, and having regard to the relevant provisions of other international instruments, States Parties shall in particular:

a)   Provide for a minimum age or minimum ages for admission to employment;

b)   Provide for appropriate regulation of the hours and conditions of employment;

c)   Provide for appropriate penalties or other sanctions to ensure the effective enforcement of the present article.

Article 33

States Parties shall take all appropriate measures, including legislative, administrative, social and educational measures, to protect children from the illicit use of narcotic drugs and psychotropic substances as defined in the relevant international treaties, and to prevent the use of children in the illicit production and trafficking of such substances.

Article 34

States Parties undertake to protect the child from all forms of sexual exploitation and sexual abuse. For these purposes, States Parties shall in particular take all appropriate national, bilateral and multilateral measures to prevent:

a)   The inducement or coercion of a child to engage in any unlawful sexual activity;

b)   The exploitative use of children in prostitution or other unlawful sexual practices;

c)   The exploitative use of children in pornographic performances and materials.

Article 35

States Parties shall take all appropriate national, bilateral and multilateral measures to prevent the abduction of, the sale of or traffic in children for any purpose or in any form.

Article 36

States Parties shall protect the child against all other forms of exploitation prejudicial to any aspects of the child's welfare.

Article 37

States Parties shall ensure that:

a) No child shall be subjected to torture or other cruel, inhuman or degrading treatment or punishment. Neither capital punishment nor life imprisonment without possibility of release shall be imposed for offences committed by persons below eighteen years of age;

b) No child shall be deprived of his or her liberty unlawfully or arbitrarily. The arrest, detention or imprisonment of a child shall be in conformity with the law and shall be used only as a measure of last resort and for the shortest appropriate period of time;

c) Every child deprived of liberty shall be treated with humanity and respect for the inherent dignity of the human person, and in a manner which takes into account the needs of persons of his or her age. In particular, every child deprived of liberty shall be separated from adults unless it is considered in the child's best interest not to do so and shall have the right to maintain contact with his or her family through correspondence and visits, save in exceptional circumstances;

d) Every child deprived of his or her liberty shall have the right to prompt access to legal and other appropriate assistance, as well as the right to challenge the legality of the deprivation of his or her liberty before a court or other competent, independent and impartial authority, and to a prompt decision on any such action.

Article 38

1. States Parties undertake to respect and to ensure respect for rules of international humanitarian law applicable to them in armed conflicts which are relevant to the child.

2. States Parties shall take all feasible measures to ensure that persons who have not attained the age of fifteen years do not take a direct part in hostilities.

3. States Parties shall refrain from recruiting any person who has not attained the age of fifteen years into their armed forces. In recruiting among those persons who have attained the age of fifteen years but who have not attained the age of eighteen years, States Parties shall endeavour to give priority to those who are oldest.

4. In accordance with their obligations under international humanitarian law to protect the civilian population in armed conflicts, States Parties shall take all feasible measures to ensure protection and care of children who are affected by an armed conflict.

Article 39

States Parties shall take all appropriate measures to promote physical and psychological recovery and social reintegration of a child victim of: any form of neglect, exploitation, or abuse; torture or any other form of cruel, inhuman or degrading treatment or punishment; or armed conflicts. Such recovery and reintegration shall take place in an environment which fosters the health, self-respect and dignity of the child.

Article 40

1. States Parties recognize the right of every child alleged as, accused of, or recognized as having infringed the penal law to be treated in a manner consistent with the promotion of the child's sense of dignity and worth, which reinforces the child's respect for the human rights and fundamental freedoms of others and which takes into account the child's age and the desirability of promoting the child's reintegration and the child's assuming a constructive role in society.

2. To this end, and having regard to the relevant provisions of international instruments, States Parties shall, in particular, ensure that:

a) No child shall be alleged as, be accused of, or recognized as having infringed the penal law by reason of acts or omissions that were not prohibited by national or international law at the time they were committed;

b) Every child alleged as or accused of having infringed the penal law has at least the following guarantees:

   i) To be presumed innocent until proven guilty according to law;

   ii) To be informed promptly and directly of the charges against him or her, and, if appropriate, through his or her parents or legal guardians, and to have legal or other appropriate assistance in the preparation and presentation of his or her defence;

   iii) To have the matter determined without delay by a competent, independent and impartial authority or judicial body in a fair hearing according to law, in the presence of legal or other appropriate assistance and, unless it is considered not to be in the best interest of the child, in particular, taking into account his or her age or situation, his or her parents or legal guardians;

   iv) Not to be compelled to give testimony or to confess guilt; to examine or have examined adverse witnesses and to obtain the participation and examination of witnesses on his or her behalf under conditions of equality;

   v) If considered to have infringed the penal law, to have this decision and any measures imposed in consequence thereof reviewed by a higher competent, independent and impartial authority or judicial body according to law;

   vi) To have the free assistance of an interpreter if the child cannot understand or speak the language used;

   vii) To have his or her privacy fully respected at all stages of the proceedings.

3. States Parties shall seek to promote the establishment of laws, procedures, authorities and institutions specifically applicable to children alleged as, accused of, or recognized as having infringed the penal law, and, in particular:

c) The establishment of a minimum age below which children shall be presumed not to have the capacity to infringe the penal law;

d) Whenever appropriate and desirable, measures for dealing with such children without resorting to judicial proceedings, providing that human rights and legal safeguards are fully respected.

4. A variety of dispositions, such as care, guidance and supervision orders; counselling; probation; foster care; education and vocational training programmes and other alternatives to institutional care shall be available to ensure that children are dealt with in a manner appropriate to their well-being and proportionate both to their circumstances and the offence.

Article 41

Nothing in the present Convention shall affect any provisions which are more conducive to the realization of the rights of the child and which may be contained in:

a) The law of a State party; or

b) International law in force for that State.

PART II

Article 42

States Parties undertake to make the principles and provisions of the Convention widely known, by appropriate and active means, to adults and children alike.

Article 43

1. For the purpose of examining the progress made by States Parties in achieving the realization of the obligations undertaken in the present Convention, there shall be established a Committee on the Rights of the Child, which shall carry out the functions hereinafter provided.

2. The Committee shall consist of ten experts of high moral standing and recognized competence in the field covered by this Convention. The members of the Committee shall be elected by States Parties from among their nationals and shall serve in their personal capacity, consideration being given to equitable geographical distribution, as well as to the principal legal systems.

3. The members of the Committee shall be elected by secret ballot from a list of persons nominated by States Parties. Each State Party may nominate one person from among its own nationals.

4. The initial election to the Committee shall be held no later than six months after the date of the entry into force of the present Convention and thereafter every second year. At least four months before the date of each election, the Secretary-General of the United Nations shall address a letter to States Parties inviting them to submit their nominations within two months. The Secretary-General shall subsequently prepare a list in alphabetical order of all persons thus nominated, indicating States Parties which have nominated them, and shall submit it to the States Parties to the present Convention.

5. The elections shall be held at meetings of States Parties convened by the Secretary-General at United Nations Head-quarters. At those meetings, for which two thirds of States Parties shall constitute a quorum, the persons elected to the Committee shall be those who obtain the largest number of votes and an absolute majority of the votes of the representatives of States Parties present and voting.

6. The members of the Committee shall be elected for a term of four years. They shall be eligible for re-election if renominated. The term of five of the members elected at the first election shall expire at the end of two years; immediately after the first election, the names of these five members shall be chosen by lot by the Chairman of the meeting.

7. If a member of the Committee dies or resigns or declares that for any other cause he or she can no longer perform the duties of the Committee, the State Party which nominated the member shall appoint another expert from among its nationals

to serve for the remainder of the term, subject to the approval of the Committee.

8. The Committee shall establish its own rules of procedure.

9. The Committee shall elect its officers for a period of two years.

10. The meetings of the Committee shall normally be held at United Nations Headquarters or at any other convenient place as determined by the Committee. The Committee shall normally meet annually. The duration of the meetings of the Committee shall be determined, and reviewed, if necessary, by a meeting of the States Parties to the present Convention, subject to the approval of the General Assembly.

11. The Secretary-General of the United Nations shall provide the necessary staff and facilities for the effective performance of the functions of the Committee under the present Convention.

12. With the approval of the General Assembly, the members of the Committee established under the present Convention shall receive emoluments from United Nations resources on such terms and conditions as the Assembly may decide.

Article 44

1. States Parties undertake to submit to the Committee, through the Secretary-General of the United Nations, reports on the measures they have adopted which give effect to the rights recognized herein and on the progress made on the enjoyment of those rights:

a)   Within two years of the entry into force of the Convention for the State Party concerned;

b)   Thereafter every five years.

2. Reports made under the present article shall indicate factors and difficulties, if any, affecting the degree of fulfilment of the obligations under the present Convention. Reports shall also contain sufficient information to provide the Committee with a comprehensive understanding of the implementation of the Convention in the country concerned.

3. A State Party which has submitted a comprehensive initial report to the Committee need not, in its subsequent reports submitted in accordance with paragraph 1 (b) of the present article, repeat basic information previously provided.

4. The Committee may request from States Parties further information relevant to the implementation of the Convention.

5. The Committee shall submit to the General Assembly, through the Economic and Social Council, every two years, reports on its activities.

6. States Parties shall make their reports widely available to the public in their own countries.

Article 45

In order to foster the effective implementation of the Convention and to encourage international co-operation in the field covered by the Convention:

a) The specialized agencies, the United Nations Children's Fund, and other United Nations organs shall be entitled to be represented at the consideration of the implementation of such provisions of the present Convention as fall within the scope of their mandate. The Committee may invite the specialized agencies, the United Nations Children's Fund and other competent bodies as it may consider appropriate to provide expert advice on the implementation of the Convention in areas falling within the scope of their respective mandates. The Committee may invite the specialized agencies, the United Nations Children's Fund, and other United Nations organs to submit reports on the implementation of the Convention in areas falling within the scope of their activities;

b) The Committee shall transmit, as it may consider appropriate, to the specialized agencies, the United Nations Children's Fund and other competent bodies, any reports from States Parties that contain a request, or indicate a need, for technical advice or assistance, along with the Committee's observations and suggestions, if any, on these requests or indications;

c)   The Committee may recommend to the General Assembly to request the Secretary-General to undertake on its behalf studies on specific issues relating to the rights of the child;

d)   The Committee may make suggestions and general recommendations based on information received pursuant to articles 44 and 45 of the present Convention. Such suggestions and general recommendations shall be transmitted to any State Party concerned and reported to the General Assembly, together with comments, if any, from States Parties.

PART III

Article 46

The present Convention shall be open for signature by all States.

Article 47

The present Convention is subject to ratification. Instruments of ratification shall be deposited with the Secretary-General of the United Nations.

Article 48

The present Convention shall remain open for accession by any State. The instruments of accession shall be deposited with the Secretary-General of the United Nations.

Article 49

1. The present Convention shall enter into force on the thirtieth day following the date of deposit with the Secretary-General of the United Nations of the twentieth instrument of ratification or accession.

2. For each State ratifying or acceding to the Convention after the deposit of the twentieth instrument of ratification or accession, the Convention shall enter into force on the thirtieth day after the deposit by such State of its instrument of ratification or accession.

Article 50

1. Any State Party may propose an amendment and file it with the Secretary-General of the United Nations. The Secretary-

General shall thereupon communicate the proposed amendment to States Parties, with a request that they indicate whether they favour a conference of States Parties for the purpose of considering and voting upon the proposals. In the event that, within four months from the date of such communication, at least one third of the States Parties favour such a conference, the Secretary-General shall convene the conference under the auspices of the United Nations. Any amendment adopted by a majority of States Parties present and voting at the conference shall be submitted to the General Assembly for approval.

2. An amendment adopted in accordance with paragraph 1 of the present article shall enter into force when it has been approved by the General Assembly of the United Nations and accepted by a two-thirds majority of States Parties.

3. When an amendment enters into force, it shall be binding on those States Parties which have accepted it, other States Parties still being bound by the provisions of the present Convention and any earlier amendments which they have accepted.

Article 51

1. The Secretary-General of the United Nations shall receive and circulate to all States the text of reservations made by States at the time of ratification or accession.

2. A reservation incompatible with the object and purpose of the present Convention shall not be permitted.

3. Reservations may be withdrawn at any time by notification to that effect addressed to the Secretary-General of the United Nations, who shall then inform all States. Such notification shall take effect on the date on which it is received by the Secretary-General

Article 52

A State Party may denounce the present Convention by written notification to the Secretary-General of the United Nations. Denunciation becomes effective one year after the date of receipt of the notification by the Secretary-General.

Article 53

The Secretary-General of the United Nations is designated as the depositary of the present Convention.

Article 54

The original of the present Convention, of which the Arabic, Chinese, English, French, Russian and Spanish texts are equally authentic, shall be deposited with the Secretary-General of the United Nations.

IN WITNESS THEREOF the undersigned plenipotentiaries, being duly authorized thereto by their respective governments, have signed the present Convention.

Optional Protocol to the Convention on the Rights of the Child on the involvement of children in armed conflict

Adopted by General Assembly resolution 54/263 of 26 June 2000.

The States Parties to the present Protocol,

Encouraged by the overwhelming support for the Convention on the Rights of the Child, demonstrating the widespread commitment that exists to strive for the promotion and protection of the rights of the child,

Reaffirming that the rights of children require special protection, and calling for continuous improvement of the situation of children without distinction, as well as for their development and education in conditions of peace and security,

Disturbed by the harmful and widespread impact of armed conflict on children and the long-term consequences this has for durable peace, security and development,

Condemning the targeting of children in situations of armed conflict and direct attacks on objects protected under international law, including places generally having a significant presence of children, such as schools and hospitals,

Noting the adoption of the Statute of the International Criminal Court and, in particular, its inclusion as a war crime of conscripting or enlisting children under the age of 15 years or using them to participate actively in hostilities in both international and non-international armed conflicts,

Considering, therefore, that to strengthen further the implementation of rights recognized in the Convention on the Rights of the Child there is a need to increase the protection of children from involvement in armed conflict,

Noting that article 1 of the Convention on the Rights of the Child specifies that, for the purposes of that Convention, a child means every human being below the age of 18 years unless, under the law applicable to the child, majority is attained earlier,

Convinced that an optional protocol to the Convention raising the age of possible recruitment of persons into armed forces and their participation in hostilities will contribute effectively to the implementation of the principle that the best interests of the child are to be a primary consideration in all actions concerning children,

Noting that the twenty-sixth international Conference of the Red Cross and Red Crescent in December 1995 recommended, inter alia, that parties to conflict take every feasible step to ensure that children under the age of 18 years do not take part in hostilities,

Welcoming the unanimous adoption, in June 1999, of International Labour Organization Convention No. 182 on the Prohibition and Immediate Action for the Elimination of the Worst Forms of Child Labour, which prohibits, inter alia, forced or compulsory recruitment of children for use in armed conflict,

Condemning with the gravest concern the recruitment, training and use within and across national borders of children in hostilities by armed groups distinct from the armed forces of a State, and recognizing the responsibility of those who recruit, train and use children in this regard,

Recalling the obligation of each party to an armed conflict to abide by the provisions of international humanitarian law,

Stressing that this Protocol is without prejudice to the purposes and principles contained in the Charter of the United Nations, including Article 51, and relevant norms of humanitarian law,

Bearing in mind that conditions of peace and security based on full respect of the purposes and principles contained in the Charter and observance of applicable human rights instruments are indispensable for the full protection of children, in particular during armed conflicts and foreign occupation,

Recognizing the special needs of those children who are particularly vulnerable to recruitment or use in hostilities contrary to this Protocol owing to their economic or social status or gender,

Mindful of the necessity of taking into consideration the economic, social and political root causes of the involvement of children in armed conflicts,

Convinced of the need to strengthen international cooperation in the implementation of this Protocol, as well as the physical and psychosocial rehabilitation and social reintegration of children who are victims of armed conflict,

Encouraging the participation of the community and, in particular, children and child victims in the dissemination of informational and educational programmes concerning the implementation of the Protocol,

Have agreed as follows:

Article 1

States Parties shall take all feasible measures to ensure that members of their armed forces who have not attained the age of 18 years do not take a direct part in hostilities.

Article 2

States Parties shall ensure that persons who have not attained the age of 18 years are not compulsorily recruited into their armed forces.

Article 3

1.   States Parties shall raise the minimum age for the voluntary recruitment of persons into their national armed forces from that set out in article 38, paragraph 3, of the Convention on the Rights of the Child, taking account of the principles contained in that article and recognizing that under the Convention persons under 18 are entitled to special protection.

2.   Each State Party shall deposit a binding declaration upon ratification of or accession to this Protocol that sets forth the minimum age at which it will permit voluntary recruitment into its national armed forces and a description of the safeguards that it has adopted to ensure that such recruitment is not forced or coerced.

3.   States Parties that permit voluntary recruitment into their national armed forces under the age of 18 shall maintain safeguards to ensure, as a minimum, that:

a)   Such recruitment is genuinely voluntary;

b)   Such recruitment is done with the informed consent of the person's parents or legal guardians;

c)   Such persons are fully informed of the duties involved in such military service;

d)   Such persons provide reliable proof of age prior to acceptance into national military service.

4.   Each State Party may strengthen its declaration at any time by notification to that effect addressed to the Secretary-General of the United Nations, who shall inform all States Parties. Such notification shall take effect on the date on which it is received by the Secretary-General.

5.   The requirement to raise the age in paragraph 1 of the present article does not apply to schools operated by or under the control of the armed forces of the States Parties, in keeping with articles 28 and 29 of the Convention on the Rights of the Child.

Article 4

1.   Armed groups that are distinct from the armed forces of a State should not, under any circumstances, recruit or use in hostilities persons under the age of 18 years.

2.   States Parties shall take all feasible measures to prevent such recruitment and use, including the adoption of legal measures necessary to prohibit and criminalize such practices.

3.   The application of the present article under this Protocol shall not affect the legal status of any party to an armed conflict.

Article 5

Nothing in the present Protocol shall be construed as precluding provisions in the law of a State Party or in international instruments and international humanitarian law that are more conducive to the realization of the rights of the child.

Article 6

1.   Each State Party shall take all necessary legal, administrative and other measures to ensure the effective implementation and enforcement of the provisions of this Protocol within its jurisdiction.

2.   States Parties undertake to make the principles and provisions of the present Protocol widely known and promoted by appropriate means, to adults and children alike.

3.   States Parties shall take all feasible measures to ensure that persons within their jurisdiction recruited or used in hostilities contrary to this Protocol are demobilized or otherwise released from service. States Parties shall, when necessary, accord to these persons all appropriate assistance for their physical and psychological recovery and their social reintegration.

Article 7

1.   States Parties shall cooperate in the implementation of the present Protocol, including in the prevention of any activity contrary to the Protocol and in the rehabilitation and social reintegration of persons who are victims of acts contrary to this Protocol, including through technical cooperation and financial assistance. Such assistance and cooperation will be undertaken in consultation with concerned States Parties and relevant international organizations.

2.   States Parties in a position to do so shall provide such assistance through existing multilateral, bilateral or other programmes, or, *inter alia*, through a voluntary fund established in accordance with the rules of the General Assembly.

Article 8

1.   Each State Party shall submit, within two years following the entry into force of the Protocol for that State Party, a report to the Committee on the Rights of the Child providing comprehensive information on the measures it has taken to implement the provisions of the Protocol, including the measures taken to implement the provisions on participation and recruitment.

2.   Following the submission of the comprehensive report, each State Party shall include in the reports they submit to the Committee on the Rights of the Child, in accordance with article 44 of the Convention, any further information with respect to the implementation of the Protocol. Other States Parties to the Protocol shall submit a report every five years.

3.   The Committee on the Rights of the Child may request from States Parties further information relevant to the implementation of this Protocol.

Article 9

1.   The present Protocol is open for signature by any State that is a party to the Convention or has signed it.

2.   The present Protocol is subject to ratification and is open to accession by any State. Instruments of ratification or accession shall be deposited with the Secretary-General of the United Nations.

3.   The Secretary-General, in his capacity as depositary of the Convention and the Protocol, shall inform all States Parties to the Convention and all States that have signed the Convention of each instrument of declaration pursuant to article 13.

Article 10

1.   The present Protocol shall enter into force three months after the deposit of the tenth instrument of ratification or accession.

2.   For each State ratifying the present Protocol or acceding to it after its entry into force, the present Protocol shall enter into force one month after the date of the deposit of its own instrument of ratification or accession.

Article 11

1.   Any State Party may denounce the present Protocol at any time by written notification to the Secretary-General of the United Nations, who shall thereafter inform the other States Parties to the Convention and all States that have signed the Convention. The denunciation shall take effect one year after the date of receipt of the notification by the Secretary-General. If, however, on the expiry of that year the denouncing State

Party is engaged in armed conflict, the denunciation shall not take effect before the end of the armed conflict.

2.   Such a denunciation shall not have the effect of releasing the State Party from its obligations under the present Protocol in regard to any act that occurs prior to the date on which the denunciation becomes effective. Nor shall such a denunciation prejudice in any way the continued consideration of any matter that is already under consideration by the Committee prior to the date on which the denunciation becomes effective.

Article 12

1.   Any State Party may propose an amendment and file it with the Secretary-General of the United Nations. The Secretary-General shall thereupon communicate the proposed amendment to States Parties, with a request that they indicate whether they favour a conference of States Parties for the purpose of considering and voting upon the proposals. In the event that, within four months from the date of such communication, at least one third of the States Parties favour such a conference, the Secretary-General shall convene the conference under the auspices of the United Nations. Any amendment adopted by a majority of States Parties present and voting at the conference shall be submitted to the General Assembly for approval.

2.   An amendment adopted in accordance with paragraph 1 of the present article shall enter into force when it has been approved by the General Assembly of the United Nations and accepted by a two-thirds majority of States Parties.

3.   When an amendment enters into force, it shall be binding on those States Parties that have accepted it, other States Parties still being bound by the provisions of the present Protocol and any earlier amendments that they have accepted.

Article 13

1.   The present Protocol, of which the Arabic, Chinese, English, French, Russian and Spanish texts are equally authentic, shall be deposited in the archives of the United Nations.

2.   The Secretary-General of the United Nations shall transmit certified copies of the present Protocol to all States Parties

to the Convention and all States that have signed the Convention.

Optional Protocol to the Convention on the Rights of the Child on the sale of children, child prostitution and child pornography

Adopted by General Assembly resolution 54/263 of 20 June 2000.

The States Parties to the present Protocol,

Considering that, in order further to achieve the purposes of the Convention on the Rights of the Child and the implementation of its provisions, especially articles 1, 11, 21, 32, 33, 34, 35 and 36, it would be appropriate to extend the measures that States Parties should undertake in order to guarantee the protection of the child from the sale of children, child prostitution and child pornography,

Considering also that the Convention on the Rights of the Child recognizes the right of the child to be protected from economic exploitation and from performing any work that is likely to be hazardous or to interfere with the child's education, or to be harmful to the child's health or physical, mental, spiritual, moral or social development,

Gravely concerned at the significant and increasing international traffic of children for the purpose of the sale of children, child prostitution and child pornography,

Deeply concerned at the widespread and continuing practice of sex tourism, to which children are especially vulnerable, as it directly promotes the sale of children, child prostitution and child pornography,

Recognizing that a number of particularly vulnerable groups, including girl children, are at greater risk of sexual exploitation, and that girl children are disproportionately represented among the sexually exploited,

Concerned about the growing availability of child pornography on the Internet and other evolving technologies, and

309

recalling the International Conference on Combating Child Pornography on the Internet (Vienna, 1999) and, in particular, its conclusion calling for the worldwide criminalization of the production, distribution, exportation, transmission, importation, intentional possession and advertising of child pornography, and stressing the importance of closer cooperation and partnership between Governments and the Internet industry,

Believing that the elimination of the sale of children, child prostitution and child pornography will be facilitated by adopting a holistic approach, addressing the contributing factors, including underdevelopment, poverty, economic disparities, inequitable socio-economic structure, dysfunctioning families, lack of education, urban-rural migration, gender discrimination, irresponsible adult sexual behaviour, harmful traditional practices, armed conflicts and trafficking of children,

Believing that efforts to raise public awareness are needed to reduce consumer demand for the sale of children, child prostitution and child pornography, and also believing in the importance of strengthening global partnership among all actors and of improving law enforcement at the national level,

Noting the provisions of international legal instruments relevant to the protection of children, including the Hague Convention on the Protection of Children and Cooperation with Respect to Inter-Country Adoption, the Hague Convention on the Civil Aspects of International Child Abduction, the Hague Convention on Jurisdiction, Applicable Law, Recognition, Enforcement and Cooperation in Respect of Parental Responsibility and Measures for the Protection of Children, and International Labour Organization Convention No. 182 on the Prohibition and Immediate Action for the Elimination of the Worst Forms of Child Labour,

Encouraged by the overwhelming support for the Convention on the Rights of the Child, demonstrating the widespread commitment that exists for the promotion and protection of the rights of the child,

Recognizing the importance of the implementation of the provisions of the Programme of Action for the Prevention of the Sale of Children, Child Prostitution and Child Pornography and the Declaration and Agenda for Action adopted at the

World Congress against Commercial Sexual Exploitation of Children, held at Stockholm from 27 to 31 August 1996, and the other relevant decisions and recommendations of pertinent international bodies,

Taking due account of the importance of the traditions and cultural values of each people for the protection and harmonious development of the child,

Have agreed as follows:

Article 1

States Parties shall prohibit the sale of children, child prostitution and child pornography as provided for by the present Protocol.

Article 2

For the purpose of the present Protocol:

a) Sale of children means any act or transaction whereby a child is transferred by any person or group of persons to another for remuneration or any other consideration;

b) Child prostitution means the use of a child in sexual activities for remuneration or any other form of consideration;

c) Child pornography means any representation, by whatever means, of a child engaged in real or simulated explicit sexual activities or any representation of the sexual parts of a child for primarily sexual purposes.

Article 3

1. Each State Party shall ensure that, as a minimum, the following acts and activities are fully covered under its criminal or penal law, whether these offences are committed domestically or transnationally or on an individual or organized basis:

(a) In the context of sale of children as defined in article 2:

(i) The offering, delivering or accepting, by whatever means, a child for the purpose of:

a.   Sexual exploitation of the child;

b.   Transfer of organs of the child for profit;

      c.   Engagement of the child in forced labour;

(ii) Improperly inducing consent, as an intermediary, for the adoption of a child in violation of applicable international legal instruments on adoption;

(b) Offering, obtaining, procuring or providing a child for child prostitution, as defined in article 2;

(c) Producing, distributing, disseminating, importing, exporting, offering, selling or possessing for the above purposes child pornography as defined in article 2.

2.   Subject to the provisions of a State Party's national law, the same shall apply to an attempt to commit any of these acts and to complicity or participation in any of these acts.

3.   Each State Party shall make these offences punishable by appropriate penalties that take into account their grave nature.

4.   Subject to the provisions of its national law, each State Party shall take measures, where appropriate, to establish the liability of legal persons for offences established in paragraph 1 of the present article. Subject to the legal principles of the State Party, this liability of legal persons may be criminal, civil or administrative.

5.   States Parties shall take all appropriate legal and administrative measures to ensure that all persons involved in the adoption of a child act in conformity with applicable international legal instruments.

Article 4

1.   Each State Party shall take such measures as may be necessary to establish its jurisdiction over the offences referred to in article 3, paragraph 1, when the offences are commited in its territory or on board a ship or aircraft registered in that State.

2.   Each State Party may take such measures as may be necessary to establish its jurisdiction over the offences referred to in article 3, paragraph 1, in the following cases:

a)   When the alleged offender is a national of that State or a person who has his habitual residence in its territory;

b)   When the victim is a national of that State.

3.   Each State Party shall also take such measures as may be necessary to establish its jurisdiction over the above-mentioned offences when the alleged offender is present in its territory and it does not extradite him or her to another State Party on the ground that the offence has been committed by one of its nationals.

4.   This Protocol does not exclude any criminal jurisdiction exercised in accordance with internal law.

Article 5

1.   The offences referred to in article 3, paragraph 1, shall be deemed to be included as extraditable offences in any extradition treaty existing between States Parties and shall be included as extraditable offences in every extradition treaty subsequently concluded between them, in accordance with the conditions set forth in those treaties.

2.   If a State Party that makes extradition conditional on the existence of a treaty receives a request for extradition from another State Party with which it has no extradition treaty, it may consider this Protocol as a legal basis for extradition in respect of such offences. Extradition shall be subject to the conditions provided by the law of the requested State.

3.   States Parties that do not make extradition conditional on the existence of a treaty shall recognize such offences as extraditable offences between themselves subject to the conditions provided by the law of the requested State.

4.   Such offences shall be treated, for the purpose of extradition between States Parties, as if they had been committed not only in the place in which they occurred but also in the territories of the States required to establish their jurisdiction in accordance with article 4.

5.   If an extradition request is made with respect to an offence described in article 3, paragraph 1, and if the requested State Party does not or will not extradite on the basis of the nationality of the offender, that State shall take suitable measures to submit the case to its competent authorities for the purpose of prosecution.

Article 6

1.   States Parties shall afford one another the greatest measure of assistance in connection with investigations or criminal or extradition proceedings brought in respect of the offences set forth in article 3, paragraph 1, including assistance in obtaining evidence at their disposal necessary for the proceedings.

2.   States Parties shall carry out their obligations under paragraph 1 of the present article in conformity with any treaties or other arrangements on mutual legal assistance that may exist between them. In the absence of such treaties or arrangements, States Parties shall afford one another assistance in accordance with their domestic law.

Article 7

States Parties shall, subject to the provisions of their national law:

(a)   Take measures to provide for the seizure and confiscation, as appropriate, of:

(i)   Goods such as materials, assets and other instrumentalities used to commit or facilitate offences under the present protocol;

(ii)   Proceeds derived from such offences;

(b)   Execute requests from another State Party for seizure or confiscation of goods or proceeds referred to in subparagraph (a) (i);

(c)   Take measures aimed at closing, on a temporary or definitive basis, premises used to commit such offences.

Article 8

1.   States Parties shall adopt appropriate measures to protect the rights and interests of child victims of the practices prohibited under the present Protocol at all stages of the criminal justice process, in particular by:

a)   Recognizing the vulnerability of child victims and adapting procedures to recognize their special needs, including their special needs as witnesses;

b)   Informing child victims of their rights, their role and the scope, timing and progress of the proceedings and of the disposition of their cases;

c)   Allowing the views, needs and concerns of child victims to be presented and considered in proceedings where their personal interests are affected, in a manner consistent with the procedural rules of national law;

d)   Providing appropriate support services to child victims throughout the legal process;

e)   Protecting, as appropriate, the privacy and identity of child victims and taking measures in accordance with national law to avoid the inappropriate dissemination of information that could lead to the identification of child victims;

f)   Providing, in appropriate cases, for the safety of child victims, as well as that of their families and witnesses on their behalf, from intimidation and retaliation;

g)   Avoiding unnecessary delay in the disposition of cases and the execution of orders or decrees granting compensation to child victims.

2.   States Parties shall ensure that uncertainty as to the actual age of the victim shall not prevent the initiation of criminal investigations, including investigations aimed at establishing the age of the victim.

3.   States Parties shall ensure that, in the treatment by the criminal justice system of children who are victims of the offences described in the present Protocol, the best interest of the child shall be a primary consideration.

4.   States Parties shall take measures to ensure appropriate training, in particular legal and psychological training, for the persons who work with victims of the offences prohibited under the present Protocol.

5.   States Parties shall, in appropriate cases, adopt measures in order to protect the safety and integrity of those persons and/or organizations involved in the prevention and/or protection and rehabilitation of victims of such offences.

6.   Nothing in the present article shall be construed as prejudicial to or inconsistent with the rights of the accused to a fair and impartial trial.

Article 9

1.   States Parties shall adopt or strengthen, implement and disseminate laws, administrative measures, social policies and programmes to prevent the offences referred to in the present Protocol. Particular attention shall be given to protect children who are especially vulnerable to these practices.

2.   States Parties shall promote awareness in the public at large, including children, through information by all appropriate means, education and training, about the preventive measures and harmful effects of the offences referred to in the present Protocol. In fulfilling their obligations under this article, States Parties shall encourage the participation of the community and, in particular, children and child victims, in such information and education and training programmes, including at the international level.

3.   States Parties shall take all feasible measures with the aim of ensuring all appropriate assistance to victims of such offences, including their full social reintegration and their full physical and psychological recovery.

4.   States Parties shall ensure that all child victims of the offences described in the present Protocol have access to adequate procedures to seek, without discrimination, compensation for damages from those legally responsible.

5.   States Parties shall take appropriate measures aimed at effectively prohibiting the production and dissemination of material advertising the offences described in the present Protocol.

Article 10

1.   States Parties shall take all necessary steps to strengthen international cooperation by multilateral, regional and bilateral arrangements for the prevention, detection, investigation, prosecution and punishment of those responsible for acts involving the sale of children, child prostitution, child pornography and child sex tourism. States Parties shall also promote international cooperation and coordination between their

authorities, national and international non-governmental organizations and international organizations.

2.   States Parties shall promote international cooperation to assist child victims in their physical and psychological recovery, social reintegration and repatriation.

3.   States Parties shall promote the strengthening of international cooperation in order to address the root causes, such as poverty and underdevelopment, contributing to the vulnerability of children to the sale of children, child prostitution, child pornography and child sex tourism.

4.   States Parties in a position to do so shall provide financial, technical or other assistance through existing multilateral, regional, bilateral or other programmes.

Article 11

Nothing in the present Protocol shall affect any provisions that are more conducive to the realization of the rights of the child and that may be contained in:

a)   The law of a State Party;

b)   International law in force for that State.

Article 12

1.   Each State Party shall submit, within two years following the entry into force of the Protocol for that State Party, a report to the Committee on the Rights of the Child providing comprehensive information on the measures it has taken to implement the provisions of the Protocol.

2.   Following the submission of the comprehensive report, each State Party shall include in the reports they submit to the Committee on the Rights of the Child, in accordance with article 44 of the Convention, any further information with respect to the implementation of the Protocol. Other States Parties to the Protocol shall submit a report every five years.

3.   The Committee on the Rights of the Child may request from States Parties further information relevant to the implementation of this Protocol.

Article 13

1. The present Protocol is open for signature by any State that is a party to the Convention or has signed it.

2. The present Protocol is subject to ratification and is open to accession by any State that is a party to the Convention or has signed it. Instruments of ratification or accession shall be deposited with the Secretary-General of the United Nations.

Article 14

1. The present Protocol shall enter into force three months after the deposit of the tenth instrument of ratification or accession.

2. For each State ratifying the present Protocol or acceding to it after its entry into force, the present Protocol shall enter into force one month after the date of the deposit of its own instrument of ratification or accession.

Article 15

1. Any State Party may denounce the present Protocol at any time by written notification to the Secretary-General of the United Nations, who shall thereafter inform the other States Parties to the Convention and all States that have signed the Convention. The denunciation shall take effect one year after the date of receipt of the notification by the Secretary-General of the United Nations.

2. Such a denunciation shall not have the effect of releasing the State Party from its obligations under this Protocol in regard to any offence that occurs prior to the date on which the denunciation becomes effective. Nor shall such a denunciation prejudice in any way the continued consideration of any matter that is already under consideration by the Committee prior to the date on which the denunciation becomes effective.

Article 16

1. Any State Party may propose an amendment and file it with the Secretary-General of the United Nations. The Secretary-General shall thereupon communicate the proposed amendment to States Parties, with a request that they indicate whether they favour a conference of States Parties for the purpose of considering and voting upon the proposals. In the

318

event that, within four months from the date of such communication, at least one third of the States Parties favour such a conference, the Secretary-General shall convene the conference under the auspices of the United Nations. Any amendment adopted by a majority of States Parties present and voting at the conference shall be submitted to the General Assembly for approval.

2.   An amendment adopted in accordance with paragraph 1 of the present article shall enter into force when it has been approved by the General Assembly of the United Nations and accepted by a two-thirds majority of States Parties.

3.   When an amendment enters into force, it shall be binding on those States Parties that have accepted it, other States Parties still being bound by the provisions of the present Protocol and any earlier amendments that they have accepted.

Article 17

1.   The present Protocol, of which the Arabic, Chinese, English, French, Russian and Spanish texts are equally authentic, shall be deposited in the archives of the United Nations.

2.   The Secretary-General of the United Nations shall transmit certified copies of the present Protocol to all States Parties to the Convention and all States that have signed the Convention.

Litho in United Nations, New York   I   United Nations publication
00-74083—November 2000—2,630   Sales No. E.00.IV.3
ISBN 92-1-130204-8